THE
BREWER'S
TALE

ALSO BY WILLIAM BOSTWICK

Beer Craft: A Simple Guide to Making Great Beer

THE BREWER'S TALE

A History of the World According to Beer

William Bostwick

W. W. Norton & Company

New York   London

Lines from the "Hymn to Ninkasi" translated by Miguel Civil. Permission granted courtesy of the Oriental Institute of the University of Chicago.

For information about permission to reproduce selections from this book, write to Permissions, W. W. Norton & Company, Inc., 500 Fifth Avenue, New York, NY 10110

For information about special discounts for bulk purchases, please contact W. W. Norton Special Sales at specialsales@wwnorton.com or 800-233-4830

Manufacturing by Courier Westford
Book design by Daniel Lagin
Production manager: Devon Zahn

Library of Congress Cataloging-in-Publication Data

Bostwick, William, author.
The brewer's tale : a history of the world according to beer / William Bostwick.—First edition.
     pages cm
Includes bibliographical references and index.
ISBN 978–0–393–23914–0 (hardcover)
1. Brewing—History. 2. Beer—History. I. Title.
TP573.A1B67 2014
663'.4209—dc23

                                                    2014016561

W. W. Norton & Company, Inc.,
500 Fifth Avenue, New York, N.Y. 10110
www.wwnorton.com

W. W. Norton & Company Ltd., Castle House,
75/76 Wells Street, London W1T 3QT

1 2 3 4 5 6 7 8 9 0

CONTENTS

My senses aren't above reproach, but they're all I have. I want to see the whole picture—as nearly as I can. I don't want to put on the blinders of "good" and "bad," and limit my vision. If I used the term "good" on a thing I'd lose my license to inspect it, because there might be bad in it. Don't you see? I want to be able to look at the whole thing.

—John Steinbeck, *In Dubious Battle*

INTRODUCTION

A guy walks into a bar. It's the oldest setup there is. But what happens next?

I was at my local pub contemplating a water-ringed beer list, a wall of tap handles, and a packed fridge. I saw a pale ale brewed 20 million gallons at a time and a triple IPA made in a jerry-rigged turkey frier in a garage down the street. I saw a traditional, light-bodied British porter and an extra-strong, cacao-infused imperial stout stored in bourbon barrels. One beer was brewed with hours-old hops, freshly plucked in an Oregon field; another had been aged for eighteen months with acidic bacteria—critters more common in vinegar and pickle brines. There were pilsners and ambers, red ales and browns, wheat beers and rye beers and spelt beers; there were three-dollar happy hour specials and thirty-dollar vintage bottles, corked and foil-wrapped like fine Champagne. Bitter or sweet, smooth or strong, fruity or dry, dark or light, it was all there, in dizzying glory. So—the bartender tapped his fingers—what'll it be?

This should have been an easy choice. I was in my element,

after all. Drinking is my job. I'm a beer critic. I cover beer for the *Wall Street Journal* and a few food and style glossies. That means when I drink I'm on duty. I put on blinders to context, story, and place. I tune out the ads, cover up the label, and focus as best I can on taste alone. My job is to translate flavor to prose, not to wonder *why* but to describe, clearly, *what*. That is, what does the beer taste like and, most important for my readers, is it any good? I'm a guide, a personal shopper. My palate is sensitive, my thesaurus well thumbed. I can flag a dirty tap line, I can distinguish tropical Calypso hops from citrusy Cascades. To me, beer is more than dry or sweet, strong or light. Not simply dark, but smoky like a campfire in a eucalyptus grove. Not just fruity, but tropically spiced like a papaya ripening in pine boughs.

There's joy in leveling judgment, sure, but I get more kicks in the describing. Flavors are rich, and it's fun to write about them, turning tastes into poetry. But staring at those taps, and my spreadsheets of tasting notes, I felt I was missing a deeper story. In my hunt for objectivity I was, ironically, getting too abstract. In ignoring context I was missing meaning. I wanted to know more than taste—I wanted to know its origins. I was done with the *what*. I wanted to know the *where* and *why*. Why does beer taste the way it does? Whence that papaya? Where did those styles, those flavors—where did beer itself—come from in the first place?

I knew that beer has been here as long as we have. What to drink? I shouldn't have been embarrassed I didn't have a good answer. We've been asking ourselves that question for ten thousand years. Humankind was built on beer. From the world's first writing to its first laws, in rituals social, religious, and political, civilization is soaked in beer. Some historians even think that beer gave us the crucial vitamins and nutrients—not to mention a source of purified water—to keep us healthy as we turned from meat-centric nomads to a settled, agrarian diet. Beer was foundational stuff, a building block of human existence. But while so much else has changed, oxen to John Deeres, wood hearths to nuclear reactors, beer has remained. How has it lasted so long, I wondered. How has it evolved, and how has it stayed the same?

What we drink says something about us, from the guy who bellied up next to me at the bar and whispered for the bitterest IPA they had, sheepishly, as if asking for the fattiest foie gras, to the folks who recoil at the thought of anything hopped—or, as my mom calls it, "flavorful." "I just want something light," she says. Some beers are revered like wines, calling drinkers on pilgrimages to Belgium just to get a taste; other are hawked on NASCAR billboards and slugged by keg-standing bros. Ever since we've been asking ourselves what's for dinner, we've also been asking what to drink with it. And it's never been an easy question to answer, even for our ancestors. Babylonian tablets recorded twenty kinds: black, red, sweet, even "beer to lessen the waist." Egyptians had rough-hewn peasant beer and beer flavored with dates and honey for the pharaohs. Dark-age tribes had spice cabinets full of henbane, ergot, and other bog-grown oddities. What we drink reveals who we are. Can it also tell me who we were?

So I kicked aside my style guides—I shut my thesaurus, I hung up my flavor wheel—and hit the history books. I traced those tap lines back to their sources. I followed IPAs into the holds of Calcutta-bound Indiamen; goblets of strong Belgian beer back to spartan tables in drafty monasteries; peppery saisons to hot days on Wallonian farms; and beer itself back, back through the murk to the beginning of time.

I couldn't just read about the beer, of course. I'd have to taste it. Which meant I'd have to make it myself. As lengthy as the bar's tap list was, I didn't see any henbane on it. To brew these beers I needed a guide. I was looking, after all, not just for a taste but for a story; I needed not just the beer but the brewer.

Because if beer's essence can be distilled to one idea, it's this: beer is *made*. Our first recorded recipes were for beer because beer was the first thing we made that required a recipe, our first engineered food. Wine, for example, just happens. A grape's sugars will ferment on their own, without a human touch; even elephants and butterflies seek out rotting fruit. But grain needs a modern hand to coax out its sugars and ferment them into alcohol. Brewing beer demands thought and skill. It demands, in a word, a creator.

As beer says something about the drinker and his tastes, it also reflects the man (or, more often, in the past, woman) who made it. Those tap lines trace back to a person. And so I couldn't just drink the beer—I'd have to cross over to the other side of the bar, to meet the Babylonian temple worker, the Medieval alewife, the monks and farmers, industrialists and immigrants who first brewed the beers over which I pondered.

So I refilled my glass and grabbed a pen. Like all the best journeys, mine took shape on coasters and cocktail napkins. A road trip through time, with eight stops along the way. I lined up eight drinking partners. The Babylonian servant, brewing liquid daily bread for the empire-building masses; the Nordic shaman, keeper of herb-infused portals into the spirit world; the monk, fueling his brothers' Lenten fasts; the farmer, turning the dregs of harvest into rustic refreshment; the London industrialists, whose factories churned out dark, rich porters and high-class, sparkling pales; the first American settlers, making due with pumpkins and parsnips; and finally their heirs, the German immigrants bringing lager to a thirsty nation and the admen taking beer into the modern age.

I augmented what recipes I found in the history books with advice from today's top pros—masters of the styles I was re-creating, experts in their eras, or simply brewers who could best translate their stories—who best understood their deeper significance. People such as Sam Calagione, who turned a 2,700-year-old potsherd into Midas Touch, the most popular honey-based booze in the country, or Brian Hunt, a modern-day shaman in the Sonoma redwoods.

And I fired up my brew pot. What bubbled up were flavors I'd never tasted before—I didn't have the vocabulary even to describe them. I was, now, out of my element; my flavor wheel was useless. Down again came the thesaurus: sweet and sour like Chinese takeout; savory spiced like mincemeat pie; viscous and tannic like the smell of fresh tar. I was an explorer mapping unknown territory. These were flavors, I thought, we hadn't tasted in millennia. Some we've missed—the rye-bread snap of a good old-fashioned saison—others, maybe, are best left where they rest.

Bringing these beers back to life, and sharing them with ghosts, those changing flavors told of changing times. Dark, spicy medieval beer was a warm blanket against the drafty chill of monastic life; bright flowery IPAs a respite from the soot of the industrial age; cloying pumpkin beer a taste of American independence from British rule. Flavors born of necessity—barley was a hassle in early America but pumpkins were plentiful—and of choice. Each new flavor told a story. Brewers are flies on the wall of history, and beers are their time capsules, each pint glass (or flagon or sheep stomach) filled with the culture, politics, and habits of its age. Tell me what you brewed and drank and I'll tell you how you lived, and when. Beers are mirrors of their times because beer is a mirror of our selves. And so it's no wonder it's changed so much. We have too.

And yet . . . in other ways, the past didn't feel so far gone. The tastes were new but the stories they told were familiar. The further back I went, the stronger the sense I got that, though *what* we've drunk has changed in big ways, the reasons *why* we drink and brew come around again and again like a barfly's bad jokes, told and retold with each new pint. From the start we've used beer to bond with friends and make up with enemies, toast our accomplishments and drown our sorrows, honor our gods and forget our troubles. Beer has been high class and low brow, sacred and profane, rustic sustenance and a rare treat. Beer tells us how far we've come and how little we've changed. Stories about ritual and transformation, about place and identity, about politics and religion. Stories, above all, about community—about how beer, varied as it is, has nonetheless always brought us together.

Brewing these beers, meeting these brewers, didn't just transport me to a former time; it bonded me to it. At first, when I looked at that long list of taps, I saw divisions: the hop head, the sour snob, the Coors-swigging frat boy. All those flavors felt like lines in the sand. How bitter can you handle? How strong is too strong? But tracing beer back to its sources simplified it for me. Beer transforms—grain to sugar, sugar to alcohol, raw to cooked, sober to enlightened, man to maker—and, as it transforms, it connects. It connects us to where we live and what grows there, it connects our present to our past, and it connects us to one another. Brewing made us human—we drink therefore we are. This isn't just my story, or beer's story, it's the story of us. This is the world according to beer, a brewer's history of civilization.

THE
BREWER'S
TALE

1
THE BABYLONIAN

A hot Egyptian dawn. The rippling air is a thick, heavy blanket, and pyramids poke up on the horizon like tucked-in toes. Date palms wilt in the haze, their fruit oozing. And into this stillness, over the dunes, buzzes the brewer.

But this isn't the brewer we're familiar with. It isn't a Carhartt-clad, rubber-booted cellarman or a fermentation specialist in goggles and lab coat. It isn't a monk in an abbey or a beer baron lording over his humming Milwaukee factory. This brewer is older than all of them. This brewer is primordial. This brewer is a fly.

Stuck in the hairs of his hirsute insect legs, this fly carries precious cargo: spores of *Saccharomyces cerevisiae,* otherwise known as beer yeast. As any brewer—human, that is—will tell you, we don't really make beer. Yeast does. Brewers set the stage, but for the performance—the transformation of grains, hops, and water into bubbly booze—we must credit this humble, hardworking microorganism. Those spores are the key to our story. Let's get introduced.

Beer yeast breathes oxygen, eats saccharides like glucose and maltose, and produces alcohol, carbon dioxide, and a host of other chemicals including flavorful and aromatic compounds called esters. The fungus lives on sugar and thrives anywhere it can find it—which is to say nearly everywhere. The soft white fuzz on past-their-prime fruits is an oft-cited example of a flourishing *Saccharomyces* colony in the wild. It's ubiquitous, and its role is crucial, but for years its identity remained a mystery. Anything sweet will ferment under the right conditions. The juice from one of those sun-plumped Egyptian dates, for example, will attract spores of yeast and bacteria from the air or passing insects swooping in for a snack (some bacteria blow on the breeze, but *Saccharomyces* in particular require a vector to travel) and slowly bubble into wine. A broth of barley, wheat, or rye—malt tea that human brewers call wort—will turn to beer. Brewers eventually learned through trial and error to reproduce those warm, oxygen-rich environments *Saccharomyces* like best, but for centuries they were unaware of to what, exactly, or to whom they were giving a home. Taming that wild bug and putting it to work has troubled and tormented brewers since time immemorial, inspiring poems, songs, libraries of how-to books, and plenty of prayers and curses. Beer fermented as if by magic, and its making was the purview of gods and goddesses, governed not by science but by ritual and faith.

Today things are different. Brewers not only know what *Saccharomyces* are but, more than that, they know how to control them. Yeast still, technically, makes beer—it just does so on our terms. By adjusting temperature, time, oxygen levels, even air pressure, brewers can manipulate fermentations to produce, say, the deep fruity notes of abbey-style dubbels, the crisp black-pepper crackle of saisons, the airy refreshment of pilsner. They even know how to breed proprietary *Saccharomyces* subspecies with their own characteristic flavor profiles, from Rogue's high-powered, extra-dry Pacman to Alchemist's citrusy Conan.

Developing those skills took time. Brewing beer is about taking control of nature, about taming that spore, transforming the raw into the cooked. The brewer's tale is the story of that transformation, and how ultimately it transformed us. This is the story that fly carried, a story I chased. And I had company, because hot on that fly's yeast-studded heels ran another brewer—human, this time—named Sam Calagione.

Sam had traveled to Egypt, six thousand miles away from his Delaware brewery, Dogfish Head, to re-create a long-lost beer, one of the first ever made, in fact. He went there to gather ingredients: emmer wheat, palm fruit, chamomile, and the key to it all, native Nile Delta microflora.

His companions were Dogfish Head's brewmaster Floris "the yeast whisperer" Delée: Belgian, bespectacled, clutching a yellow, hard-shell suitcase packed with petri dishes and sterile swabs; and Ramy, their driver: an Egyptian Indiana Jones resplendent in cowboy hat and remarkably clean white shirt, unbuttoned, his chest hair billowing in the breeze. Back home at mission control there was Patrick "Dr. Pat" McGovern in his artifact-packed office at the University of Pennsylvania's Biomolecular Archaeology Laboratory for Cuisine, Fermented Beverages, and Health. And, at the brewery in Milton, Delaware, lab technician Katrinka Housley scowling into her microscope over iodine-stained fingers, providing the sweet but stern voice of reason. And me? I was there in spirit—all brewers are brothers, especially those like Sam and me, sharing an odd fascination with the old and obscure. But really, I was on my couch. This was the fifth episode of *Brew Masters*, a short-lived

Discovery Channel TV series that chronicled the trials and adventures of running a brewery.* Adventures like fly hunting.

As the fawning film crew—if not the lengths to which Sam has gone to re-create this ancient Egyptian beer—reveal, Dogfish Head isn't just any brewery. And Sam isn't just any brewer. He's a godfather of craft beer. Dogfish Head is one of the first and most successful craft breweries in the country, founded as a brewpub in 1995 and now a 200,000-barrel-a-year operation. But Sam's beers are famous not only for their longevity in a temperamental industry, but because they're, well, *weird*. Sam brews with cilantro and apples, with raisins and chicory and brown sugar. He flavored his Choc Lobster stout with, yes, lobsters and chocolate. Even Dogfish Head's "normal" beers come with a twist. Take 60 Minute IPA, the brand's flagship. Almost all beers, but especially IPAs, get their bitter flavor from the resins of a leafy plant called hops, which brewers extract by boiling the fresh or dried buds in wort. Most IPAs, even the strongest of the style, are hopped in short bursts—a dash here, a dash there, during a boil that usually lasts about an hour. Bitter, piney 60 Minute, on the other hand, gets its name from the continuous stream of hops pumped into it during its entire hour-long brew. It's a trick Sam learned from cooking shows: soups are more flavorful slowly spiced over time than powdered with pepper right at the start. (For an extra boost, some versions of the beer are dispensed at the bar through a specially made hop infuser Sam calls Randall the Enamel Animal. Brewers and beer fans shorten it to Randall and use it as noun and

---

* *Brew Masters* ran for only five episodes. The Discovery Channel cited poor ratings, but many speculate the decision not to renew it for another season had more to do with tension between Sam, his army of die-hard craft-beer fans, and the show's main sponsor, MillerCoors's craft-seeming brand Blue Moon.

verb—as in, "Did this beer get Randallized?") Against the odds, Sam's "off-centered ales," as he proudly calls them, have paid off. He has a thrumming brewery, media coverage from beer snobs and mainstream rags alike, and even his own TV show.

Back in the desert, Sam and his crew swung into a date farm where workers with black-nailed, fly-specked hands tossed the fruit onto straw mats to pucker and dry in the sun. With a smile, Floris set his traps among the mats: Petri dishes smeared with date juice, a sticky agar jelly to catch the spores, and isoamyl acetate, a brilliant lure whipped up by Katrinka that smells irresistibly (to the fly) like rotting banana. And then they waited.

A single spore, like a single spark—everything pivots on this. The course of history sometimes swings on the tiniest fulcrum: Newton's apple, Edison's filament. And upon this spore we built everything. But first we needed fire.

Night in the desert. Thunder cracks and then there was light. For millennia humans were hunters, gatherers, and scavengers. We grabbed meals where we could, from the occasional speared megafauna, picked-over carcasses left by keener hunters, or wild fruit plucked as we wandered the plains. Then we found fire.

With a smoldering, lightning-struck branch we could bring wild nature under some kind of order. With fire, we could chase away the big cats and we could herd game. We could clear fields and we could plant crops. And we could cook. Deep in an African cave, maybe, or high on a mountain in northern China—archaeologists aren't exactly sure where—someone had the bright idea of throwing a carcass on a pile of embers and thus fire turned to tool. Danger was harnessed, flame became kitchen, and kitchen became laboratory. For eons, "What's for dinner?" had meant whatever was around. Now, man had options.

Meat was first on the menu. Buffalo, aurochs, and other wild beasts evolved to depend on fire-pruned land, and so-called cattle cults grew up around these domesticated herds. The cow was venerated, its meat a sacred delicacy for kings and gods. Archaeologists have since dug up sacrificial tombs packed with piles of cow skulls. While the wealthy ate cattle, most learned to subsist on a brand-new food: grain. We joined our livestock at the trough.

Caked in a Neanderthal molar discovered deep in a Belgian cave, a single charred kernel of barley, last munched some thirty thousand years ago, is our earliest record of that agricultural revolution. The story of that kernel unfolds poetically in the *Epic of Gilgamesh*, a Mesopotamian creation myth about the adventures of the noble, godlike king of Uruk. The poem opens on his foil Enkidu, a wild man barely distinguishable from an ape.

Made by the gods from clay and spit, Enkidu is "shaggy with hair." Like an animal, "he knew neither people nor settled living." He ate raw grass and "his thirst was slaked with mere water." A fateful trip to the whorehouse would change all that. The temptress Shamhat saw Enkidu jostling the wild animals at the watering hole and lured him away to Uruk, and civilization, with a striptease, bread, and beer.

> *Enkidu had not known*
> *To eat food.*
> *To drink wine**
> *He had not been taught.*

---

* This translation from the 1920s interprets the Akkadian *šikaram,* or Sumerian *kaš,* as "wine," but modern scholars tend to agree that it meant, instead, a grain-based beer.

The woman opened her mouth and
Spoke to Enkidu:
"Eat food, O Enkidu,
The provender of life!
Drink wine, the custom of the land!"
Enkidu ate food
Till he was satiated.
Wine he drank,
Seven goblets.
His spirit was loosened, he became hilarious.
His heart became glad and
His face shone.
[The barber] removed
The hair on his body.
He was anointed with oil.
He became manlike.
He put on a garment,
He was like a man.

The myth is true. Eating plants changed us. From pottery to politics, art to architecture, modern life grew from grain. In a way, we didn't control plants; plants controlled us. Grain put us to work. Mesopotamia was fertile but that doesn't mean it was a grocery store. Agriculture took effort. Before we could eat, we had to clear, plant, and irrigate fields. We accomplished this with a massive feat of infrastructure, connecting the Tigris and Euphrates rivers with a network of canals. That project didn't just feed us, it united us, bringing together loose, nomadic tribes under a shared purpose. Once that irrigated grain was harvested and stored, the tribes stuck around. Those settlements became our first cities.

Records of what grain was kept where, and for whom it was allotted, became the first writing; the organized distribution of that grain evolved into the first laws and political systems. The more we settled, the larger those settlements grew until two main powers emerged: the Sumerians and the Akkadians. They eventually united to form the first civilizations on earth, a grain-fueled Babylonian empire that would last for millennia until conquered by the Persian king Cyrus the Great and then swallowed into Ancient Greece by the wine-sated Macedonian Alexander.

Babylon was built on grain. The Greek historian Herodotus wrote, awestruck, that "in grain [the land] is so fruitful as to yield commonly two-hundred-fold, and when the production is the greatest, even three-hundred-fold." Barley, spelt, millet, and rye, emmer and einkorn wheat piled up in heaps. But once harvested and packed into storage the work was not over. Raw, dried grass seeds are inedible. To get at their brain-boosting nutrients and energy-rich sugars we had to learn to make malt, in another transformation, a half step from grass to bread, or grass to beer. Malting is trickery. By soaking and warming kernels of grain we can fool them into thinking they've been planted. Their engines of growth flick on, and enzymes come alive, unpacking the grain's starches and turning them into digestible sugars, maltose and other monosaccharides. In nature, the grain will eat those sugars itself, and use the energy to send out tiny roots called chits and a nubbin of a sprout called an endosperm, reaching for the sun. Unless we cut the process short. After we trick grain into growing, we stop it from doing so by drying it out—killing its sprouts but preserving the sugars. These sugars we can then eat ourselves or feed to yeast.

Malting unlocks grain's potential. Those latent sugars, now set free, can be used for pretty much anything, and an explosion of recipes followed the discovery of the process, most of them for bread. A bilingual tablet from the second millennium—a kind of Akkadian-to-Sumerian food dictionary—lists a staggering two hundred kinds of bread, differentiated by flour type (emmer wheat, barley, spelt), add-ins (dates, nuts), and cooking techniques. Some loaves dried slowly in the sun. Others, more elaborate, were slapped on the walls of an oven to cook tandoori-style. But the basic daily loaf, called *mersu* or *bappir,* was a simple, gritty, granola-bar-like hardtack.

I easily whipped up a batch myself, gleaning ingredients and techniques from a smattering of archaeological reports and a fascinating little book on Mesopotamian cooking by the French Assyriologist Jean Bottero, *The Oldest Cuisine in the World.* Mix a rough dough of malted grain, honey, water, and a dash of spice— pepper, if you're so inclined, or cinnamon. Then bake or dry it out, however you can. I opted for low and slow, leaving a few cakes in my oven overnight, the pilot light a dim stand-in for the Mesopotamian sun.

If the flour is ground fine, mixed wet, and the dough left out in the open for a while, it might catch some wild yeast and begin to leaven, or rise. Otherwise, baked soon after mixing, it comes out looking like a week-old sun-cracked cow pie or an adobe Frisbee. In other words, about as good as it tastes. "Like health food," said a friend of mine, choking down a mouthful of my first batch. And indeed it was: foundational stuff, a nutrient-rich brick, just as tasty and just as durable.

Mesopotamian cooks were clever though—their experiments didn't stop with bappir. Dried and crumbled, the dough thickened soups; rolled thin and stuffed, it became pie crusts. In fact, pretty much everything we ate had bread in it somewhere. Every piece of meat was wrapped in bread; every root, every berry was encrusted in dough. Stag, gazelle, and mutton; onions and leeks; baked in pastry crust or simmered slowly in a bappir-richened stew, then seasoned with heaps of garlic, doused in vinegar, and dusted with mint and other herbs. Dishes were pungent but, on the whole, surprisingly edible-sounding. Take this recipe for pigeon pot pie etched in cramped cuneiform on a 1600 BC tablet: "After removing the pigeon from the pot, I roast the legs at high heat. I wrap them in dough and I place the pigeon filets on the dish. When it is all cooked, I remove the pot from the fire and before the broth cools, rub the meat with garlic, add greens and vinegar." Doesn't sound too bad.

Eating meant bread, literally. The Sumerian verb "to eat" was a cuneiform combination of an open mouth and a chunk of bread. Bread was indeed everything. Even beer.

Back in Egypt, while Floris continued the fly hunt aboveground, Sam plunged below, into the 2400 BC tomb of Ti. There, his lamp illuminated a telling series of hieroglyphs painted on the mausoleum walls. They showed a group of squatting figures sifting, grinding, and mixing grain, soaking bappir loaves in water, and drinking the gruel. Bakers? Brewers? No: both. The processes were linked. Bread was just baked, dehydrated beer. Beer was liquid, fermented bread.

With this window to its origins, and a suitcase full of ingredients—palm fruit, chamomile, Egyptian wheat to bake into bappir and add to the brew, and Floris's precious spore, which Katrinka would culture into a healthy, full-size colony of cells—Sam returned to Delaware to re-create the beer. He called it Ta Henket, Egyptian for "bread beer."

Before I tasted his version, though, I would try to make it

myself. Luckily, I found a more descriptive recipe than those hiero-glyphs. Unluckily, it was a poem. The "Hymn to Ninkasi" is a 3,800-year-old ode to the goddess of beer. It rambles through the requisite honorifics, praise, and family history. Beautiful Ninkasi was born "by the flowing water" to this king or that. Then, down to business. While "the noble dogs keep away the potentates," the poem reads, Ninkasi sprouts grain, dries it, grinds it, mixes it into dough, and bakes it into loaves of bappir. (Done that, I thought, still picking stray husks from my teeth.) These, she blends up "in a pit" with honey and "sweet aromatics."

At first glance, it makes sense. Whip up a batch of bappir, crumble it into boiling water, spice to your liking, and let the gods—wild yeast and a thirsty fly—take care of the rest. But once I started brewing, things got a bit more complicated. It's one thing to sing about beer, it's another to actually make it. What kind of dates? What kind of honey? What were those "sweet aromatics" anyway?

I thought of the old German saying *"Wer die Wahl hat, hat die Qual"*—with choice comes torment. Sam could chase a fly to the Egyptian desert, hunt palm fruit in a Cairo medina. With his resources, he could brew anything. My options were slightly more limited, making my recipe simpler, if not, perhaps, as historically pure. I got some zahidi dates from the toothless date vendor at the farmers' market and some bulk orange-blossom honey from the local grocery store. For my spices, coriander and black pepper seemed accurate, and potable, enough. I opted against mint and vinegar—a bit too close to salad dressing, I thought, in an ironic premonition, it turned out. Obviously, I wouldn't be brewing in a pit or even a clay urn, or using whatever long-lost strain of wheat Ninkasi had, so I rationalized that I could cut other corners. I'd get as close as I could to the real thing; Ninkasi would have to smile on the effort.

And she did. I baked and steeped and stirred. As the wort came to a boil in a soup pot on my stove, I sprinkled in my spices and some chopped-up dates. Then I poured the slop—chunks of soggy grain cakes, swollen waterlogged fruit, and all—into a big glass jug. Home brewers call it a carboy, and they're usually tightly stoppered with an airlock to keep fermentations sealed and sanitary. I used a piece of hose called a blow-off tube, wide enough to let any wayward date pieces bubble up and out of the jug without clogging it, but not as secure as a specially made lock would be. I didn't want an explosion or, as the poem reads, a river of beer "like the onrush of the Tigris and Euphrates." I set the jug in a safe corner and left for a well-deserved postbrewing brew, imagining dates stuck to my ceiling when I got back. But instead I came home to a welcome sight—foam. The carboy bubbled with froth, the blow-off tube pleasantly gurgled burps of carbon dioxide. Not a rushing river but active enough, I thought, that if I didn't know any better I'd think spirits were happily at work.

Things seemed to have gone off hitch-free. I had brought an ancient beer back from the grave. I had reanimated an untombed corpse. But what would my Frankenstein monster say when it spoke? I had channeled the brewer, but Ninkasi's story wasn't over. Its climax—whether tragic or triumphant—would come in the drinking. I'd brewed with a ghost. Now it was time to share a pint with her.

Well, it tasted fine. There's a reason we don't make beer like this anymore, but Ninkasi's brew was at least drinkable. A little sweet, a little thin, a little tangy but, judging by how liberally Mesopotamians sprinkled vinegar on their dishes, they could handle a sour kick. The dates gave the booze a deep, molasses-like sugariness; the honey just a touch of light florals. If I really concentrated I could even taste some orange blossom. I didn't bottle it, stealing my sips by dipping a turkey baster into the jug, so it wasn't carbonated. And I drank it room temperature, as they must have in the balmy desert. Still, for a time it was, more or less, beer. And then, quickly, it wasn't.

Ninkasi's dogs turned on me. I hadn't sanitized anything—no OxiClean in Babylonia. Boiling my wort would be enough of a deterrent to serious infection, I thought, and, anyway, the glass and food-grade plastic equipment I was using was much cleaner than a pit or a porous clay pot. One of beer's benefits in prehistory was being relatively safe to drink, thanks to the purifying effects of the cooking process and alcohol's natural preservative qualities. Still, without sealed and pasteurized bottles and refrigerated storage, beer—well, anything—left out in the desert sun has a short shelf life. If my beer got a little funky, I thought, I'd chalk it up to the taste of history. Instead, it got really funky. This wasn't the rich, balsamic smoothness of Flemish reds or the refreshing pucker of lambics, beers made sour on purpose, but something closer to salad dressing. Downright acrid, saccharine sweet and sour like cheap Chinese food with a side of vinegar.

I couldn't blame myself—I had followed the recipe as best I could. And I didn't want to curse the gods. This wasn't Ninkasi's fault. Instead, I blame the fly. What likely happened was that some wild bacteria less friendly than the *Saccharomyces* I was used to had landed in the sweet but unsanitary brew. The boiling had killed any bacteria latent in my dates and bappir loaves but, once cool, the wort was vulnerable again. What's more, I had fermented my bread beer not with a cultivated, professional-grade strain of

Saccharomyces but instead with an envelope of trusty Fleischmann's baker's yeast. The organisms are more or less the same, though bread yeast is designed to work best with the sugars in wheat flour—not dates, honey, or cracked malted barley—and to ferment quickly and vigorously, lifting dough into airy loaves. Brewing yeast is used to more complicated sugars, and is raised more for its flavors and alcohol-producing ability than for its other by-product carbon dioxide. I figured, though, that bread yeast's rougher, workaday characteristics would be closer to what the pharaoh's servant knew than today's modern strains. Problem was, that humbler yeast must have pooped out before finishing its job, leaving some sugars unfermented, awaiting new scavengers, such as acid-producing lactobacillus and acetobacter.

No one would want to drink this, not even a vinegar-loving Babylonian. Our taste buds haven't changed much since then— sour beer is sour beer. I thought I understood Babylonian brewing, but maybe I needed to change how I thought of Babylonian drinking. If this was humble daily bread, it should be enjoyed like it. A fresh baguette left out for a couple days will get stale; why shouldn't it be the same with beer? This was a brew at its prime when fresh. In fact, it probably tasted best while it was still actively fermenting in the jug—a kind of proto beer, low-carbonated, low-alcohol, and full of live, active yeast for a bit of fruity flavor and a healthy boost of vitamins B_6 and B_{12}. I could picture each Babylonian home with a gurgling jug in the corner, like the ever simmering stew pot in an Italian farmhouse, the barrel of kraut in a Russian root cellar, or the steaming Mr. Coffee slowly tarring into sludge on the counter. A good wife, a Sumerian saying went, was a good brewer: "The house where beer is never lacking, she is there!"

Beer might have been born and raised at home but its story, of course, doesn't end there. And neither does ours. As settlements grew into towns, and towns into cities, beer making grew with it. Rare foods stayed rare: wine and mead will occur naturally, fermenting seemingly out of thin air like the juice from that plump, sugar-packed date. But that made those drinks—at least before the Greeks and Romans figured out large-scale viticulture—pearls, not produce, randomly occurring treats impossible to capture or control. One of the beauties of brewing, though, is how easily it scales. Once you have the infrastructure in place for malting, baking, and boiling, making more beer is just a matter of building a bigger brew pot. It's a magical art, but it can also be a business.

As the first cities bloomed, especially in Egypt, brewing became an industrial-scale operation built for the thirsty masses. In the second millennium, the city of Nuzi on the Tigris, in modern-day northern Iraq, had a centralized bakery that delivered thousands of loaves a day—records include an epic one-day 5,600-loaf rush. Meanwhile on the Nile, the Sun Temple of Nefertiti included a factory-sized brewery-slash-bakery within its walls and the Hierakonpolis brewery churned out a daily torrent of 300 gallons of beer. Government-issue beer was doled out like workhouse porridge to laborers: Assyrian temple workers got about four pints a day; Giza's pyramid builders were allowed ten. But the river of *hqt* or *heqa* pouring out of Hierakonpolis was the lowest-quality swill, the bulk-made Wonder Bread of its day. Low-alcohol, high-carb plebeian fuel.

As brewing scaled up, though, it diversified and specialized. While large-scale factories like those at Hierakonpolis took care of the masses, smaller taverns catered to more discerning clientele. These *bît sabîti,* as they were called in Babylonia, were run by housewives with home brew to spare. Boozy hangouts for the leisure class, they were vilified by the early kings Samsi-Addu and Hammurabi as dens of sex, crime, and rebellious plotting. But the beer was good. A series of laws to ensure the government's monopoly on cheaper, low-end brews saw to that. The Hammurabi codes—the world's first written laws—fixed prices on what taverns served. Undercut the government to draw a crowd, read code 108, and you'll "be prosecuted, and thrown into the water."

Temple laborers couldn't pick and choose their gruel but taverns provided options. They served multiple kinds of beer, low end to high. Records and recipes list beers "of nice appearance," "of good quality," and "of superior quality." White beer, red beer, or black beer, depending on the grains used, or sweet beer, very sweet beer, and even "beer to lessen the waist" (the first light beer?), according to how much it was diluted with water when served. As cities started trading with one another, imported foreign ingredients spurred an appetite for the exotic, and Ninkasi's "sweet aromatics" diversified. The rarer the spice—saffron, say, plucked stigma by stigma from the fragile crocus blossom—the more special the beer. Flavorings grew from pepper and radish to include basil and thyme, spicy cubeb berries, bitter hallucinogenic mandrake root, and the sweet resinous sap from the acacia tree. When the pharaoh Scorpion I was buried around 3150 BC, his tomb was stocked with jugs of sorghum beer flavored with grapes, savory, thyme, and coriander, and its stone walls were etched with a prayer for "beer that never turns sour."

"We assume early humans had essentially the same sensory organs we do," Dr. Pat told me when I asked him if my acrid brew would have passed the test in ancient Babylon—or gotten me tossed in the Tigris. Some might have drunk it, he said, but only by necessity. No one wanted sour beer but not everyone could afford the good stuff. "In societies with more hierarchy, more specialization," Dr. Pat went on, "you get finer beverages with finer ingredients. If honey is rare, if grapes are rare, the only people who have access to them are the upper class."*

That hierarchy was even more pronounced when it came to food. "The delights of the table," Bottero states in his Mesopotamian cookbook, "were less accessible, more refined, and, moreover, in their highest and most succulent state, not for the common man." The fanciest ingredients—from exotic spices to milk-fatted calves and rare birds—were reserved for the rulers or sacrificed as burnt offerings to the gods. One temple records a daily offering of "seven choice sheep, fattened and without flaw" ceremonially burned in what Bottero calls a "negative gesture" to deprive penitent worshippers the pleasure of a good meal. Beer too came in degrees of quality, from watery Lite to pharaoh-grade grape-and-coriander. But while the gods and kings got most of the good stuff, their servants could at least sneak a taste. Offerings of beer were communal, "poured and received." Along with the sheep, that same temple was stocked daily with 170 gallons of beer, offered to the gods, then enjoyed by the faithful. Unlike food, beer was, at its core, for all, and it brought the same pleasure to gods, kings, and commoners alike.

The very nature of these ancient beers demanded mutual enjoyment. For one thing, they were all unfiltered. Like mine, they

---

* Prowling the Khan el-Khalili spice market, Sam and Ramy gawked and tasted—dried lizards, deer horn, doum palm fruit. Also called gingerbread palm, doum palm's woody globules look like oversized dates and are, Sam attests, "explosively sweet." When Sam eventually decided to use it he discovered importing the fruit was a bank-breaking legal mess. The dried lizards, he joked, would have been easier.

brimmed with date pieces, barley husks, bits of grain, and who knows what else—a wayward fly or two. The ancient Greeks would later joke that Babylonian drinkers strained out that detritus through their bushy beards and mustaches. In fact, they used straws made from hollow marsh reeds or, for the kings, rolled from hammered gold or bronze and fitted with a filtering end piece through which they'd drink beer straight from the fermenter, like me with my turkey baster. Huddled around a jug, Babylonian drinkers would all dip in a straw. As at an office water cooler, drinking was communal. And nowhere was that more apparent than at a feast.

When the Assyrian king Ashurnasirpal II held a ten-day feast to celebrate the renovation of his capital city Kalhu, he served the seventy thousand guests a thousand barley-fed oxen, fourteen thousand sheep ("from the flocks belonging to Istar my mistress," the menu read), a thousand lambs, five hundred deer, and ten thousand jugs of beer. "At a feast, like the funeral for King Midas, everyone would be given a little taste" of special, regal-quality beer, said Dr. Pat. "Shared feasts led to social interaction." Midas's tomb in central Turkey was "maintained," in one historian's words, with 157 beer-filled bronze urns. Dr. Pat salvaged the residue caking one of them and, with Sam's help, re-created the brew as Dogfish Head's Midas Touch—letting modern drinkers share in the revelry. If making beer made us human, drinking it made us an "us." Sharing these brews linked the masses with kings and gods; offering them at funereal celebrations joined past and present, the living and the dead.

So it was that on a windswept Atlantic seaboard night I found myself at the Dogfish Head Ancient Ales dinner in Rehoboth Beach.

This humble boardwalk bar was where Dogfish Head got its start in the early 1990s. In its tiny kitchen, on a twelve-gallon home-brewing setup pieced together from old kegs and a turkey frier, Sam would whip up test batches, swiping ingredients and inspiration from the pantry to make experimental brews like a chicory-infused stout or raisin-and-brown-sugar abbey ale and share them with whomever happened to be on the other side of the bar. Dogfish Head started as a neighborhood pub, and that focus on personal connection remains a key part of its ethos. The brewery prints its phone number on every six-pack, and Sam jokes that he's often greeted at the office on Monday morning by a blinking voice-mail box stuffed with drunk dials from adoring if overindulgent fans.

The bar that evening was warm and crowded, relaxed but charged with the kind of sun-dazed vibes that energize all beachside bars, even in the off season. I was, though, a little apprehensive. My Babylonian beer wasn't as compelling a link to the past as I hoped it would be. The brewer I conjured, I imagined, sniffed my middling wares and wandered to the next *bît sabîti*. My own tale too was a little muddled, this book still embryonic in my mind. Offering it to Sam felt like placing a jug of my beer before Ninkasi herself. Go easy on me, I thought. I'm just a humble brewer trying to tell a story.

With my girlfriend close behind for moral support, I squeezed through the bar to a small, wood-paneled dining room upstairs and approached the hostess. This feast wasn't a funereal free-for-all. It had a guest list, and ours were just two names in a select group of devoted fans lined up for a taste of royalty. Or so we thought. Then we were shown to a table up front and introduced to Sam's wife, Mariah. Sam would be over in a minute, she said. We wouldn't be simply tasting his beer; we were eating with the king.

Sam sauntered over, wearing faded khakis and a shawl neck sweater stretched tight over his former footballer's chest. We shook hands. "Let's drink," he grinned, eyeing the glasses and easing my nerves. "What are these?" Dogfish Head makes dozens of regularly available beers, in addition to a dizzying torrent of one-off experimental releases. But Sam's puzzlement was unexpected. He was the boss, after all. How could he not know his own work? He held the glasses up to the dim, dinnertime mood lighting, judged their colors—all shades of sun-baked gold—and took a few tentative sips of each. There was Midas Touch, made with saffron and honey. Birra Etrusca, an ancient Etruscan brew Sam, Pat, and a pair of Italian craft brewers based on ingredients collected near a 2,800-year-old tomb, featured myrrh and hazelnut flour. Theobroma was an Aztec-style beer made with chocolate; Chateau Jiahu, Chinese, with rice and hawthorn berries; and Sah'Tea, from Scandinavia by way of Japan, steeped with juniper and tea leaves. Sam was looking for Ta Henket, the Egyptian beer that Floris's single spore of captured date-fly yeast eventually became. This one, he said. No, wait, this one. We laughed, we drank, and I settled in even more. And then we started talking about Ho-Hos.

Hostess had just gone bankrupt—the news was all Twinkie stockpiles and runs on Little Debbies. We joked about our favorites. Sam wouldn't dare cop to swigging a Bud Light after a day's work brewing lobster-chocolate beer but, hey, even the king of craft enjoys a shrinkwrapped brownie now and then. As the chef explained the menu—not bappir but a fluffy sweet semolina cake called basbousa and topped with whipped cream; not dough-caked pigeon but honey-rubbed caprid, a goat-antelope hybrid shot on a private Texas wild-game ranch—Sam commented that tasty food can come in humble packages. Even cellophane, sometimes. In between mass-made junk and high-class indulgence, true luxury is artisan made. "We pay more for a taste of home," Sam said. "Wood-hearth-baked bread. Good coffee. People are realizing, 'I can buy the big SUV or I can get some great cheese.' We're getting our priorities back."

Handmade goods, warts and all, give us a taste of home—a taste, more specifically, of the kitchen. While an airy slice of Wonder Bread is as bland as the factory system that churned it out, a crusty loaf or, for that matter, a crusty tip of goat rib, says in its complexity—even in its mistakes, in its char marks, or slightly underdone center—something about the hand that made it. "It's good to have context," Sam says. Good food tells a story of its creation, the process leaving some residual mark, a patina of taste.

We finally figured out which stemmed wineglass held Ta Henket. It was, surprisingly, the most bland of the bunch. Its context, the story of its creation, was rich—Egypt! fly hunts!—but it tasted simple. Birra Etrusca was earthy and tannic, with a bite that reminded me of birch beer. Chateau Jiahu was juicy with sweet grapes and cherries. Ta Henket, though, tasted like bread. Bread and, perhaps, a little salt. I was, for a minute, confused. And so were customers when Dogfish Head later packaged and released the beer. It tasted no more profound than a piece of toast, but it was priced and packaged like cake, in a big, corked champagne-style bottle, with a label finely printed on heavy card stock. The beer was a flop. "Yeah, we fell on the sword of authenticity with that one," Sam said.

By that, Sam meant that though the packaging might have been a symbolic miss, the beer worked. It wasn't cake but it was more than just toast. It was peasant bread, hearth-baked and chewy. It wasn't simple, it was artisanal. Its story now made more sense. Bread beer—the name, at least, was accurate. It was peasant fuel, a quick source of calories for the masses of thirsty workers who built the pyramids. And it tasted like the gruel it was. But drinkers used to the big, bold flavors of today's expensive craft beer expected something more exciting. It told a story, not one stuffed with processed vanilla cream, but not one topped with hop *gastrique* either. Drinkers wanted strength; they got subtlety. They expected a chocolate lobster; they got a bread basket.

After dinner, I took a detour down to the ocean. The foam in the moonlight fluffed into phosphorescent pillows, the dark blanket of sea rippled on, it seemed, forever. Looking out at the infinite nothingness, I thought about dinner and about the journey ahead. Beer's dual nature is bread and beverage; the brewer's is part maker, part storyteller. Each flavor carries a context, like that date fly carries the spore of a story. It's my job to catch those flies and let their cargo ferment. Midas Touch's saffron speaks of the purple robes of the powerful king; Jiahu's sweetness evokes what Sam called the "booze-fueled hootenanny" that accompanied its drinking. (The residue on which that beer was based caked urns found buried with the world's first musical instrument, a bird-bone flute.) The tastes traced back to a brewer, even if he or she was sometimes hard to see.

I met Sam again at the brewery the next morning, my head a little woolly from the deep quaffs and deeper thoughts the night before. His seemed so too. He had forgotten his keys and had to buzz the intercom. "It's me," he said. "Sam."

We walked in, flicking on the lights as we went, and Sam showed off the brewery's new lab, giddy over the million dollars' worth of gleaming tubes and wiring. But he's even more excited about the small-scale system they're installing. "I don't even know how to brew on the big system," he admits. "The biggest I can brew on is the five-barrel system [about 160 gallons]. And now, at the brewpub, we're building one even smaller, downgrading to two barrels. It's more like an ancient setup." A kettle over a flame, simple fermentation tanks without fancy pressure controls and glycol cooling jackets. Not a factory but a home kitchen.

Even the full-size system, though, is hands-on. When I visited that day, Dogfish was brewing Midas Touch, and I chatted with the workers as they hefted bucket after sticky bucket of wildflower honey into the kettle. "We hook the handle onto the boiler door and let it drip out," one of the safety-glassed and rubber-booted staffers told me with a sigh. He loves to drink it but, he admits, "it's my least favorite beer of ours to brew. It's the hardest one." The taste of honey in the finished brew tells not only a story of wealthy King Midas who could afford the pricey golden sweetener, but also a story of the human effort it takes to brew with it. Dogfish Head's unexpected flavors aren't just gimmicks—they give the beers context.

Flavors tell a story of process, a process dictated by ingredients. Take the myrrh in Birra Etrusca. Sam knew he wanted to use it but didn't know how. Myrrh comes in little rock-hard resin clumps—as impossible to brew with as unmalted grain, packed with flavor but locked up tight. Sam bought a bag of the stuff at an Ethiopian grocery store and, for days, he and his brewers attacked it with every trick they knew: dissolving the lumps in alcohol, cooking them, pulverizing them. The answer was a combination of all three. Effortful but effective. On a tour of the sensory lab, Dogfish Head's QC manager got me a couple of the lumps to taste. I warmed up the crystals in my hands, breaking them apart for a faint whiff of licorice, spearmint, and bergamot. Nothing's off-limits, Sam said. You build a process around what you want to make. And that makes it authentic, no matter the packaging. When drinkers taste those flavors, they taste the story, whether in a laboratory or a private dining room or, say, a strip mall pizza joint like the one Sam and I retired to after our brewery tour. They knew Sam here. Everyone seemed to know Sam. We ordered burgers, fries, pizza, and the waitress even threw in an off-menu cheese dip. The "cheese" was spelled with a Z. A round of 60 Minute IPAs washed it down. No stemware here, of course. The glasses flashed the Bud Light logo. Like hearth bread wrapped in cellophane, it's not the package, it's the taste.

And it tasted great. It tasted like the hop dust billowing out of the boil kettle; it tasted like the process. Why chase a fly to Egypt, why add hops for an hour, why pay for genuine myrrh when a chemical imitation would do as well? Out of respect for the past. If that's how the pharaoh's servant brewed, that's how Sam would too. I felt better about my failed brew, a failure I now knew I surely shared with those brewers of old. Making beer by hand, the old way, was hard work. But the work was noble. "The challenge makes it real," Sam said. In big bottle or small, in stemware or Bud Light pint, the ocean of history roared. Faintly, maybe, but listen close. The brewer is talking.

2

THE SHAMAN

Brian Hunt and I sat under a redwood tree in his rutted, gravel driveway. We were in rural Sonoma County, California, somewhere around Santa Rosa. Where, precisely? Neither I nor my dashboard Garmin was sure. Among the towering trees and gnarled, rolling vineyard hills, cell signals fizzled, GPS was useless. I was lost.

I had come here to find a recluse. Brian runs Moonlight Brewing Company, and his beers, though available only in the Bay Area, are cult favorites for those in the know. His black lager Death and Taxes is a craft-beer-bar staple around these parts. Brian says he specifically engineered its iced coffee–like roasty kick to pair with carne asada tacos. It's the coal-hued yin to the bright, citrusy yang of other local standards, hop bombs such as Lagunitas IPA from nearby Petaluma. Death and Taxes is, as the name implies, a reliable classic. But I had heard that, if you can find it, Brian's hidden forest brewery traffics in more curious wares. Some call him a curmudgeonly loner, others a shaman. Either way, Brian doesn't reveal his tricks easily. He can be gruff on the phone; e-mails are curt. His first to me, when I asked for an interview, began "I am difficult to pin down." "E-mails are unreliable," he wrote. "Chaos here now." I could come if I wanted and if I could find the place. No promises.

To visit the shaman I had to make a pilgrimage. I drove north on Highway 101, pulled off around the manicured Kendall-Jackson winery château, and jogged west on a furrow-straight, farm-country lane, past billboards advertising local vineyards' gold medal pinots and tasting-room hours. I turned onto a signless dirt road, then another, even dirtier road (was it a road or a driveway?), bouncing between pine trees and hop trellises, and parked next to a dusty Dodge Sprinter van and even dustier pickup truck. I glanced at the license plates: HALFBBL and CRZYLUN. I met Brian in the brewery, squeezing around a pile of empty kegs into an airless barn stuffed with buckets and kettles and hoses, all seemingly half operational or half broken, depending on one's perspective. On the wall, a stained scrap of paper read "beer is not an industrialized product." As if, here, under the trees, where Brian and I now slouched in weathered Adirondack chairs among a pile of open bottles, there were any other choice.

Brian slumped deeper in his chair. He seemed to get more feral from the top down, his neat, close-cropped white hair giving way to a scraggly beard that drained over his neck into the frayed collar of his T-shirt. Below that, washed-out jeans, out of which poked a pair of bare, hairy, Hobbit-like feet, as if he were growing roots. Brian toed aside an open can of gasoline, saying its fumes were interfering with our beer tasting, and opened a new bottle. Number five? Number six? Our drinks, too, had gone off the grid. What they were, exactly, was hard to figure. One beer tasted like Coca-Cola, another like Twizzlers. One like peach fuzz, musty and sweet; another minty, cedar-like and cool.

"Taste this," he said. The beer opened bready and dark with a hint of hazelnuts, like a slice of rich, country toast. And then something odd. Licorice? A touch of grated orange peel? A sprinkle of sage? "Nope," Brian said, a glint in his eye, and plucked a branch from overhead. "Now, nibble on that."

I'd munched raw brewing grain, crushed open hop cones to smell the fresh resin, slurped bubbling beer straight from the fermenter. But in all my brewery tours—in all my life—I had never eaten a tree. Brian seemed disappointed at this, as if I had confessed to never listening to *Sgt. Pepper* all the way through. With a frown, he patiently walked me through the process. "Back where it's barky, you get tannins, like when you leave a tea bag steeping for too long. The palest growth, the tips, are very citrusy. Crunch them with your teeth so you crack them open," he told me. "When the weather is cooler, the twigs come up light green. Fluorescent, almost. This year, 'cause the weather was so different, I couldn't get as much of that as I wanted. I got more of the dark green, piney flavors. It tastes like a Christmas tree, or even a little licoricey, like an adult Dr. Pepper." He smiled—the first time today. "I don't think they use redwood, though." This, then, was the secret to that beguiling beer. Brian calls it Working for Tips, and he brews it with these very branches. Picking bark from my teeth I felt brave enough to gently wonder at his methods. Where'd he get such a crazy idea? From whence this deep-rooted understanding, this friendliness with flora? I asked. "Just by chewing," he said with a shrug. "You can't find an iPhone app to tell you when to pick the twigs. You gotta chew the tree."

Brian likes tasting Working for Tips with self-described hop heads, IPA-mad craft-beer geeks who might pass by Brian's two-bit setup without even noticing it on their pilgrimages to Russian

River, a brewpub down the road in Santa Rosa. Russian River is best known for its outrageously hoppy double IPA Pliny the Elder, and its even hoppier, limited-edition sibling Pliny the Younger. The Plinys are classics, Younger often cited as the best American IPA, if not the best American beer, if not the best beer, period. It's available for only a short time, and only on tap at the brewery itself. If Brian's beers are cult hits, Russian River's are secret obsessions of which fans whisper with Skull and Bones–like reverence. Release-day lines clog traffic downtown. Devotees have been caught filling water bottles with the precious nectar to take home as a trophy or, worse, to resell on eBay. Uber-citrusy, packed with acidic strains of hops like Cascades and Simcoes, Younger tastes, to me, like a bitter Orange Crush. Faced with a beer that tastes, instead, like tree branches, the nerds scratch their heads and try to guess what secret variety of hops Brian is using. "Their mind goes, 'oh, it's not Cascade. Is it Galaxy?'" Brian laughs. "'Is it that new one, code-name R-12-37?'"

Tricking nerds is one thing, but sharing his beer with the uninitiated is even more fun, those lucky souls who think they know what beer *is* but don't yet know what it *can* be. "So much of what people describe in beer is what they're thinking they're supposed to say, one of the hundred and thirty-three 'approved beer words,'" Brian said. No, there aren't *actually* one hundred thirty-three official sensory terms, but flavor wheels and beer descriptions do tend to lean heavily on a select few: pine, citrus, spice, coffee, dark fruit. "But we all have different memories of flavor. I remember one woman said about Tips, 'Wow, this reminds me of being in Vermont eating a maple candy lollipop,'" he went on. "She's tasting the tree sap. How perfect is that? And tree sap, that's not one of the hundred and thirty-three approved words. But even a person who tries it and goes, 'oh God,

no!' I put a crack in them. I broke something, like breaking a bronco."
He points a hairy toe at the unlabeled bottles strewn about the
driveway. "I showed them that this is possible."

Brian is a barefoot, Pan-like trickster, and his beers are magic.
They exist in this world but gesture beyond it. Rooted in one place,
they transport the drinker to another: out to the Sierras, back to
memories of family trips to New England, up into the treetops in
Brian's yard. Brian is a shaman and this is his medicine. Beers of
transformation.

On that bright dusty afternoon, Working for Tips sent me
deep into northern pine forests. As I sipped, the wine-country sun
flickered off behind the boughs above, the air cooled and deadened, the world muffled in mist. Brian's yard was already off the
grid; now, I was completely off the map. Here, there be monsters.
A beer that tastes like trees? This isn't beer . . . is it?

Today's hop heads are yesteryear's Greek and Roman wine
snobs, obsessed with catalogs and categories. Now, the world of
drinks is parsed into IPAs and double IPAs, International Bittering Units and alpha acid percentages. Back then it was divided
into wine—and everything else. The Greeks listed and described
more than fifty kinds of wine, based on both their tastes and their
uses (or purported effects). The one-eyed Athenian playwright
Hermippus wrote that Saprian wine smells like violets and roses.
Wine from Arcadia was supposed to help induce pregnancy,
Zante wine to be especially potent. Exotic foreign wines from
Crete, Ionia, and Rhodes were prized, mixed with water (seawater
added smoothness, the Greeks believed) and savored slowly. In *De
Agri Cultura* the Roman writer Cato intersperses recipes for pick-
les and cakes with tips on everything from appropriate vineyard
size (ninety *iugera*, or about sixty acres) to food and clothing

allowances for winery slaves (not very much). Cato's protégé Columella updated his master's text with rough genetic information,
mapping some twenty different vine species. As their empire
expanded, so did the Romans' knowledge of grapes: which kinds
grew best where, what flavors came from what soil and weather.
Thracean whites were poor. Phanean reds from the island of Chios
were delicious; Virgil called it the king of wine. The Romans
understood *terroir*. Different land made different grapes, and different grapes made different wine.

Then there was beer. On the fringes of their empire, Roman
legions bumped up against a new kind of drink, one that didn't fit
into Cato's nor Columella's taxonomy. By the dawn of the Common Era the factory-scale breweries of Egypt and Babylon had disappeared into the sands. But the brewers themselves didn't vanish;
they dispersed to Europe's borderlands, the eastern mountains
and steppes and the northern bogs and forests, where Romans
rediscovered them on the edges of their known world.

In Rome, wine was God given, of the earth. So were its effects.
Romans grouped wine with opium, mandrake, and other naturally
narcotic plants: potent but wholesome. Beer was different. Perhaps
because beer ferments more vigorously than wine, throwing off a
startling, foamy head later brewers would dub a *krausen,* or perhaps because of the malting process needed to prepare grains for
brewing, Romans considered it manufactured and thus inferior. It
had to be engineered, it required a process. It didn't just spring
forth, ready-made. Romans said the grains were "rotted" or
deformed and called the drink "that which is brewed"—in other
words, a product. Unlike wine, beer was not of the natural plane.
It wasn't a gift of the gods; the hand of man gave it a sullying stamp.
Entire books have been written about how the tension between

raw and cooked, nature and culture ripples through our modern lives everywhere from lawns to literature (Michael Pollan's *Second Nature*, Leo Marx's *The Machine in the Garden*). Beer is a perfect embodiment. Where does magic end and art begin? Is the brewer bound by nature, or in control? Writing in *Lapham's Quarterly's* Nature issue, the poet and critic Frederick Turner draws a line from the artifice of genetic engineering back to, yes, humankind's first tinkerings with brewing yeast. When we shape the world, we play God, and so move further from the naturally divine. And yet, Turner says, quoting Shakespeare, "This is an art / Which does mend Nature, change it rather; but / The art itself is Nature." Which is to say, it's complicated.

Roman critics had a point though. Wine just . . . happens. Making it can be as easy as letting fruit juice sit out too long. Beer brewers had to put in more effort, especially in places where grapes, for instance, and their easy-to-access sugars were scarce. In chillier climes, far from the Mediterranean, people used what they could find. In the seventh century BC nomads from the eastern steppes settling Europe on felt-padded horseback got their kicks where they could, scavenging what wild grass and fruit they found along their way, adding honey, even horse milk, and fermenting the gruel in their saddlebags as they rode. This was a drink born on the road. Beer was an orgy of grains, fruits, honey, and herbs. "Can it be then that the Celts because of a lack of grapes made you from cereal?" Julian wrote in a satire of the barbaric drink.* In Virgil's *Georgics*, his ode to agriculture, the nomadic

---

* Not knowing quite where to put beer in their map of the universe, many thought it was just a poor man's imitation of wine. As Emerson wrote, "We are always at the mercy of a better classifier than ourselves."

Eurasian Scythian tribes "copy vine drinks with wheat and sour rowanberries." Farther eastern tribes in what was once Babylonia, taking cues from their Sumerian ancestors, used dates. In the *Deipnosophists*, a third-century account of Greek life—fifteen volumes pretty much entirely devoted to describing lavish dinner parties—the Greek wit and critic Athenaeus contrasted his own civilized ways with savage tribes who drink, he wrote, "a beer made of wheat prepared with honey, and oftener still without any honey."

Where nomadic tribes crisscrossing northern Europe stopped, the grains they carried, stuffed in a rawhide pouch or tangled in a horse's mane, took root. Germanic tribes were cultivating wheat and barley by 5000 BC and Celtic bands on the British Isles soon after. It wasn't long before the first breweries emerged. The earliest found to date is at a 3000 BC village in Skara Brae, in the Orkney Islands off the north coast of Scotland. Others anchor equally inhospitable corners: Balfarg, Ashgrove, Machrie Moor, and as far afield as Kinloch on the Isle of Rum.* These weren't Egyptian megafactories; these were outposts. Brewing might have been a settled, structured operation now that the nomadic age had passed but it was still rough. Malting grain and drying, or kilning it, to preserve the kernels through the winter was an especially rustic procedure. Often, grain was simply piled into trenches and covered in hot ash to roast and pop in the smoke. But those kilns are rare—we have evidence of only a few, around Hochdorf in northern Germany.

---

* Stranded on the wind-racked Scottish border in fortresses at Bearsden and Vindolanda, Augustan legions, wine snobs or not, warmed their toes with ale. "When in Scotland," the saying might have gone. The first brewer in British history we know by name, in fact, was a Roman: Arrectus.

Northern Europe's rugged climate and landscape just didn't support enough grain for that kind of infrastructure to make sense. Plus, these Germanic and Anglo-Saxon tribes were far less centrally organized than the massive Babylonian city-states that irrigated the desert. Better here to build a fortress than a bakery.

Brewers augmented what little grain they could grow with the same gleanings as their nomadic ancestors: tree sap, honey, cherries, cloudberries, lingonberries, and, when they were lucky enough to get it, even a nip of Roman wine.* Beers were mixed bags, down to the language used to describe them.

Tracing the etymology of modern brewing terms back into the Neolithic plunged me quickly into a tangled thicket of cognates, derivations, and plain old guesswork. *Beer* links all the way back to the Latin *bibere*, "to drink," but also, perhaps, to words for barley, or even bee. In Ancient Greek, *methe* means mead but also, simply, strong; Indo-Aryan *madhu* can mean honey, mead, or just "sweet drink." The Norse wrote of drinking *medu, ealu, win,* and *beor*—mead, ale, wine, and beer. Maybe. Or maybe not. Old English *beor* (and Old Norse *björr*) could, in some cases, refer to any sweet, alcoholic beverage. The word might share a root with barley, or it might have originally meant something entirely different—cider or, some linguists think, even a kind of freeze-distilled liquor.

---

* Indeed, they weren't all unwashed rubes. Even barbarians appreciated the finer things. Rome escaped a Goth siege in 408 by tempting the barbarian King Alaric with 5,000 pounds of gold, 30,000 pounds of silver, and 3,000 pounds of fancy black pepper. Alaric and his noble kin drank wine. It was rare, and priced accordingly. In Gaul, cheap rotgut cost eight dinarii, while beer went for four or even two. A slave for a jug of wine was a standard trade. Romans mixed theirs with water, but the Goths took it straight, a show-offy gesture of virility and wealth.

To make matters worse, the language surrounding Neolithic European drinking is preserved mainly as poetry—no handy bilingual food dictionaries or agricultural textbooks here—and artistic license blurs linguistic lines even more. Poets seemed to use the gamut of alcoholic terminology interchangeably, based on the requirements of meter and rhyme. In *Beowulf*, for instance, King Hrothgar's stronghold Heorot is, at different times, a wine hall, a mead hall, and a beer hall. One single verse of the tenth-century Anglo-Saxon poem *The Fortunes of Men* uses all three: *"Sumum meces ecg on meodubence / yrrum ealowosan ealdor obþringeð, / were winsadum; bið ær his worda to hræd"* (One the sword shall slay / as he sits in the mead hall / Angry with ale; it shall end his life, / Wine-sated warrior: his words were too reckless).

Cato would never play this fast and loose with terminology. But then again the Norse were more interested in drinking than in defining. "Almost all the compounds of [the word for] mead are emotive," the historian Ann Hagen put it in her compendium of Anglo-Saxon cuisine. The words *medu, meodu,* and *ealu* don't necessarily refer to specific drinks but were used instead to conjure a mood, "the revelry associated with drinking." Mead—or *ealu* or *win* or *beor*—wasn't simply a beverage, it was more of an idea. Like Brian's beer, what mattered was not what it *was* exactly but how it tasted, and what it did.

Nordic beer parties weren't the good-natured, wine-fueled symposia of the Romans. Hieronymus of Rhodes said that "to do the Scythian" was to get flat-out wasted: those horsemen, he said, drank by "pouring [beer] over their clothes." The Latin poet and early Catholic bishop Venantius Fortunatus crashed a similarly raucous sixth-century German drinking bout. The drinkers, he said, "were carrying on like mad men, each competing in drinking to the other's health. A man had to consider himself lucky to come away with his life." Writing in the eighteenth century, the Swedish botanist Carl Linnaeus reported on a traditional Scandinavian wedding that served a beer infused with fennel-like yarrow flowers so strong it "makes one lose one's balance." Drinking all night, he wrote, "the guests became crazy."

To get a better sense of these feasts, I sifted through the morning-after leftovers: charred cannabis seeds in the stone fire rings left under Scythian sweat lodges, giant goblets and drinking vats in Nordic bog tombs, poetic references to forgotten hallucinogens. These tribes drank for more than sustenance or status. On beer like this you wouldn't feed an army, build a pyramid, or impress an honored guest. You would get skull-crushingly drunk.

Enter the shaman. Fringe societies weren't entirely orderless. Many had kings and chieftains, generals and commanders. Religion too. But without the temples and other edifices of ritual that defined more settled civilizations, like those in Sumeria, Greece, and Rome, their religious practices revolved around a shaman. The shaman was a sort of multipurpose community leader. Not simply a healer or a priest, but a medium, a translator between the physical and the spiritual worlds. "The shaman is both healer and sorcerer, human and divine, human and animal, male and female," the ethnographer Piers Vitebsky explained in his guide to shamanic belief systems around the world. The shaman was a gatekeeper, and beers were his keys into another realm.* "Shamanic

---

* Another bit of etymological evidence: the word *hag*, for witch, comes from the ancient High German *hagazussa*, meaning the fence between a cultivated garden and the wild forest beyond.

logic starts from the idea that the soul can leave the body," Vitebsky goes on. That journey to the spirit world was by nature destructive, a breaking of physical ties. Shamanic rituals involved dismemberment, torture, fasting, trance states, and almost always some altering of consciousness, often with drink. "As he drinks, man assimilates the soul of something else, and he loses his own soul in proportion to his drinking," the cultural historian Wolfgang Schivelbusch wrote. The shaman, and those under his, or her (or its), spell, became bears, deer, monsters, wild men—Enkidu, in other words, not Gilgamesh. This wasn't enlightenment through sophistication but through devolution.

Alcohol was a doorway, or what ethnographers call an entheogen. From the Greek for "creating god within," an entheogen is a substance used in a religious context, a tool or a pathway to mystical understanding of the sacred or spiritual dimension. Drunk in ritualistic communion with the recently killed, for example, in what the Norse called a *totenfolge,* or "following into death," potent beers were, one historian explains, acts of solidarity. The drink wasn't just celebratory, as at Midas's feast, but transformative. "It puts those who remain among the living into a kind of transcendent, paranormal state." But alcohol wasn't the only magic in these drinks.

Though they might have lacked for grapes, northern European shamanic brewers made use of a substantial apothecary. At that first brewery site in Skara Brae, for example, archaeologists found residue of a beer made with henbane, hemlock, meadowsweet, and nightshade. Fortunatus was right. He was witnessing no simple drunken revelry. Beers like this are heady indeed. Hemlock is a well-known poison; henbane is mildly narcotic, supposedly producing a feeling of flight, and was a common component in witches' flying potions. Nightshade, or belladonna, disrupts the nervous system, causing delirious hallucinations. (Ironically, it was used during the Inquisition to torture some of those same potion-wielding witches into confessing.) Meadowsweet, the mildest of the lot, still isn't entirely benign. It contains some of the same anti-inflammatory chemicals as aspirin.

Entheogenic beers could be even more potent than that. Some Nordic shamans were fond of a parasitic fungus called ergot, *Claviceps purpurea*, that grew on rotted barley and rye. Archae-ologists have found its telltale bloated purplish grains in the guts of buried bog bodies. Ergot is powerful stuff. The fungus shares some of the same chemical compounds as LSD. The good side: wild hallucinations, ecstatic dancing—doctors call it "convulsive ergotism." The bad, "gangrenous ergotism," causes abdominal pain, convulsions, a sensation of burning limbs called Saint Anthony's fire, and, ultimately, death. Gangrenous ergotism is caused perhaps by a different strain of the fungus, though we apparently lack for test subjects to figure it out conclusively.

Mushrooms were another common addition. A nineteenth-century explorer in eastern Russia wrote that the Koryak tribe on the Kamchatka peninsula "invented a drink equally potent [to brandy] which they extract from a red mushroom." One has to wonder what kind of brandy he meant. The mushroom was likely *Amanita muscaria*, which contains ibotenic acid, a neurotoxin that causes, according to *Poisonous Mushrooms of the Northern United States and Canada*, "inebriation, derangement of the senses, manic behavior, delirium, and a deathlike sleep." Some especially dedicated mycophiles say this last effect—sort of a

THE BREWER'S TALE

temporary coma—is the basis for the metaphor of resurrection in Western religion. Indeed, we've found images of mushrooms in shamanic religious art everywhere from the antennaed and fungus-toting "bee man" cave drawing in the Tassili n'Ajjer mountains of Algeria to carved stone heads in the Guatemalan jungle. Some even say Stonehenge was based on a circular mushroom bloom called a fairy ring.

And then there's soma. Ancient texts from the eastern Vedic and Zoroastrian religions mention a ritualistic drink called soma, strained through sheep's wool and spiked with a hallucinogenic and energizing plant. What plant, exactly? No one really knows. Like *boer*, soma is awash in endless and delighted confusion. The base drink was probably koumiss, or fermented horse milk. But the plant itself is elusive: milkweed, cannabis, or maybe the stimulating herb ephedra, also called Mormon tea. Or *A. muscaria*, perhaps, or another mushroom like *Psilocybe cubensis*. The Vedic hymnal the *Rigveda* includes 114 odes to the drink—"God for Gods" or "Creator of the Gods," it is called. "We have drunk soma and become immortal," one hymn reads. "We have attained the light." Like the Norse sagas, though, writings about soma are poetically obscure. "Fragmented descriptions in a long-dead language," the ethnobotanist Terence McKenna writes in his own hymn to mushrooms, *Food of the Gods*.

Still, soma's legend has persisted. As Eastern traditions migrated north through the centuries, the Norse transposed soma's power onto mead, mixing its stories with their own gods, myths, and drinking culture. Soma became the Mead of Suttungr, brewed from the blood of the wise man Kvasir (himself made from godly spittle). Like the original drink, this divine brew made anyone who tasted it a poet. Slurped up by the god Odin and spit back to mankind, the mead enlightened humanity.*

Though both cultures had their own systems of divinity, the Romans better understood their world by digging in, defining and ordering what they found; the barbaric tribes by dropping out. Soma or ergot beer altered the drinker's consciousness and perspective, offering a way of understanding the familiar, physical world by moving beyond it. Getting drunk gave new meaning to sobriety, experiencing death (temporarily, one hoped) helped us better appreciate life. McKenna called this breakdown a "ritual of reversal" or "drunken degeneration"—an opening "between semicontrolled debauchery and the sacred spirit world."

As these shamanic brewers mapped the hard edges of reality by moving beyond them, they also defined social roles—us and them, drunk and sober, healthy and sick—by bending them. Drinking let these cultures commune with the dead, the spirits, and, maybe most important, with each other. It wasn't chaos—not quite Sam Calagione's "hootenanny" or Fortunatus's "mad men"— it was ritual, an important form of social bonding.

Drinking was, first of all, a group activity, and as dangerously mind-altering as the drinks were, drinkers stayed safe within the tribe. No wonder poor, wallflower Fortunatus, watching the fun from the sidelines, felt so threatened. Within the circle, though, gathered around the cauldron, rules could be safely bent, or even

---

* Norse mythology is full of stories of men—literally—drowning in booze and finding nirvana on the way down: the Swedish kings Hundingus and Fjölnir; both Odin and his son Veraldur; the Irish king Diarmaid; the Duke of Clarence. There are so many, in fact, that folklorists Antti Aarne and Stith Thompson categorized the story type as "Tale 943A."

broken. In a *New Yorker* article about alcoholism research, Malcolm Gladwell tells the story of a pair of Yale anthropologists who traveled to the Bolivian jungle to study the drinking habits of the native Camba tribe. The couple joined the tribe in their weekly binges, fueled by 180-proof rotgut rum—"laboratory alcohol," Gladwell writes, "the concentration that scientists use to fix tissue." And yet the Camba, in general, were a healthy, peaceful tribe. "There was no social pathology, no arguments, no disputes, no sexual aggression, no verbal aggression. There was no alcoholism." Why? "The Camba did not drink alone. They did not drink on work nights. And they only drank within the structure of their elaborate ritual."

Rituals writ in drinkware. If every civilization leaves a telltale residue, from Native American oyster middens to our great Pacific Gyre trash patch, Neolithic Europe wrote its culture in its cups. Amphorae, flagons, strainers, and jugs; Auroch horns and enemies' skulls; corded bell beakers and loop-handed Scheibenhenkel tankards—the ancestors of today's dimpled glass *masskrugs,* standard issue at every Oktoberfest. And then, of course, giant cauldrons. In a tomb near Stuttgart lies a forty-year-old man decked out in the trappings of the good life: pointy leather shoes trimmed in gold, a three-foot-long, one-and-a-half-gallon drinking horn, and, if that weren't enough, a 130-gallon cauldron. (It's still not the biggest ever found: a 317-gallon behemoth was unearthed next to a comparatively puny Nordic ballerina.)

From these cauldrons toasts were made and healths were poured—"a sacrificial offering," Schivelbusch put it, "not to the divinity but to other human beings." Drinking equalized as well as established hierarchy. "The order in which each is served shows relative rank between the participants, with the king coming first, then men of higher rank, and finally the youngest and lowest rank-ing," another historian explained of Viking mead-hall structure. Passing cups built structure. Draining them dissolved it. When King Hrothgar first meets Beowulf, he invites the warrior to loosen up with him at a banquet, to "unbind thy words" with mead. The king and his subjects became brothers in drink.

And so it is today. Drinking is bonding, from the happy-hour pint with colleagues to the frat house keg stand—a cauldron full of Keystone Light. Or, if you know the right shaman, one spiked with monarda leaves and yarrow. Brian's burly, nose-ringed assistant brewer Jeff Barkley remembers taking a keg of a beer they made with Labrador tea to a New Year's Eve party. Labrador tea, in the rhododendron family, contains the mildly narcotic chemical, or terpene, ledol. Athabaskan and Inuit people would chew the leaves as a painkiller for toothaches or brew a medicinal tea from them. In a beer its effects are noticeable, if slightly vague. "You could feel the mood change," Jeff said, trailing off, unwilling or unable to offer any specifics.

Laborador tea is just one of the tools in Brian's medicine bag. I asked for a peek inside and we hauled ourselves out of a near recline and shuffled over to a shed down the driveway. (On the way, an overdue stop at the bathroom, a yellowed Budweiser can strung with twine between two trees. "If you're really good," Brian said, "you can make it spin.")

Brian, still barefoot, crunched on the gravel without a wince and slid open the shed's door. Inside were boxes and bags, piled high overhead, obscuring a rudimentary and slapdash shelving system. Bags stuffed with what, exactly? "Those don't look like hops," I said. Brian smirked. "They aren't.* That's mugwort in the far corner. And these leaves that look like rhododendron leaves, or olive leaves the way they curl up, those are Labrador tea. I think. That's yarrow. These are monarda leaves, or bee balm. We have some burdock root here somewhere." He pulled down a clear bag of wood shavings. "This is incense cedar," he said. "I've always loved the smell of this since I was a kid and spending a bunch of time in the Sierras. This was a bad year for it, though. It's missing its high, ethereal notes." Lacking an "approved beer word," he flutters his fingers dreamily, then stomps his bare feet on the ground. "It's heavier—*tromp, tromp, tromp.*"

As Brian expounded on seasonal changes in the flavor of red-wood, about the difference between eastern cedar and western cedar, I realized that as much as these beers are about entheogenic transformation, they are also about specific spaces and times. Beer made with that cedar sends Brian back to his childhood (others, maybe, to a hamster cage), but it also grounds him in this place. "You use what you have. Every beer happened for cultural, economic, governmental, political reasons. When we try to copy a style from somewhere else, it's totally bogus," Brian said. Hence Death and Taxes, a dark beer suited to light California cuisine, not the roasts and schnitzels of its heavier, European relatives. So instead of chasing exotic ingredients to far-flung corners of the globe, Brian uses local herbs. He chose them with the help of an herbalist he knows at a nearby homeopathic medical school. "I

---

* Legally, Brian has to use *some* hops in his beers, otherwise they wouldn't be beer. He'd have to call them "malt beverages," and they'd be regulated by the FDA instead of the TTB, a logistical snafu Brian would rather avoid. "So I want to inform you," he told me with a glare, "that all these beers have half an ounce of hops per barrel."

went to the school and we tasted all the native plants," he told me. "She said, 'You oughta check out this farmer, three miles away. She grows monarda and mugwort.' So now I get it from her. If I had all this stuff shipped in, then how would I know what I'm getting? That's my version of *terrior*." If the yellowed can of Budweiser is an apt symbol of Brian's stance on industry, another cast-off bottle embodies his take on localism. I noticed, half-buried in a pile of dead leaves, an empty Westvleteren XII—what some call the best beer on earth. For a beer lover, finding such an exotic jewel in this unkempt forest felt as out of place as Gucci at a Goodwill, its foreign charms toothless here in the native dirt.

Cato and his countrymen saw status in imported wine. They would have swooned for that rare Westy. But Brian and his shamanic brewing brothers draw their power from the world around them. And so, for a different take on—and taste of—this kind of beer, I couldn't phone it in. I'd have to make another pilgrimage.

I met my second shaman three thousand miles away, in a Cambridge, Massachusetts, office park lit by a bright fall sun and the polished glass of MIT lab buildings. This was the straitlaced home of Cambridge Brewing Company, makers of some very unconventional beers. For a medicine man, CBC's brewmaster Will Meyers looks surprisingly put-together: parted hair, clean plaid button-down tucked into neat brown Carhartts. He's a product of his cultured, collegiate environment, like Brian going wild in his woodland grove. Will's bar was quiet that afternoon, just a couple guys tucking into big, late-lunch salads and half pints of Charles River Porter. But when the herbal beer is flowing—odder brews named Arquebus or Brett Semetery—things change. "People don't go crazy," Will admits. "But it's interesting to see."

The bar for now was sedate, but there was magic brewing

underground. I followed Will into his basement barrel room, stooping low beneath the five-foot ceiling. "Watch it," Will said. "I lost three discs in my back to this barrel room." The basement felt like the secret burrow of some booze-hoarding troll. It was stocked with rows of barrels, bubbling carboys and buckets, some jugs dusty, sealed tight, and covered. Others—dustier—left wide open to the musty air and the spirits therein. "Sometimes I come down and read them a bedtime story," Will smiles. He names his beers after Shelley poetry ("Ozymandias") and Phish lyrics ("I Am Nitrogen"). He reads Arthurian legends for fun. He's the quintessential Ivy League hippie. In school, Will told me, "If they had taught chemistry with home brewing as a lab, I'd have known what I wanted to do with my life a lot earlier." When he decided to make some Nordic herbal beer, then, he was diligent. He wanted to do it right. At first, he tried getting his herbs from mail-order catalogs. "I'd call the hippie herb dealers out in California looking for sweet gale. 'How much do you have?' I said. 'I'll take all of it.' But prices could be sixty dollars a pound. So I found a friend who has some marsh property. We hacked out the skunk cabbage and brought in a truckload of plants. Now I grow most of it myself."

Will grabbed a pair of pliers and, with a squeak, pulled out a nail from the head of one of the barrels. A stream of beer squirted into our glasses. Ozymandias was tart and syrupy sweet, Cerise Cassée bright cherry with a minty, back-of-the-throat tingle. Weekapaug Gruit, brewed with gale, yarrow, and rosemary, was earthy and tannic, like red wine in a bog. Heather Ale, made with the shrub's delicate flowers, was faintly, beguilingly coniferous, pine on a sea breeze, like smelling a coastal forest from a sailboat. "I wanted to go find a field and pick heather flowers," Will remembered of the first time he made that beer. "It took years of calling gardeners and asking, 'Can I come to your field this spring and cut the flowers?' They all hung up on me. 'Why would you want to do *that*?' I finally found someone who said yes. It's a great day. Some friends and I meet up at the brewery, drive out, and spend the morning harvesting. We get two or three grocery bags full, about twelve pounds." Heather was common in medieval Scottish brews, and I asked if Will had heard the tales of pickers hallucinating from a fungal moss called *fogg* that sometimes grew on the blossoms. Of course he had. Were the stories true? He wouldn't say. He and his friends got their kicks the local way. After a day of harvesting, "we go for a swim and then we go eat lobster rolls. Just like the Vikings," he laughed.

Will and Brian became my mentors. But they had a teacher too, Stephen Harrod Buhner. Bearded, bespectacled, beret-ed, Buhner is a self-described Earth Poet, and his book *Sacred and Herbal Healing Beers* acts as a sort of Satanic Bible in the fringes of the beer world. Mentioning Buhner is its own kind of entheogen, a secret door into the weird world of herbal ales, ancient meads, and, everyone's favorite chapter, "Psychotropic and Highly Inebriating Beers." I found my copy in a backwoods home-brew store in upstate New York. The shop clerk winked when I brought it to the counter. Will and Brian both had well-thumbed copies in their libraries.

Buhner in hand, a recipe dog-eared, I headed to the natural food co-op. I was looking for mugwort, wormwood, bog myrtle, gale, and yarrow. A throng of shoppers mobbed the bulk spice rack, stocking up on chia seeds and rose hips, sniffing the garam masala, filling hemp satchels with hemp seeds. Checking a shopping list of potential hallucinogens, I had anticipated sidelong looks. But among this crowd my herbal mix was as commonplace as parsley and sage. So common, in fact, that the grocery store was out of mugwort. Between the marshmallow root and nettle leaf stood an empty jar. Dejected, I headed home. *What would a shaman do?* I wondered. And then I turned a fragrant corner and perked up. Rosemary grows wild in San Francisco's Mediterranean climate, and I surreptitiously snipped a few sprigs from a neighbor's front yard. My senses alight, on that short walk I found sage, yarrow, eucalyptus, and pine. Back home, like a Nordic brewer supplanting a bit of Hochdorf grain with lingonberries and wine, I mixed up a kettle of malt smoked over peat moss, a little honey from my beehive, and some frozen cranberries. I added my herbs and poured it into a gallon jug—the biggest cauldron I had. After a week of fermenting it was time to drink. But I couldn't worship alone. Sharing these beers, after all, was a ritual as important as brewing them. I gathered a few friends and opened a bottle.

The beer came out piney and warming, a bit like a campfire, but drawn with an unfortunately heavy hand—more like the "wild-crafted desert piñon" incense from aisle twelve than the subtly sweet trees I passed under on my walk home. The rosemary was especially potent. Undried, unmeasured, wild-foraged, I couldn't guess how much to use. I overdid it. "It'd go well with chicken," a friend said.

Brian was more diplomatic. Back in Sonoma, under his redwoods, after making our way through his medicine chest, we opened a vial from mine. We filled our glasses and added another empty bottle to the pile in the gravel. He paused to think—my tape recorder was beer-sticky by this point in the boozy afternoon but it was still running. This was on the record, and Brian chose his words. "It's got a lot going on," he said. Another pause, and then he hoisted his hazy, yeast-flecked glass with the best compliment he could give an aspiring shaman. "If you give this to someone they might say, 'This isn't beer. What is this?'"

Brian keeps a study of sorts in a cramped outbuilding next to the combination brew house–tractor barn. A desk filled one corner, drawers flung open and piled with papers. In another was a bed with a strange lute-like instrument on its rumpled sheets. And everywhere, everywhere, books. "I remember things, I don't even know where I read them," he said, handing me a hefty Xeroxed copy of Odd Nordland's *Brewing and Beer Traditions in Norway.* "I have books from 1880 in here. Some are in German. I can read them with a dictionary." He told me about his biggest score. "I was in Denmark looking for brewing books in this half-underground bookshop. Just stacks of books. The guy there said, 'We have a bunch of books from when the Carlsberg brewery closed.' They had found a Dumpster full of their corporate library." Brian bought the lot.

While at brewing school, at UC Davis, Brian lived in the library—he maxed out his card. The school in those days was a feeder for big breweries, and when he graduated in 1980 Brian went to work for Schlitz in Milwaukee, Wisconsin. "I learned the opposite of what everybody else who left the brewing program and went to work in a big brewery learned," he said in his defense. "I learned the beauty, the poetry. Schlitz had buildings they didn't use anymore. I loved to walk through them. The walls were crumbling, they had wooden tanks, wooden fermenters. When I joined them, Schlitz was run by accountants, and using these horrible, disgusting shortcuts. But the architecture of the old brewery was made with flair, made with personality, made with pride. It wasn't a computerized factory." That was where beer's spirit lived.

"Beer is poetry," Brian went on. If Buhner is an Earth Poet, Brian said, "I'd like to be called a Beer Poet. Beer chose me. I don't know why." The legend of Soma lives on, the Mead of Inspiration hasn't lost its power. You just need to know where to look for it. Brian raised a guru-like finger. "Someone said to Jerry Garcia, man, I have every Grateful Dead recording there ever was. And Jerry said, if that's all you got you ain't got nothing."

In the Viking age, a "beer keeper" was a good storyteller. Riding the razor's edge between drunk and sober was an art. And after a beer-sated day, with the bird of unmindfulness fluttering and the Budweiser can spinning, after I spill even more beer on my recorder, then turn it off altogether, with notebooks closed and words unbound with potent brew, Brian seems less like a trickster and more like a guide. Beer is a journey. Get on the bus; he'll drive.

3

THE MONK

Tasting Westvleteren XII is not easy. Forget your corner beer store, no matter how hip it is. Finding a bottle is an adventure. First, wake up at 9 a.m., Central European Time, and call the beer phone at the Saint Sixtus Abbey. (Yes, it's called the "beer phone.") You'll probably get a busy signal. The abbey can get 85,000 calls an hour during the short window the beer phone lines are open. Call again. Still busy? Keep at it until a monk picks up, who tells you in clipped, accented English when you're allowed to come to Belgium. Then go to Belgium. Fly to Brussels and drive an hour and a half west, toward the French border, to the town of Vleteren. Find the monastery (you have a map, right?), pull around to the loading dock (no visitors are allowed inside), and for 40 euros and a solemn promise not to resell on the black market (would you lie to a monk?) carefully load up your four dozen precious bottles. Two cases per car, that's all. Now move aside for the next in line. And there *will* be a line. Hours long, sometimes; fistfights have broken out among impatient drinkers. That's because this isn't just any beer. This is the best beer in the world.

Craft beer's ship seems sometimes to sail on hype—not the flavors in the glass but the stories told around them. Stories of potency, rarity, and expense. And no beer is heaped with more discussion, debate, and praise than this one. Online forums continually rank it as number one: 100 points on RateBeer (2,905 reviews and counting); 100 points on Beer Advocate (3,795 reviews). Entire message board threads are devoted to tips, tricks, and horror stories of finding a bottle. One response to a novice's question on the difficulty of getting those crates begins, "Have you seen the film *Hostel*?" Then there are the reviews themselves. The praise is profound, as if poetic extravagance could validate the effort it takes to get a taste. Call it the adjective defense; a Herculean task demands the epic mode.

The descriptions start tame. Plums, nougat, pound cake, nutmeg, walnuts. Then, they veer into the ecstatic, the reverent, the beatific. "Baked banana forests," one reads. "Leaf and truffle," claims another. "My holy grail." "Transmogrific." "Makes me consider moving to Belgium and becoming a monk."

Joe Tucker, who runs RateBeer, tried to explain the hype. "A beer brings more than just flavor," he told me. "It's more than the molecules in the bottle, there's a genie in there too. That whole story of how you got the beer, and where and when you're drinking it, that's part of the experience of tasting it." Years ago, Joe bought his first taste of Westy, as devotees call the beer, on the gray market from a company specializing in imported Belgian delicacies. Weeks later, a bottle arrived on his Texas porch (shipped illegally, considering it was alcohol) in a deceptively labeled crate marked "From the Belgium Coffee Company." There are other loopholes in the supply chain—easier ways to heaven.

There are eBay's bottles, with their hefty price tags, moral and monetary (one recently went for $450 and presumably the monks' eternal opprobrium). A small café near the monastery called In de Vrede pours samples. And, shortest cut of all, Westvleteren's twenty-one monks, who've brewed a tightly capped 3,800 barrels a year since 1945 (that's 117,800 gallons), temporarily upped production in 2012 and sent a limited supply to the United States to help finance some repairs to the roof of their abbey. Lucky customers could pick up a gift-boxed six-pack (with commemorative glass!) for $84.99. The 15,000 boxes Westvleteren released sold out in under twenty-four hours.

All this suggests one special beer. And it's true: Westy is delicious. It tastes like a mix of blue cheese, roasted bananas, and rum-soaked raisins. But you don't wait in line for hours just to eat a raisin. Transmogrification can't be gained from taste alone. So where lies Westy's power?

At first, the answer seems simple. It's old. Its legend is its longevity. Westvleteren is called an abbey ale, part of a loose family of beers connected by flavor (a fruity yeast, lots of sugar, not much bitterness), provenance (generally from Belgium, though plenty of other brewers have adopted the style, from Colorado's New Belgium to California's Lost Abbey), and, most of all, tradition. The most popular abbey ales have been around for centuries. The Trappist Abbaye Notre-Dame d'Orval was founded in 1132; Rochefort in 1230. Leffe proudly prints its birth year on every golden label of its beer: "Anno 1240." Sweet, rich, and strong, abbey beers' flavors conjure a distant past of drafty stone churches and hearty Christmas feasts. As read the ads for Leuven's Stella Artois—not from an abbey but still iconically Belgian—under a sudsy gold-rimmed goblet: "It's a chalice, not a glass." When we buy these beers we're buying a long story. Wouldn't you pay $84.99 for an eight-hundred-year-old time capsule?

Tasted with a clearer mind, though—forget the year on the label, ignore the ads, toss out the chalice—those flavors speak less to preservation, and more to change. Do Westy's raisin notes eerily remind you of another abbey beer? The Abbey of Saint Benedict's walnut-hued Achel 8, say? They should—the breweries started sharing yeast in 1970. Does Westmalle's pale, potent Trappist Tripel seem especially light for something so medieval-sounding? Thank the brewery's postwar effort to compete with bright-bodied pilsners. The story of abbey beers isn't so much a brewing story as it is a story of brands: how tradition evolves and congeals into trademark, how the past can be preserved through reinvention, how things change and stay the same.

The story starts with the merging of two heritages, Christian and pagan, as monks reclaimed beer from the shaman, codifying his belief system and marrying it to their own.

Early church leaders were reluctant to stoop to the beer drinker's barbarous level. Writing in the fifth century, the Christian theologian Theodoret of Cyrus called *zuthos* (literally, "barley wine") "vinegary and foul-smelling and harmful." And yet he and his brethren knew they couldn't simply write off beer as the other man's drink, not if they were going to scrub those pagan races into godliness. They had to compromise. So the church fathers launched a campaign to win beer-drinking converts.

First, they synced calendars. The church lined up its own Christian holidays with pagan drinking parties: Christmas with the yuletide feast of Odin, All Saints' Day with the Dísablót harvest festival, the Feast of Saint John with the bonfire-lit solstice rituals of midsummer. Pagan symbols of herdsman morphed into Jesus as the Good Shepherd. The cloven-hoofed shamanic Krampus shed his goat horns, gained a few pounds, and became, eventually, Santa Claus. Abbeys started holding church ales, fund-raisers like today's church-basement potlucks, only with more beer. Some church ales refilled the holy coffers in general, but others were linked to a specific cause or a construction project. The monks at Saint Sixtus must have heard of the Old Norse *taklagsöl,* or barn raising—literally, "roofing ale."

Early church dogma was lenient even toward drunkenness. Theology students—notoriously bibulous—played drinking games like Herring in which one tipsy brother tied a dead fish to another's habit and tried to step on it as they walked their abbey's halls. Their superiors looked the other way, as long as the drinking was done, according to a rulebook penned by the seventh-century archbishop of Canterbury, "for the joy of Christmas or Easter or any of the feasts of the saints." Just try not to get more drunk than the abbot—and, please, begged another monastic primer, don't "vomit the Eucharist." (Forty days' penance if you do, one hundred if a dog licks it up.)

Church tolerance grew with its flock. In the century following Theodoret's dis, monks revised doctrine and even some scripture to shine more pleasantly on beer. They treated it now with a mix of reverence and humility. Beer was both as wondrous as wine and as commonplace as bread. In Irish lore, Saint Brigit turned water into sacred suds; in some British monasteries beer was penitent enough to drink while fasting. "Liquida non frangunt ieiunium," monks said as they sipped—liquid doesn't break the fast.

Beer eventually moved from a gesture of acceptance, to—

especially during those fasts—a critical piece of church practice. When Saint Benedict decreed in his book of precepts that monasteries following his Benedictine order welcome passing travelers with food and drink, and that his monks stay self-sufficient, living "by the labor of their hands," that work included brewing.

Like the Cistercians, who started the long and fruitful tradition of great winemaking in Burgundy and the Rhine, Benedictine monks made some damn fine beer. Tithes from farmers on church land stocked the granaries. The money those church ales raised bought top-notch equipment such as copper kettles, large fermentation casks, and kilns to dry out malted grain for storage. Brewed for sustenance to warm tired travelers and fasting monks, the beers were rich and packed with nutrients, made hearty and sugary strong with loads of grain. (If you imagine making wort as steeping a pot of grain-based tea, think of these as double-strength brews, with more malt as an extra scoop of leaves.) But most of all the beers were safe. While shamanic brewers were more concerned with their beer's spiritual potency than its health or cleanliness, abbey brewers took care to make sure their liquid daily bread wasn't lethal. The monks kept their brew houses clean, passing laws that, to take one example, made it illegal to drink a beer in which a mouse had died. Small steps, yes, but they made a difference.

The church no longer scorned the pagan drinker but his dark-age practices, what the eleventh-century monk Aelfric Bata called "the shameful sorceries" shamanic brewers relied on. No backwoods, cauldron-on-a-fire setups, abbey breweries used revolutionary technology. Take Switzerland's monastery Saint Gall, renovated in the ninth century by King Louis the Pious to serve as a model church that the Benedictine order could replicate around the rest of Europe. "Here the sustenance of the brother shall be taken care of with thoughtful concern," his plans for the new abbey read. They included three brew houses, making beer of different strengths and quality (the best, *prima melior*, for the monks, the worst for the thirstiest and least discerning travelers), plus a granary, malt house, kiln, mill, cooperage, and, most impressive of all, spice garden. The Saint Gall stores burst forth in fragrant splendor: dill, chervil, mint, parsley, rocket, horseradish, rosemary, rue, sage, savory, tansy, bay, cumin, lovage, houseleek, pennyroyal, fenugreek, coriander, poppy, agrimony, betony, wormwood, mugwort, white horehound. Why would humble monks need such an exotic array? For their beer, of course.

In previous centuries, the Romans had built a vast web of trade routes that pulled into their capital from the fragrant, far-flung corners of their empire spices in variety and amount that would put even Saint Gall to shame. "Roman tables bloomed with shades as violent but not so harmless as those in a modern seed catalogue," M.F.K. Fisher wrote in *Serve It Forth*. "One course of a Roman meal would lay us very low, probably, and strip our palates for many days of even the crudest perceptions of flavor." A simple boiled chicken, for example, in a recipe from the Roman cookery collection *Apicius*, came in a sauce of anise, mint, mustard seeds, dates, fermented fish, vinegar, oil, and asafetida, a pungent, onion-like spice also known as "devil's dung." Guests at Roman banquets gawked over the flavorful extravagance of their hosts, gorged themselves on its luxury, then retired to the vomitorium. But when the empire fell and Europe shattered into tribes and other isolated pockets of civilization, those lines of trade contracted, or snapped entirely. The piles of devil's dung dried up, forcing dark-age brewers to resort to foraged flavorings like bog myrtle and heather. The medieval mind-set expanded, though, as the power of the church illuminated the world's shadowy corners. Once forgotten spices began to trickle back into kitchens, bringing with them the older traditions of their use, Roman and to some extent even pagan. Those spices, and the beers they made, did not open shamanic doors to the spirit world but were instead status symbols and health tonics.

With our modern picture of the dreary muck of medieval life, it's tempting to think that spice was deployed simply to mask the taste of rancid meat and sour beer. But it's more likely cooks instead used spice to temper salt—the day's only preservative. Lent's mountains of dried fish must have been a particularly penitent affair, making a sprinkle of pepper seem, well, divine. One salad recipe was a pungent mixture of garlic, scallions, onions, and leeks. A little spice did a lot. A lot did even more. "Prepared foods were virtually buried under spices," Wolfgang Schivelbusch wrote in *Tastes of Paradise,* his treatise on indulgences of all sorts. "Food was little more than a vehicle for condiments." Used in vast quantities, spices, as in Roman times, were signs of wealth. Some lords would will their spice-cabinet stores of pepper and ginger to their heirs. One medieval banquet for forty featured a table spread with one pound of columbine, a half pound of cinnamon, two pounds of sugar, an ounce of saffron, a quarter pound of cloves, another quarter of grains of paradise, and an eighth of a pound each of pepper, bay leaf, and nutmeg.

To the medieval mind, spices were "emissaries from a fabled world," Schivelbusch wrote. Before their true geographic origins were discovered by Columbus, de Gama, and Marco Polo, spices arrived at the medieval table after a bafflingly circuitous journey.

A single clove, say, was picked from a myrtle tree in Indonesia's Maluku Islands, then pinballed to and fro in the archipelago and scooped up by a Chinese trader. Brought to India, it went out through the Malabar coast, via dhow into the Persian Gulf, by caravan through the Arab sands to the Mediterranean, and north into Italy before finally being funneled into Amsterdam's brimming Herengracht Market or, farther, out past Gibraltar and up to London, where it was unloaded on the docks, "above the knees; whole rooms full," wrote an awed Samuel Pepys in 1665, high-stepping among the brimming kegs. "As noble a sight as ever I saw in my life." With origins so strange and distant, most assumed spices grew in paradise. (Hence the eponymous grains, actually from West Africa.)

Back on the table, spices hadn't lost all their spiritual power but they became more symbol than device, stand-ins for the divine, not entheogenic paths to it. Daisy-like tansy flowers, for example, became a symbol of the Virgin Mary. Angelica, an aromatic herb related to carrots and a common flavoring in traditional Scandinavian drinks, manifest as the sacred root of Archangel Michael. The mythical phoenix, reborn in a pyre of cinnamon, was often etched into early Christian sarcophagi—the fragrant yet unassuming bark symbolizing not only rebirth but also divine humility, inner worth valued above outer appearance. While mandrake and ergot induced shamanic trances, Christian spices were more benign—most just smelled nice. Spices' scent became a mark of saintly purity, from church floors dusted with the gingery wetland grass sweet flag to Tolstoy's Father Amphilochus, "who led so holy a life that his hands smelled of incense."

On laymen's tables, spices were signs of wealth. In the church, with its vow of humility, though, the spices that weren't used as symbols took on the new aura of science. The church codified and regulated the medieval spice rack into an official apothecary that preserved, by modernizing, its traditional shamanic use. Each abbey had an *infirmarer* where monk botanists such as the ninth-century Walafrid Strabo organized spices in books called herbals or leech books. Strabo's *Hortulus* praises the medicinal virtue of sage, rue, and rose—"flower of flowers," he called it— among other plants grown in his abbey plot. Strabo and his followers made order out of the natural world instead of shamanically embracing its chaos. Educated by the church's research, the shaman now became a "spicer," employed by medieval manors like an on-call doctor. Hot and dry in a cold, wet age, ginger and pepper balanced the humors, these proto-doctors thought. Blessed thistle gets its Latin name, *Carduus benedictus,* from its use in Benedictine tonics. During the plague years, fifteenth-century spicers sloshed through cities' pestilent muck clutching pomanders, or oranges studded with cloves (think on that as you deck your mantelpiece this Christmas). But most often medicinal spices were delivered in beer. Specific beers were said to cure specific ailments, from coughs to tumors, from "the stone" to "the itch." Ale with garlic, sage, and the bitter evergreen shrub rue treated a rabid dog bite. Bee balm, wrote the sixteenth-century Italian naturalist Pietro Andrea Mattioli, "purgeth all melancholy vapours."

The most commonly prescribed cure-alls of the day were the marsh shrubs gale and mugwort and the weedy yarrow flower. The blend, called *gruit,* was held as *Gruitrecht* by each local church, which controlled the uncultivated land on which these wild plants grew and monopolized their trade. In medieval towns the church wasn't just a brewery and friendly inn—the social, political, and economic furnace powering daily life—it was grocery store and pharmacy too. And each one doled out its gruit mix to spicers and home brewers with a firm, taxing hand. Saint Arnold of Metz reportedly saved his town from a sixth-century plague by serving them the monastery's own spiced beer instead of water. Now, he's the patron saint of brewers.*

Arnold and his followers brewed beer for sustenance and for what the saint called its godly "gift of health." They were deep, hearty, and strongly spiced, brewed from impressive abbey gardens and stuffed grain stores. And yet Westvleteren XII doesn't owe its "burnt banana forests" to gale and wormwood. Today's abbey beers are worlds different from those medieval brews. Thirteenth-century Leffe might have been a potent sludge of sacred tansy and medicinal horehound; today, it's flavored with hops alone and brewed not by monks but by employees of Anheuser-Busch InBev. Clearly, traditions have changed. What happened? Martin Luther, Napoleon, World War I, gin, lawsuits, buyouts, leaky roofs. But first hops, the unassuming pale green flowers of a weedy, creeping plant, and bitter symbol of rebellion, trade, and a modern brewing revolution.

Made from bursting granaries and groaning spice racks, monastic beers were brewed meaty and flavorful, not just for health

---

* Of course, with these brews, the carrier probably did more work than its contents, the spoonful of sugar more effective than the castor oil it chased. Of all the day's ailments (and the list is long and frightening) the most studied were hangovers. Cures ranged from the tame, betony in water, to the punishing: five slices of roasted pig's lung. The physician Andrew Boorde's sixteenth-century *Breviary of Health* advised the whole gamut, in all its self-evident futility. "If any man do perceive that he be drunk," Boorde wrote, "let him take a vomit with water and oil, or with a feather, or a rosemary branch, or else with his finger, or else let him go to his bed to sleep."

and sustenance but for the sake of preservation. Extra grain meant extra sugars for yeast, which produced extra alcohol. Alcohol, naturally antibacterial, keeps stronger beer from going sour. Still, these beers didn't travel well, and those loads of grain and herbs it took to produce the potent brews made them expensive to make. Monastic brewers' goal was quality and self-sufficiency; their batches were small, their brewing time limited by prayer and study. Abbey beers—as many still are today—were rare, available only in limited amounts, and often only at the abbeys themselves.

Hops changed all that. If monastic beer has its foundation in cloistered purity, hopped beer was based on trade. Hops are a much more effective preservative than other traditional spices thanks to a bitter, antimicrobial acid in their flowers called humulone. Beer that kept longer could travel farther, and so hopped-beer brewers could command a wider market than their spice-using competition. Hops also meant beer could be made weaker—and cheaper, with less grain—and still last as long. Most important for medieval brewers working outside the church, hops were largely ignored by the faithful. The abbess, mystic, and early Christian botanist Hildegard of Bingen said in her twelfth-century herbal that hops "were not very useful." They "make the soul of man sad, and weigh down his inner organs."* And so hops fell outside the church's *Gruitrecht*. The powerful plant—*Humulus lupulus*, or climbing wolf; it spreads vigorously if left unchecked—was untaxed and free for the plucking.

As nascent governments knit together once-separate, church-

---

* What did she know? Hildegard liked beer for the healthy, rosy complexion it gave her nuns, yet her herbal guidebooks *Physica* and *Causae et Curae* also prescribed deadly black nightshade as a cure for toothaches.

run city-states into better delineated political realms, beer, now fit to travel, became an international commodity. Visiting dignitaries were gifted bottles of the local specialty: red beer from Gdansk, white from Hamburg, sour cloudy *broihan* from Hannover. Einbeck, which had seven hundred breweries by the seventeenth century, was famous for its strong, crisp bock. Goslar, in north-central Germany, made a salty, sour brew called *gosa*, still its specialty today. Quality concerns became not health but business matters, and beer testers flocked the ports. Not every brewing center was famous for the right reasons. Danish beer came in two types, one contemporary beer critic wrote: "ordinary beer and worse than ordinary beer." Antwerp's tasted, on good days, like "reboiled water," on bad like "a mixture of water, beer, pitch, pinewood, soapsuds, vinegar, treacle, and a few other things."

Where ingredients were plentiful breweries flourished. As early as the 1300s Hamburg, in a geographic sweet spot between Elbe Valley grain fields and Baltic hop yards, boasted more than four hundred breweries and a fleet of twenty ships to carry all that beer around northern Europe. Half the city's income came from brewing. The church, once the economic bedrock of urban life, was becoming irrelevant.

Its flock dispersed to bars, shunning the cross for the broom, a symbol hung by alewives outside their inns as a makeshift sign for good beer, a warm bed, and maybe some company. The fifteenth-century Benedictine monk Robert Rypon complained that, even during Lent, his congregation skipped church-sanctioned *drynkynges* for the tavern, "thinking and saying—'Fishes must swim!'" If brewing's new wealth made the church's economic power irrelevant, inns and taverns dissolved its social glue. All walks of life mixed in their warrens of rooms: drunks in the basement, whores upstairs, merchants on the ground floor. Chaucer captured that tumult in his *Canterbury Tales,* which gave a then revolutionary common man's perspective of the tavern as neighborhood gossip hub. It was a place—like the Viking mead halls and Roman symposia before it—to hear the news and a good, if secular, story. In sixteenth-century, post-Reformation London, former religious halls shuttered by the new government filled their cellars with kegs instead. The city's thirteenth-century Carmelite monastery became Ye Olde Cheshire Cheese. The fifteenth-century Bermondsey Priory is now the Angel. Others of the city's oldest bars still echo their churchly origins in name: the Mitre, the Blackfriar.

Like the beer they served, these taverns were quality-controlled—pour swill, or overcharge, and, as in the Babylonian cities Uruk or Bad-tibira millennia before, you'd get a governmental talking-to. Not dunked in the river but slapped with a fine. King Henry III's 1267 assize on bread and beer set early standards for sizes and prices: quarts, half gallons or "pottles," and, for a hefty half penny, full gallons. Regulation like this pushed brewers to form guilds—early brewing-industry lobbies—to stay the government's hand. Brewing was becoming a business, and brewers were learning to preserve not only their wares but their investments.

When Protestantism arrived on the scene in the 1500s, the organs of the Catholic Church still controlled, through both symbolism and their *Gruitrecht* taxes, the bulk of the medieval herb garden, so the new religion, like the age's burgeoning community of secular, money-minded brewers, championed the hop.

Hildegard was on to something when she fretted over those heavy innards. Humulone is just one of many chemical compounds contained in the acids and resinous oils tucked into hops' seed cones. Another, the volatile alcohol dimethylvinyl carbinol, is relaxing, and even hypnotic in high enough doses. (Stuff a hops-filled sachet in your pillowcase for richer sleep, old wives say.) Hops' sedative properties made them a mellow, temperate alternative to the excesses of church ales and gruit's cackling echoes of hallucinogenic Nordic grog. Even with their trappings of health and godly purity, spices such as radish, henbane, wormwood, and hemlock—a monk-approved cure for insomnia—could have worse effects than a sleepless night. Even yarrow, wrote Odd Nordland in his guide to traditional Scandinavian brewing, was "in no way innocent." It supposedly made beer more intoxicating. Some of the plants Catholic spicers employed were borrowed from the shamanic medicine chest and had powerful properties beyond their newly bestowed attributes of health or religious symbolism. Fueled by these potent concoctions, church ales could be as boisterous as the Germanic drinking bouts church elders once frowned on. And so, to distance themselves further from papal excesses, when Protestants drank beer they preferred it hopped.* Martin Luther was hardly a teetotaler. "When the devil says to you, 'Do not drink,' answer him, 'I will drink, and right freely,'" he wrote. "Sometimes we must even sin a little to spite the devil, so that we leave him no place for troubling our consciences with trifles." During his first bout with church authorities at Worms in 1521, he sipped from a keg of hoppy bock beer, a gift of solidarity from the duke of Brunswick.†

---

* A note on the names: some beer writers are sticklers about the difference between beer and ale, saying beer refers to a drink made with hops and ale to one without. I find that distinction arbitrary and etymologically suspect and will ignore it.

† Luther's followers were more strict. Temperate texts such as Ludwig Haetzer's *On Evangelical Drinking* and Sebastian Franck's *Concerning the Horrible Vice of Drunkenness* used the Protestant idea of consubstantiation—wine as

Beset by ideological attacks on one side and economic pressure on the other, the church's power waned and the head went flat on monastic beer. The political tumult of the Renaissance didn't help matters, least of all in Belgium. The country, if one could call it that at the time, was more a loose net of states and provinces before it finally succumbed to Napoleon's domineering rule. By the turn of the twentieth century Europe's monasteries were in ruins, their breweries shuttered, their kettles melted into girders and bayonets or simply left to rust.

In December 1930 a caravan of Rolls-Royces bounds over the Spanish plain, helmed by a sunburned bright-eyed William Randolph Hearst. The deep-pocketed (for now) newspaper magnate was prancing around the countryside scooping up relics to bedazzle his castle retreat at San Simeon on the central California coast. A pile of stones catches his eye—remnants of Santa Maria de Ovila, a thirteenth-century monastery sacked in 1835. A swoop of his fountain pen, eleven freighters, eight thousand ocean miles and a million dollars in inter-hemisphere shipping costs later, the stones land in San Francisco, to rise again, he hopes. A cinnamon-scented phoenix: death, then rebirth.

But there was trouble in Hearst's imagined Eden. Picture now the barren, golden nothingness of Vina, in north-central California. Brown hills, cropped by tired cows, flatten out exhausted into the earth. Tumble-down barns and rusted tractors, scuttling quail and wild turkeys peeking through the grape vines. Then, olive and

---

a vehicle for divinity, not Christ's actual blood—to disassociate themselves from Catholic drinking entirely.

almond trees, plums and oranges: an orchard. And through the trees a glimpse of familiar stones. This is Hearst's monastery, or part of it, slowly being rebuilt seventy years later. Just beyond it sits a drafty, high-beamed hall, in which I shivered on a late-fall day, wondering how those stones, like a bouncing clove, got all the way out here. And, more to the point, wondering where the beer was.

This was the Abbey of Our Lady of New Clairvaux, a Trappist monastery of twenty-one monks about three hours north of San Francisco. Bill Smith, a volunteer docent, was patiently waiting for me when I arrived. Tall and split-rail thin with big, wire glasses, a baseball cap, and a fleece jacket, Bill looked like an organic chicken farmer. "I'm not a monk," he said, by way of introduction. "I just like history, and I'm Catholic. I've been coming to Mass here since I was a kid. And," he added ominously, "I love to blather." With that, Bill hefted an NRA-logoed tote bag, dumped a pile of Post-it-studded books and grainy, Xeroxed photos of ruined churches, habited monks, and extravagantly sideburned businessmen, and launched into the history of this place.

We were sitting, it turned out, in the entryway to Leland Stanford's wine cellar. Stanford bought this land in 1881 from a man named Henry Gerke. Gerke was a master vintner and a recluse. He'd lock himself in his basement and blend his wines in secret until dawn. The results were as spectacular as his business acumen was lacking, and Gerke couldn't keep his farm afloat. Stanford had bigger plans. Gerke was an artist but Stanford was all business. He wanted to introduce the country to low-cost, everyday table wine and raise a new generation of Americans on the pleasures of the grape. He braced for success. The cellar Stanford built stretches for nearly two acres under a massive vaulted roof. After only two years on the land his harvesters were pulling in two million pounds of grapes a season. But he had planted the wrong kind. Stanford had the drive but not the touch. Without Gerke's sorcery, Stanford never filled his cavernous halls and finally was forced to distill his mediocre wine into brandy. With Prohibition looming, though, brandy was too stiff for Stanford's investors and in 1915 the winery burned—mysteriously, needless to say. His faulty vines were ripped up soon after. The land lay fallow and became on Stanford's death a prime, if uncultivated, piece of university property.

Then, in 1955, a Kentucky monastery looking to expand—its forty-some monks feeling too cramped on their two thousand bluegrass acres south of Louisville—heard about the land for sale and sent its abbot out to take a look. The abbot had a free day in San Francisco before heading to Vina, and he spent it as a tourist, on a walking tour of Golden Gate Park. In the Japanese Tea Garden, he noticed something odd: sixteenth-century stones from a Cistercian monastery lining the paths. With a fortuitous clang, past and present collided.

As Hearst's stones sailed to California, he lost his fortune, and his nerve. The ten thousand stones arrived in San Francisco in 1931 to an empty dock, and for years there they sat, carefully boxed and labeled. Finally, rather than continuing to pay to store what had become a 2,200-ton white elephant, Hearst turned the stones over to the city, which let them molder more. San Francisco had little interest in a pile of old rocks, and even less after a warehouse fire ruined the numbering system that had kept the crates in order. The city abandoned divinity to more practical matters—it used the rocks as curbs, pavers, and some as stairs in Golden Gate Park's Tea Garden. But some holy spirit must have remained therein, some mustard-seed-sized faith only an abbot could see. So in 1994 he bought for his order both the land in Vina and the stones that remained in storage and entered the long monastic tradition of fund-raising.

Today, the monks at New Clairvaux grow plums, mandarins, walnuts, and almonds. (Bill calls them *eh*-monds, in California Central Valley vernacular. "It's not *sahl*-mon, is it?" he said. Then laughed: "As we say here, the fall from the tree knocked the 'el out of 'em.") But they needed something a bit sexier. "An elixir," Bill said, "something exciting, to get people to come here." Wine? The monks still make it, but Bill steered me away from a tasting. Vina's hot nights make growing grapes a challenge, Bill explained. Stanford's struggle remained. The monks needed a new Gerke. They found him in beer.

Down the road from Vina in nearby Chico lies the Sierra Nevada Brewing Company. An icon of American craft beer, Sierra and its flagship Pale Ale, gets credit for starting the trend of citrus-forward IPAs loaded with Cascades and other West Coast hops. What Westvleteren is to abbey beer—the one to beat, the gold standard, the picture in the dictionary—Sierra is to new-school American.

Sierra Nevada is no leaking monastery. The brewery sprawls out off the Golden State Highway, enormous, aglow with serene corporate confidence. On a drizzly December morning the lobby, decked in tinsel, plastic holly leaves, and strands of chilly LED Christmas lights, was quiet. Out-of-date copies of *People* and *Sports Illustrated* sat stacked on end tables. Phones rang and a trio of middle-aged women in sensibly short haircuts and conservatively funky, cool-mom glasses took turns answering in singsong: "Sierra Nevada Brewing Company, this is Barbie. One moment please." Closer to a dentist's office than an abbey. Except, instead of cool-mint antiseptic, the faint fresh-bread-and-honey scent of bubbling beer filtered through the air ducts. This was, unmistakably, a brewery. I signed in with Barbie, got my clip-on name tag, picked up a *People,* and waited for Steve.

Sierra's brewmaster Steve Dressler flashed a card key and buzzed into the lobby. He's been here since Sierra's beginning. "Thirty years next month," he says with pride. That patient confidence, combined with Steve's scholarly, wire-frame glasses and ruddy cheeks set off by chin-length hair so blond and limp it looks steam-cleaned, gave him a monastic air, wise and kindly, if distracted by a higher calling. No robes, though. Not even the standard-issue brewer's uniform of Dickies, rubber boots, and an oversized hoodie. Sierra employees wear fancy fleece jackets and Gore-Tex vests stamped with the brewery logo: hop vines and barley sheathes twined 'round an alpine stream, babbling down from snowcapped peaks.

In Steve's thirty years Sierra has grown from a scrappy pioneer of the craft-beer movement into a thrumming battleship. The country's second biggest craft brewery, and sixth biggest brewery overall, Sierra just finished constructing a new $108 million, twenty-acre brewing complex in North Carolina. It makes close to a million barrels a year, most of it Pale—the best-selling pale ale in the country. This brewery, and this beer, coined much of the craft-beer industry's language: stubby brown bottles, forest green tap handles, sylvan imagery, and, most important, an insatiable taste for hops. When Founders Brewery in Grand Rapids started in 1997, it declared itself part of the scene by using Sierra's iconic short bottles. In London, Camden Town Brewing uses green tap handles for its IPA—a symbolic gesture understood even on that side of the pond.

Order a Pale Ale anytime, anywhere, in any of the sixteen

countries to which Sierra distributes, and it will taste the same. Steve is proud of that. He calls Pale a "historical" style, meaning that here at Sierra it's respected and preserved. Sierra is the biggest brewery to still ship all its beer under refrigeration. Not even Anheuser-Busch does that, Steve said. If a Sierra employee happens to taste a Pale past its prime at a bar or beer store, he has carte blanche to buy the lot and dump it, saving any other drinkers the suffering of a mediocre pour. While the first batch of Pale Ale took founder Ken Grossman a legendary twelve tries to get right, after those experiments little has changed. The brewery has grown but Pale is still brewed with whole, uncrushed hop cones, not processed pellets; fermented in open square tanks, not modern, pressurized cylinders; and carbonated with living yeast, not CO_2 gas. A traditional, all-American classic.

But I wasn't here to drink a Pale. Still hunting Westvleteren and the story of abbey beers, I came to Sierra to taste Ovila, an incongruous adoption of monastic style by the very type of brewer—corporate, international, and, most significantly, hop-focused—that brought its demise in the first place. If Sierra Nevada can brew an abbey beer, then anyone can. And if anyone can, then what makes Westvleteren so special?

When New Clairvaux asked Sierra for fund-raising help, the two neighbors decided to collaborate on a line of beers, special-edition brews that would combine the monks' tradition and Sierra's crafty creativity. This wouldn't rehash what others like Westvleteren have already mastered. "We didn't want to pay tribute by cloning. These beers are very historic," Steve said. Meaning, like Pale, they're icons of their style. Sierra didn't want simply to ape their language, it wanted to translate it anew. "What are we going to do to put a twist on it? I want some nuances that'll make it our beer." The Ovila series includes three editions: a dark, malty dubbel, a light, peppery saison, and a strong golden ale called a quad, or quadrupel, in the Belgian style of numbering beers by strength. (Westvleteren XII is a quad too—the "12" refers to degrees plato, a European way of measuring alcohol content. It translates to about 10 percent ABV.) All three of Sierra's riffs have a bit more hops than their Belgian brothers, and incorporate some fruit from the monastery's orchards, a gesture to the Benedictine tradition of self-sufficiency. The saison uses mandarin oranges, the quad plums. Some batches were even aged in New Clairvaux wine barrels—a better use for them, perhaps, than their original purpose. None is your typical abbey beer, whatever that is. "Nothing is sacred," Steve put it.

I arrived in time for the year's final brew of the Sugar Plum Quad. Steve took me into the old brew house to explain the process. Old, here, is measured in decades, not centuries. Twenty years ago, Sierra made its first batches of Pale Ale in this pair of burnished copper kettles, but these days that's done in the factory. This brew house now bubbles with small batches like the Ovila series. The smaller system makes it easier to play around with new styles and unfamiliar ingredients. Even for pros like Steve there's always more to learn, and having a small system dedicated to side projects helps with that. A storage room usually filled with hops today is crammed with barrels of dried plums and tubs of sugar syrup they'll add to the beer for flavor and extra potency. We grabbed a handful of the knobby fruits and popped them in our mouths to taste.

"I've never brewed with fruit like this," Steve said as we chew (and chew) the rubbery sugar bombs. Boiling fifty pounds of dried plums for an hour and a half must do something to the beer. But what? At first, Steve and his brewers worried that oils from the pit would kill the head (put a drop of olive oil in a foamy beer and you'll see the idea). But the foam was fine. Clarity, though, was another issue. A brewer in Carhartts and a knitted Schlitz beanie—finally, a traditional uniform—was eyeing the beer's "first runnings" as they began to leave the boiling kettle through a clear pipe called a sight glass, and he moved over to let us take a look. "Oh, nice rich color," Steve said, peering at the murk. It had a woody, purple hue, like stained mahogany. "Yeah, it's cloudy as hell. I have no idea how this is going to filter. I have faith it'll be fine. But you never know." Then he zipped up his vest and headed back into one of Sierra's fermentation rooms.

The room's cold, tiled floor was blindingly clean, as if it had just been hosed down. This, I would learn when we'd spray it out with sanitizer before leaving, was exactly the case. Sierra is no abbey but they take sanitation just as seriously. Not a dead mouse in sight, I thought. (Wandering back to the fermentation room, though, I picked up an unfamiliar, slightly meaty aroma. "Yeast?" I asked Steve. "Nope. Bacon." The brewery's restaurant kitchen was just down the hall.) Cleanliness counts, especially with a beer like Pale that ferments as it has since its first brewing, in low, uncovered rectangular tanks. The rest of what Sierra brews ferments in steel silos that rise sixty feet tall, like a stubbly field along the brewery's roof. The bottoms of the fermenters taper into cones from which brewers can drain off dead yeast and other sediment and pull out tasting samples. Those cones hang down from the fermentation room's ceiling like stalactites, or unexploded warheads fallen through the roof. Steve strolled over to one and thunked it with his knuckle.

"This is a brand-new creation. I still don't know what the flavor is going to be," Steve said. "So I get a glass, come in here, and play with it on my palate." Should it taste old? Should it taste new? Was he aiming at banana forests—at transmogrification? Simpler than that, he said. "I'm looking for a beer that I like. I'm not trying to emulate anybody or anything I've had before."

Out of the cone poked a nipple-like nozzle called a *zwickel*. Steve spritzed it with sanitizing solution from a plastic spray bottle and screwed in a corkscrew-shaped spout, called a pigtail, to draw off a sample. Another spritz, a twist of a knob, and a bright stream of beer hissed into his glass. He held it up to the light and frowned. "It's dark," he muttered. He tucked his hair behind his ears and stuck his nose in his glass. "Dry, dark fruit. That's the plums and sugar." Finally, he took a sip. "I'm getting a lot of caramel notes. A little bit of chocolate." I grab a glass and follow his lead. I taste chocolate plum pudding with a burnt caramel crust, like a crème brûlée. Steve paused, swished, satisfied. It tastes traditional, it tastes new—it tastes *good*. Dark roast and fruitcake conjured hearth-warmed nights in New Clairvaux's drafty stone halls. But a twist lurked: the slight bite of citrusy hops, the acid sweetness of the plums. And that's fitting. What's new for Sierra is new—well, newish—even for Belgium. Those numbered styles—dubbels, tripels, even Westvleteren's famous quad—might seem like dusty relics but they're actually twentieth-century inventions. At the dawn of the modern era, Belgium's beer culture was in ruins. By the end of World War I half the country's breweries had vanished. Belgian beer was dead. And then it was reborn. Abbey ales, as we know them, are a recent brand.

Stan Hieronymus is the reigning expert on Belgian beer—he wrote *Brew Like a Monk*, the bible for anyone tracking down these brews or making them at home—but, despite the curiously medieval-sounding surname, he's a Marylander. I called him in Baltimore and he gleefully shattered the icons. Palm Breweries' amber-hued flagship Speciale, one of the most popular Belgian brews in Europe, isn't a vintage classic but a calculated crowd-pleaser. It was an entry in a twentieth-century contest for "The Improvement of Belgian Beer." Though the venerable Duvel Moortgat brewery dates to the 1870s, it started brewing its vivacious strong golden ale only in 1923, using a British yeast. The Trappist abbey Orval, sacked in the 1790s, wasn't rebuilt until 1926. The monks there added a brewery to help finance construction and hired a German brewmaster to run it. "There's a rich tradition," Stan agreed. "But the tradition has constantly evolved, reset because of wars, changing tastes. Some abbey beers have links to the nineteenth century, but no recipe in use now is really more than seventy years old."

When the sulfurous dust of World War I settled, the modern drinker, the modern Belgian, had changed, and as Belgium's breweries retooled, they catered to new tastes.

Reeling after the war—in need, surely, of a stiff drink—Belgium succumbed to a calamitous gin craze. Of the 130 murders in 1900, the nation's foreign minister Emile Vandervelde reported in a plea for temperance the following decade, 101 were committed drunk. While "Belgians drink much beer," he went on, "there is hardly any intoxication not caused by hard liquor." So swayed, in 1919 a reform-minded government banned spirits from bars (a prohibition not lifted until 1984). Belgian drinkers missed their kicks. Meanwhile, elsewhere in early twentieth-century Europe, light, clear pilsners were gaining popularity. Gdansk's syrupy, dark brown *joopenbier* and other meals-in-a-mug had fallen out of favor, relics of a dimmer age. The modern drinker wanted light cosmopolitan beer, and he wanted it strong.

Brewers scrambled for a solution, and they found it in sugar. Sugar adds strength without weight, fermenting directly into alcohol without the body-building proteins barley and other grains leave behind. Those proteins give beers what brewers call "mouthfeel," a tongue-coating unctuousness popular with monks looking for filling, grain-rich brews but anathema to drinkers hoping for bright refreshment. Pure sugar leaves little or no trace in finished beer, and brewers can ferment it by the ton, making extra-alcoholic brews, without worrying about adding mouthfeel. Revisiting our metaphor of beer wort as a kind of tea, imagine strengthening your mug with a dose of straight caffeine instead of adding more tea leaves. Sugar refining technology improved in Europe in the late nineteenth century when the Napoleonic wars' shipping blockades made importing cane from the Indies a hassle. Acres of sugar beets and the ability to transform them into that prized white powder turned what was once a luxury as rare as any spice into an additive as common as salt in breads, jams, and candy. By the early twentieth century brewers could finally join the saccharine fray. Westmalle was probably the first to the party, adding sugar to its beer in the 1920s and '30s. The lightest and strongest Westmalle made was called Superbier, later renamed Tripel.

This new kind of fermentable food demanded a new kind of yeast with a new kind of appetite. Old-fashioned, slow-burning yeasts used to casually munching through heaps of barley and rye can't handle the jittery boost of refined beet sugar—they'd literally gorge themselves to death on its more accessible nutrients, producing so much digestive heat they'd self-immolate. So the yeast used to produce this new generation of abbey beers is unique. Though technically the same species as yeast in any other ale (lager yeast, in pilsners, is a different beast, as we'll see), this abbey yeast evolved to ferment simpler sugars and thrive at the higher temperatures such fiery fermentations produce. High temperature kills most other kinds of yeast, or stresses them into emitting undesirable off-flavored chemicals like soapy-smelling phenols and nose-burning fusel alcohols. At 70 degrees Fahrenheit and up, though, abbey yeasts emit a bouquet of fruity compounds called esters. Westvleteren's fermentations can peak well into the 80s, producing bananay isoamyl acetate, wine-like ethyl caproate, and the clove-flavored molecule 4-vinyl guaiacol that make its beers so flavorful.

Belgian yeasts are powerful little engines too; they ferment more fully, leaving the beers, though flavorful, not especially sweet or filling, stripped of most of their residual sugar. Brewers call this attenuation—the higher a yeast strain's attenuation, the more sugars it can consume before tuckering out. British yeast, for instance, is traditionally lower-attenuating than Belgian, leaving porters and brown ales, for example, relatively sweet.

That strain makes abbey beer, on the whole, light on body and big on booze. Why the commonalities? Belgian abbey yeasts, for the most part, are all the same. "It all changed in the fifties," Stan told me, "when Father Thomas went into Westvleteren and cleaned up." Father Thomas was a traveling consultant and he, along with Jean De Clerck, who worked at Duvel and De Koninck, modernized Belgium's breweries. Thomas switched Westvleteren from wooden fermentation tanks to steel ones and introduced the Westmalle yeast strain, which Westvleteren still uses, delivered fresh each brew day.* Achel, which began brewing only in 1970, uses the same.

---

* Other abbey yeasts have similarly unexpected provenances. Duvel got its first cells in the 1920s from Edinburgh's McEwan's brewery. Inheritors of the

Today, "abbey" can mean anything—Brassiere St-Feuillien's world-class Abbey Tripel comes, indeed, from a small monastery, but Affligem's equally stellar beer is brewed by Heineken and Leffe's popular blonde by AB-InBev. "Trappist," though, has specific meaning. In fact, it's the rare word that's actually worth money, like "organic" and "Champagne." The Trappists go back some two millennia, to Saint Robert of Molesme, in France. Fed up with the laxity of his black-robed Benedictine brothers, the abbot started the stricter, white-robed Order of Cistercians in 1098. One of those monks, the abbot Armand-Jean de Rancé, founded La Trappe monastery in France in 1656.* The monks fled Napoleon's persecution to Switzerland, then into Russia, before finally settling in Belgium with a well-earned skill for self-preservation.

Like any good monks, Trappists brewed. And like good brewing monks everywhere, they made great beer. It was so good that secular brewers tried to cash in on their reputation. One was Leu-

tradition, Colorado's New Belgium got its from a bottle of Chimay the brewery's founder Jeff Lebesch bought on a bike trip through Belgium and smuggled home. The original Westvleteren yeast, beer nerds say, lives on in a mutated form at St. Bernardus. When Westvleteren temporarily shut down its brewery after World War II, it continued making beer at the St. Bernardus brewery five miles away, bringing yeast and even kegs of its own well water. Westvleteren restarted in-house operations in 1992 with a new strain, the original cells still lurking in each Bernardus bottle.

* The Cistercians knew good taste; they just didn't want anything to do with it. One story tells of a white-robed monk named Bernard, peering from his leaky-roofed abbey to the spicy excess of a neighboring Burgundian monastery, where he saw "a thousand such types of seasonings, which delight the palate but inflame the libido."

ven's Veltem Brewery. In 1960, it released a beer it called Veltem Trappist and the Cistercian monastery Notre-Dame d'Orval sued. Two years later, the Belgian Trade and Commerce Court drew a legal line around "Trappist," differentiating it from the broader term "abbey." And in 1997 the International Trappist Association established the brand Authentic Trappist Product with its corresponding hexagonal logo, now burned into the side of every precious Westvleteren crate.

Legally, "Trappist" means the beer is made by or under the supervision of monks at a certified Trappist monastery. It's specific on one level but vague on almost every other. That auspicious seal can appear on almost anything, from cheese to honey to Kentucky's Abbey of Gethsemani's chocolate bourbon fudge. The definition says nothing about what the monastery looks like, where it is, or how it brews. Westvleteren uses old-style, rectangular fermenting tanks; Chimay, modern hop extract syrup. The Engelszell Abbey in Austria—the newest Trappist brewery, and one of only two outside of Belgium so far—makes its dark, strong Gregorius beer with honey from its own hives, in a state-of-the-art German-made brew house.

When Sierra's brewers went to Belgium to research the Ovila series, they dove into this deep palimpsest of tradition and change.

Sierra's head brewer Scott Jennings won't forget the trip. Scott, Steve, Sierra's founder Ken Grossman, and a few other lucky employees took New Clairvaux's then-abbot Father Thomas and went to five breweries. ("It always helps to bring an abbot," Scott said. Keep this in mind the next time you ring Westvleteren.) They hit Rochefort their first morning. "The sun was shining through the stained-glass windows. I wanted to get on my knees and pray," Scott said. And yet Rochefort wasn't a relic. None of the abbey breweries were. "Some of them are beautiful, state-of-the-art breweries with laboratories like we have," he told me. The rays through Rochefort's stained glass illuminated modern, cylindrical fermentation tanks—the same kind Sierra uses. "Before I went on the trip, I read about [some abbey brewers'] trepidation with newer tank designs," Scott said. The choice sounds arbitrary, but it actually matters. Less contact with air means that special Belgian yeast puts out fewer of its characteristic esters. A traditional low, rectangular tank, with a greater surface-to-height ratio, gets fruitier than a tall cylinder, where only a small percentage of the fermenting beer is in contact with the air. And though some, like Westvleteren, stick with older fermenters—Sierra does too, with its Pale Ale—Rochefort and Orval have both updated.

"They're not against using modern equipment," Scott said. "Neither are we. As long as the approach is traditional." Abbey beer, then, is less about a place than a process, less about equipment than attitude. Tradition is a mind-set—styles, equipment can change, as long as the thought, the purpose stays true. Does it make good beer? Does it, as Sam Calagione said, get me closer to the gods?

Sierra Nevada isn't all that far from the abbeys after all. Pale isn't changing any time soon, but the brewery is. It's updating but, Steve says, updating in order to stay the same. This did not immediately make sense until Steve showed me the Torpedoes, ten-foot-tall metal tubes that look like miniature corn silos. In a sense that's what they are, though stuffed not with grain, but hops. "We needed to increase production of Celebration [Sierra's popular, dry-hopped holiday beer—like Pale, another historical style, brewed since 1981]. But we didn't have the infrastructure. It's a tank-intensive beer," Steve explained. Dry-hopping requires extra time in the fermenter, as the beer soaks up the oils of a fresh dose of hops after it has finished brewing. "We didn't have enough space [for more fermenters]. So Ken came up with this on a cocktail napkin." The Torpedoes work like giant French presses: fill with hops, add beer, steep, and strain. Instead of tying up a fermenter for another week the beer is pumped through the Torpedoes in a few hours, then it's ready for bottling.*

You can keep an old beer tradition alive by imbuing what you make with new flavors (plums, say) or with a modernized process (Torpedoes) so long as the original idea of the beer remains. Brewing can be a science—codified, manipulated—but beer's flavor is an art. It can't be rated objectively or measured with a computer. Or can it?

That question hits home in Sierra's quality control lab. The lab is a strange mix of technology and humanity, of computers and adjectives, hermetically sealed agar dishes and open Red Vines tubs. When I arrived, glasses of water were set out on a long table, cluttered with pencils and scrap paper. Palate cleansers, perhaps? No—Sierra's beer testers even taste their water. The computers they use aren't calibrated to handle water tests, so the tasting panel gathers and sips. They've caught things, sensory specialist Cathy Haddock tells me proudly.

---

* Sierra uses the Torpedoes on a number of its beers, including the 7.4 percent ABV Torpedo Extra IPA, the best-selling IPA in the country. It's dosed with nearly a full pound of fragrant Citra hops per barrel and bursts with the acidic sweetness of zested orange rind. Torpedo became so popular with drinkers and brewers it sparked a run on the hop—at the time of the beer's first brewing in 2009, a little-known experimental strain grown on just three acres in Washington State. The crop sold out faster and faster each season. California's Knee Deep Brewing eventually had to rename (and re-hop) their Citra IPA. It's now called, aptly, Hop Shortage.

"We taste the incoming city water, then it gets zapped with a UV light and we taste it again. Then it goes through a carbon filter and again we taste, because it should be cleaned up of any aromatics at that point. There are some computer tests, but sensory is the best way." She points to a pair of pitchers at the end of the table labeled "line one jetter" and "line two jetter." After beer bottles are filled, but before they're capped, a machine called a jetter purges the last bit of air in the bottle neck by blasting the beer with a high-pressure stream of water. The beer foams up, and that burst of CO_2 empties the bottle of air, readying it to be sealed. "We noticed some off aromatics coming from the jetter, and it turned out that [the nozzle] needed to be broken down and cleaned out."

Of course they taste beer too: fermenter samples before and after filtration, samples from the line as it goes to the bottler, packaged beer at different ages. Today, they were tasting this year's batch of Celebration, or Celly, as the testers familiarly call it. In a small separate room lined with a waist-high countertop, brewers pace in silence, pausing at clusters of cups to sip, swirl, spit, and scribble. "We set a maximum capacity in there at seven, to keep a focused environment," Cathy says as we peer in through a window. She tells me the tasters are looking for "true to brand—does that beer meet our expectations?" Subtle changes year to year are okay, Cathy says. A major flaw (eggy, hydrogen sulfide flavors from a fermentation that got too cold, for instance) is a "no go" that triggers a dramatic attack plan to clean up the beer or, in the worst cases, dump it.

Then, the testers return to the table for a Red Vine or two and run through their notes. Here, again, a human is better than a computer or, at least, has more flourish. "Stemmy. Almond Joy.

Spritzy. Brothy," the tasting panel riffed. I waited for someone to drop a "transmogrific" but the scientists kept it mainly in the real world. "Line two jetter. Tom, you say lotiony?" Cathy asked. "What brand of lotion?"

Plus, humans are better at tracking how tastes change over time, cross-referencing beers with data and memory both. I mention to Cathy that Celebration Ale has always been my favorite Sierra beer—my mom's too, in fact. "Celly over the years has gotten more rosey," Cathy says. "Last year it was more resinous."

And so what do you taste in Ovila's plums, in Celebration's rose? A decades-old orchard, a shiny new hopping tank. Tradition and twist, past and present, change and continuity. You taste the transmogrific story.*

If I could make abbey beer on my stove, then surely nothing is sacred. Like Sierra, I didn't want to make a clone, but I could have. Plenty of recipes, either shared by the breweries themselves or pieced together by resourceful home brewers, exist for even the world's most revered brews: Sierra's Pale, yes, and even West-

---

* When Sierra first released Ovila, it was branded as a completely independent beer. Sierra's designers used different bottles (no stubby "craft" icons), no bucolic imagery, and barely even a Sierra logo. Instead, a yellowed illuminated manuscript–style label with "Ovila" written in medieval blackletter type. The beers flopped. No one knew who made it. Ovila felt new, without the stamp of approval from an established name, and, priced as it was, it seemed a risk for most buyers. So when the 2013 Ovilas came out, Sierra rebranded them to look more like the rest of its line, with a roughly drawn hooded monk and, over his shoulder cherub-like, the Sierra Nevada logo sending blessings from on high. A brilliant move: the design makes the new beers seem old, makes change seem like staying the same.

vleteren. I could have taken a shortcut to greatness. But I wanted to chase it myself.

I laid my foundation with historical stones: a classic Belgian yeast, White Labs WLP500. "Fruity, moderately phenolic," the company promised. Home brew forums speculate it might have even been cultured from the yeasty dregs of a Chimay bottle. Its provenance was ancient. On it, though, I built a modern chapel.

I used sugar to boost the alcohol content, but instead of the expensive syrups Sierra and the abbeys use I stuck with regular old brown. Belgian candy sugar, as those professional-grade syrups are known, is an inverted beet sugar, which means its molecules have been broken down into pure fructose and glucose, saving yeast a digestive step during its fermentation. American table white and brown sugars are likely made from corn, not beets, and are raw sucrose, which yeast has a harder time processing. But the price is right. Instead of ordering a vial of European syrup, I popped down to the corner store for a box of Domino crystals. While there, I decided to emphasize the yeast's fruit notes with a pack of golden raisins—my KitchenAid hand blender providing a little modern sorcery when I pureed them into a mush I added to the beer as it boiled.

Sun-Maid raisins, not monk-grown prunes. Corner-store brown sugar, not fancy Belgian candy-grade. These were my nuances, my twists, like Engelszell's honey or Sierra's plums. Held up to Westy, even to Ovila, my abbey ale was unique. Cloudy and lighter than both, not quite as strong. The iron and salt in the molasses, which colors unrefined brown sugar, added a bit of a sour, ferric tang. The raisins came through subtler than Ovila's meaty plums. And yet drinking it I smelled warm, stewed fruit. I tasted oozing, syrupy sweetness. A light body was chased by a warm, boozy kick. I tasted differences, yes, but connections too. The beer told a story, its own take on tradition, its own interpretation of the scripture.

Beer is more than its molecules; a church is more than a pile of stones. I had my epiphany in New Clairvaux's chapel house, slowly being reconstructed from Hearst's reclaimed rocks—and Sierra's sales of Ovila. A foreign tradition, transplanted, growing again. No sunlight through the stained glass, though. Instead, a sprinkling rain through the scaffolding. Is reuse better than life in a crate? I wondered. Is updating tradition better than letting it molder, a relic under glass? Here, shivering in this half-made house, part old stones and part new, ancient methods and modern money, the answer is obvious. Bill Smith pointed out that the new stones filling in the missing gaps in the chapel house walls weren't made artificially old-looking and patinaed. You could tell what rested on what. And the five arches coming together in the central column sit on an ancient hunk of rock. Bill nodded: "There's a lot of history resting on that one block."

4

THE FARMER

A tired farmhand trudges back from the fields, pushing through heavy curtains of grain to join his friends, lounging under a tree after a hard day's work. A woman tears into a loaf of bread, a few others sip porridge from wooden bowls. One, entirely beat, sprawls passed out under a tree; another, quickly headed there, slugs a drink from a giant earthen jug. This is the bucolic scene in Pieter Brueghel's *The Harvesters,* painted in Antwerp in 1565. Or, more accurately, a postcard of it from the Met, sent to me by my dad. I'd recognize his crisp, architect's handwriting anywhere. On the back he asked, simply, "Beer?"

Had to be. As my winemaking friends joke, it takes a lot of beer to make good wine. The same must have been true for whatever those peasants were up to. After a long day crushing grapes, or a hot, late-summer's grain harvest, you don't want to kick back with a meaty Côtes du Rhône. You want something light and easy. You want rustic refreshment. To those peasants, as my dad put it, the solution was simple: farmhouse beer.

Farmhouse beer is a catchall category defined by two catchall styles, saison and lambic. Today, their nuances are endlessly picked over and debated by connoisseurs, but in essence the beers are simple. That is to say, wide open. Both kinds of beer were traditionally made on farms from grain scraps—post-harvest leftovers, last year's unsold stores, anything would do. That dissonant amalgam of flavors and ingredients was knit together by long aging in wooden barrels and a unique fermentation process. Light, bright saisons are fermented by zesty and powerful yeast strain brewers slowly honed and trained over many seasons. Sour, funky lambics, on the other hand, use a unique blend of microorganisms and wild bacteria—not a specific yeast at all, really, but the same kind of complex, spontaneous fermentation behind kimchi, sourdough bread, and old-fashioned pickles.

Both kinds of beer are common today, though they're hardly the cheap, laborer's day ration they once were. Saisons are one of the latest craft-beer trends, tarted-up darlings of the hippest new brewers, some of whom—Logsdon Ales in Washington or Stillwater in Maryland—specialize in nothing but. I've had dry-hopped saisons, black saisons, saisons flavored with hibiscus, sage, and even one (less successfully) with pennyroyal. Their lambic siblings are some of the most revered and sought after beers around. When a broken furnace overheated at Brussels's legendary lambic brewery Drie Fonteinen in 2009, ruining a hundred thousand bottles of its precious nectar, the beer blogosphere reeled on its axis; more than a few wept at the loss. And yet saisons and lambics have humble origins. These are beers born not in churches or in labs, neither factories nor corporate corner offices, but down on the farm.

Saisons come from Wallonia, Belgium's Jekyll and Hyde–like southern half, a region split between farm and industry, fields and mines, the granaries of Condroz and the coal pits of Charleroi. Brewed for the working masses, these were beers made out of necessity and drunk for sustenance. Saisons varied around the region, their flavors altered to suit local tastes. Miners and smelters liked them rich and strong; farmhands, or *saisonniers*, preferred something light and dry. Those preferences split Wallonia's beer, like its economic activity, in two: the malty Bière de Garde ("beer to store," so called for its longevity) and its crisper cousin known simply as saison, for the seasonal farmworkers who most enjoyed it. Flavors changed, too, based on local ingredients. Bière de Garde, made with thick-husked French barley and dark, licorice-tinged hops, came out richer than its rural brothers, which used a peppery, nitrogen-rich winter barley called *escourgeon* and lighter, more delicate hops, augmented sometimes with ginger, anise, and other spices. You'll occasionally find Bières de Garde labeled as such, but these days both subclasses are usually lumped together as saison, regardless of their grains or hops. What matters is yeast. Brewers fermented that jumble of ingredients with a powerful strain they would harvest from the actively fermenting foam of one batch and transfer to another in special metal tanks called *guilloires*. This top-skimming technique, which captured only the healthiest, most vigorous cells, combined with the yeast's scavenged diet of grain scraps, over time raised superstrains capable of eating up every last sugar from whatever brewers threw at them, making beers crisp, light, and peppery dry. Perhaps the most famous saison brewery, Brasserie Dupont, uses a house strain often compared, in its strength, to wine yeast.*

---

* Traditionally served from the barrels in which they aged, most saisons were drunk flat. But when sealed in bottles that yeast built up incredible pressure,

Saison brewers didn't use codified recipes or church-ordained ingredients. They weren't even really brewers; they were farmers. That made me wonder, then, what made saison saison? What story does that mishmash of flavors—not one taste but innumerable ones; not specific but infinite—tell? I was living in a small apartment on the fourth floor of an old, battle-scarred building, cracked walls and chipped ceiling paint, perched on a hill over San Francisco's bustling Mission District, as far from quiet Belgian grain fields as it seemed possible to get. I couldn't find saison's secret here, I thought. First things first: I needed to find a farmhouse. So I went to Rogue.

Rogue's production brewery is in Newport, Oregon. The Rogue Nation World Headquarters, as employees call it, makes dozens of beers that ship all over the globe—ninety thousand barrels a year in forty-some varieties, from their flagship boozy Dead Guy to spicy Chipotle Ale to a bacon-and-maple-syrup beer based on Portland's most popular doughnut. But I wasn't interested in one-off whimsy or factory-scale production. Rogue has another story to tell, a story set seventy miles east of the World Headquarters, on a forty-two-acre farm outside of sleepy Independence, Oregon. And that's where I headed.

I hitched on to a guided tour for a dozen other west coast beer journalists—a proper PR junket, from the passenger van to the branded tote bags. On the typical press trip these bags come stuffed with laser-jet–printed pamphlets of press releases, USB

---

making the beers intensely carbonated. The champagne-like fizz and rich, bone-white head of foam we associate with today's saisons emerged only once brewers started distributing their beers off the farm, to compete with foreign imports (mostly pilsners) in the 1920s.

drives (containing, for good measure, digital files of said press releases), and XL T-shirts. Ours were filled with beer. The van rolled south out of Portland on a spring morning and it wasn't long before I heard the first *phsssst* and was handed a Solo cup of Single Malt Ale, a small-batch brew made with Rogue's own farm-grown barley. Bready, fluffy, and English-muffin sweet, it was not a bad way to start the day.

We reached Independence by noon, the day just starting to heat up. The former hops-growing capital of the world was quiet, with that desolate, exhausted air you find in Midwest factory towns or former Borscht Belt resorts. The road stretched taut through the center of town, then scrunched into right-angled kinks as it entered the fields in the farm country beyond. Produce signs dotted the view: peaches, plums. One was painted "berries" and modified for the latest crop with a tacked-on piece of paper reading "rasp." Green hills hunched into farther distant mountains. The fields, painted in the dew-wet green of fur-topped cornstalks or the worn-out khaki of sun-baked hay stubble, gave way to fluffy, Seussian towers of hops waving in the breeze. And then a line of faded green metal barns emerged, stamped with the brewery's trademark red star. We had reached Rogue Farms.

All breweries are a little disheveled, even the big ones. The wear and tear tells a story. At places like the Miller factory in Milwaukee, ticket stubs and hot dog wrappers heap the parking lot like a public beach, evidence of the crowds of tourists they draw. At San Francisco's Anchor Brewing, a packaging-room floor strewn with caps belies the growing pains of a newly installed, finicky bottling line. At Rogue the dirt is dirtier.

We pulled in and sent scurrying a flock of multicolored chickens with fluffy, pantaloon legs. Two guys kicked a couple of empty barrels down the gravel drive; they bounced, crunching the stones. An ATV puttered up to a stack of dinged mailboxes. Hopping out of the van, buzzed and blinking in the sun, I wandered through the yard, plucked an apple from a tree, and sat on an old barrel to take it all in. The barrel smelled like warm vinegar and grape juice, pine and lemon blew through on the breeze, the big trees whispered overhead. No bottling lines here, no need for ear plugs.

Rogue's farmers grow barley and rye—scraps of this year's slug-ravaged rye crop lay drying in the sun. They grow roses that they use in a flowery wheat beer called Mom's Hef. They have raspberries, marionberries, a tangled pumpkin patch, nineteen beehives, at last count, and a couple of jalapeño plants in a little plot next to the chicken coops. But mostly Rogue grows hops.

Hops climb up twenty-foot-tall wire trellises in leafy towers called bines—not to be confused with vines. A vine inches its way, starfish-style, with suckers; hops, instead, climb with cat-tongue hairs. In an especially hot, dry summer they can grow a foot a day. We wandered through green walls so dense and fragrant you could almost feel them breathe. A guy in a *Brew Your Own* magazine T-shirt, stretched tight over a gourd-like belly, plucked a thumb-sized hop flower, a soft, pale green pinecone dotted with yellow clumps of fragrant resin. "Yeah, that's a good one," he sniffed.

That resin makes fresh hops wet and sticky and the bines' scratchy hairs turn hand harvesting into tough work indeed. "If I pulled one of these down, I'd look like I was in a fight with a cat," our guide and Rogue's farm manager Natascha Cronin said, delicately petting a bine. Still, in the hops industry's premechanized heyday, before the introduction of the tractor-pulled pickers Rogue uses, harvests were family affairs. Clans would follow the season north, and summertime farms were tent cities of migrant pickers.

The largest camps boasted dance halls and boxing rings to lure more hands. One early-twentieth-century picker remembers the scene like this: "For weeks, the hop grower's good wife has been preparing. Beds, rough but comfortable and clean, are set up in every building on the farm. Bread is baked by the barrel, doughnuts are fried by the bushel." Pickers at work walked the rows of bines, filling fifty-pound sacks. Kids were paid in soda, their parents in tokens or hole-punched tickets: one sack, one punch. During the harvest, these tickets were legal tender at local groceries for beans, bread, or a new pair of gloves. Shop owners traded them back for cash at the end of the season, when farmers were flush.

That was the golden age, and the industry around Independence boomed. Between 1895 and 1899 the United States exported 15,827,630 pounds of hops, most grown in either New York State or the Pacific Northwest. In 1909 the United States Brewers Association gushed over Oregon's weather and soil, "so deep and rich and virginal that the yield of hops is exceptionally good, both in quantity and quality." Chimay and other Belgian brewers started sneaking American-grown Galenas and Clusters into their beers; even some British breweries looked past the fabled fields of Sheffield and Canterbury to Yakima and the Rogue River. Little old Independence became the hops capital of the world. Twenty thousand acres of hops grew here, and kept growing even through Prohibition, flavoring the nonalcoholic near-beers and nerve tonics Bevo and Medico Malt. In the 1950s, though, the so-called Big Three—Anheuser-Busch, Miller, and Coors—decided they didn't need dainty, lemon-and-hay-scented homegrown Horizons. Specially bred, highly efficient crosses of hardy, if bland, German strains would do just fine. The small farms around Independence sold out and specialized or vanished altogether as huge monoculture fields took over.

But thirty years later a new generation of craft brewers looking for more interesting flavors—the region's *terroir* especially suited the intense pine and citrus that characterize trendy Imperial IPAs—reopened the market for small-scale growers, and little farms began to dot the landscape once more. Little farms like this one. Rogue planted its first twenty acres in 2008 and twenty more the next year. It grows seven proprietary varieties—each unique enough, in fact, that they've earned the area a government appellation, like Chianti or Rioja. (Rogue doesn't do much to protect its prize, though. Healthy hops grow like weeds, and lucky local home brewers might find, er, rogue Rogue bines taking root in their front yard.)

No harvest-time doughnuts anymore, but little else seems to have changed. Rogue's tractors are fifty years old. They trudge down the rows armed with mechanical claws that snip the trellises at their base and carry them, like a bird dog with its quarry, over to a conveyor belt, which flips the bines into the processing barn. Hop cones are delicate bundles of petals, but you wouldn't guess it from this torture chamber of a barn: tangles of crisscrossing leather belts, greasy gears and pulleys, stairs weaving in between, leading no one knows where, it seems, but the forty-year-veteran hop grower who built it all by hand. "The first tour I gave, I got lost," Natascha said as we made our way through this labyrinth. Everything inside was sticky with dust and resin from pulverized cones. A deep breath clogged the throat. It smelled like warm wood, burlap, orange blossoms, and diesel.

Once mechanically sheared from their bines, the cones are

piled for drying in kilns, windowless rooms pumped full of hot air from big, gas engines.* Kilns used to be heated with wood fires, and hop barns all had emergency water tanks on their roofs. Fires were common. These days, Rogue worries more about birds. After drying, the hops cool on the floor of yet another lofty barn. Farmhands regulate the temperature by opening the doors on dewy dawns, letting in the breeze—and hungry birds. Every few minutes the barn echoes with the screech of a computerized hawk, meant to scare off intruders. Finally, the dry cones are packed into two-hundred-pound bales and sent to the pelletizer, which crushes them into rabbit-food-like nubs. Some die-hard traditionalist brewers like Sierra Nevada prefer to use whole cones, but pellets dissolve faster, keep longer, and take up less space. Most of what Rogue harvests gets palletized and sent to the World Headquarters for brewing. 7-Hop IPA uses every strain the farm grows, plus its own barley, proprietary yeast, and, the label jokes, "free-range" water. The leftovers go to Natascha's husband, Josh, the farm's resident beekeeper and brewer, or, in Rogue's own lexicon, "Deputy Undersecretary of Agriculture, Department Bee."

Josh gets his own barn. It's low and dark and cool inside, and clouds move past the spaces in the pale green siding like a tongue behind gap teeth. Books—*Beekeeping for Dummies, How to Brew*—are piled next to beehive boxes, a cider press, and a hand-cranked machine, still dripping with goo, for spinning hive frames to empty their combs of honey. Bee suits hang on pegs with spare pipes, a copper coil used to chill freshly boiled wort, some empty grain sacks, and a shovel, caked with (surely) manure. Broken barrel staves,

---

* The technical term for these drying rooms is *oast*, a longtime favorite of crossword puzzle makers.

which Josh turns into furniture, heap in a corner. Somewhere in this tumult is a twenty-five-gallon home-brew system. "This is a working brewery," Josh said, shrugging at the mess. "It is what it is."

Josh poured us one of his creations. A brown ale, grainy, but a little thin, like cheap diner toast. Not quite carbonated enough, he admitted, and in truth not that great. "I wish I had more kinds for you to taste," Josh said, "but we had a heat wave and my fermentations got all screwed up. The only thing working is this brown." It's not quite a saison. Not by the book, at least. But is it farmhouse? You bet. "When I started brewing here," Josh said, "Jack Joyce [Rogue's owner] told me, 'Brew whatever you want, but it's gotta be farmhouse.' He didn't tell me what that meant. I made a dark, German-style doppelbock—that's not farmhouse, Jack said. Scottish ale—that's not farmhouse. After a while, I realized that farmhouse wasn't a style. Farmhouse means not brewing on the hottest day of the year. Brewing when you have time. Things get busy on the farm," he sighed, pointing to the sticky bee suits. "I'm harvesting honey now. Farmhouse brewing means being lazy. Using what's in season, using what you have. I don't really use recipes. Some work, some don't. I learn as I go." He calls his beers the Chatoe series, and that tongue-in-cheek hillbilly-ese carries over into their names: Dirtoir, or Good Chit (a "chit" is the first growth of a barley sprout). Josh brews when he has time, with what he can scrounge: spare hops, rye the slugs didn't get, leftovers, scraps. He brews mutts. He doesn't call them saisons but, then again, neither did Brueghel's peasants. It's just beer.

Farmhouse beer doesn't need a farmhouse after all. It doesn't need a special recipe or a cultivated provenance. All it needs is the right attitude—a farmhouse of the mind. And that, though still barn-less, I had. Whenever I scrap together a brew from previous batches' leftovers, poking around the freezer for the dusty dregs of half-used hops packets or, running low on pilsner malt, make up the difference with a handful of rye or, why not? some flaked spelt, I'm making saison. I've made a rye saison, a smoked saison, a wheat saison. One, dark as Guinness but brightened by the saison yeast's trademark snap and smoothed by six months of aging, forgotten in the back of my fridge, was sweet and fizzy like chocolate soda. Another, brewed with chipotle peppers, had mellowed into the slow-building burn of a perfectly simmered chili. All different, and all delicious. Brewed to no target style, with no recipe, no label, no name, these beers were made and enjoyed under no pressure to be anything other than their nature: beers trying to be only what they are, a refreshing mess of what's at hand.

Another postcard: a hay field, a babbling stream, a dirt drive-way, a lazing hammock, and a tiny, pale blue cabin, like a robin's egg dropped in forest duff. This was summer in the Hudson Valley, at a little house on Store Road I shared with my girlfriend, my books, and my brewing equipment. There wasn't much space in its two small rooms for anything else. The street's namesake, a short walk away, stocked country-life staples: cans of Skoal and Folgers, cases of Bud Light, unlabeled tubs of jerky. I stopped shaving. We perfumed ourselves in woodsmoke. We ate farm-stand strawber-ries and doughy pizza from the strip mall off the country highway. We read, wrote, hiked, brewed, and, when the sun swung low and the deer came out to graze, we drank home brew.

A month into our stay the car was shellacked in dust, my beard a mane—we had gone feral. The beer-labeling system we had been using, promising ourselves we'd spend the summer meticulously honing our craft, had dissolved as well. It was a mess. What had started as screenprints and stencils, custom-made stickers and punning names, had become vaguely color-coded bottle caps and Sharpie-marker scribbles. We'd note the style—actual or attempted—perhaps a brewed-on date, maybe a Post-it note of the hops we'd used. We had other things to do than spend a summer keeping books. The hammock beckoned. Our lackadaisical approach made brewing an adventure, and drinking one as well. On a fateful afternoon, while setting the table out back for a picnic lunch of farm-stand salad, grilled corn, and crusty bread, I reached deep into the back of the fridge and grabbed the coldest bottle. "SSN" was all it said.

The mystery brew poured cloudy into our jelly jar glasses. But a sip dispelled all doubt. Bitter and refreshing, fizzy and cold, grainy but dry, like a crunchy rye cracker: perfect for lunch on a hot afternoon in the country. Perfect for what it was. Perfect for that moment, perfect for the season.

I had made passable, even delicious, saisons without much thought, without even knowing it. Lambics, I feared, would not come as easily. Today, these beers are revered. Cheek suckingly sour, funky as stinky cheese, complex as old wine, lambics are not for everyone. But for those who've acquired the taste, lambics can become a life's pursuit, like scotch or Burgundy. Aficionados horde bottles and age them for years. Hip bars display their cellar inventories like treasured wine lists. It's hard to picture parched farmhands knocking back jugs of a beer sometimes served by the ounce in miniature snifters. Lambics aren't forgotten in the backs of fridges; opening one is a special occasion, not mere afternoon refreshment. Lambics today aren't mutts. These beers have pedigree.

What makes them so special? The same things that make their Belgian homeland unique. The sun, the rain, sea winds over the orchards, frost on the barley, cherry trees in bloom. Climate, soil, superstition: *terroir*.

Lambics were born on the banks of the Senne River, in the Pajottenland region, southwest of Brussels. Some pinpoint the town of Lambeek, once home to six hundred lucky residents and forty-three breweries. Farmers first, brewers second, the folks there made everyday table beer. From wheat-and-oat *walgbaert* to red barley *roetbier*, these were all-purpose workhorse brews— mash-ups, like saisons. What made them unique was what they omitted: yeast. Saison brewers carefully harvested, preserved, and strengthened their strains from batch to batch; lambic brewers just threw open a window.

Lambic's secret—the magic in the brew—is called spontaneous fermentation. Left to cool in the breeze overnight in open tubs called *koelschips*, the freshly boiled, unfermented beer incubates a host of hungry microorganisms, wild yeast, and bacteria. At this stage lambics—all beers, in fact—are syrupy sweet grain soups, a rich feast for any hungry critter. Most brewers are careful to make sure only brewing yeast gets a seat at the table. They do this through careful sanitation and selective culturing. They chill their wort quickly (a beer too hot will kill its yeast) and add a pure culture of their desired strain. If they're not careful that wort will ferment *au naturel*, like Floris Delée's date or a crock of shredded cabbage, with a potent cocktail of slow-moving microorganisms. These vagabond gourmands give lambic its characteristically sour kick. It's a sharp—mythically so—edge on an otherwise unremarkable blade. With lambics, that's the point. To make sure the deep, wine-like notes from its complex fermentation really shine, the rest of the beer's components are kept simple.

The grain is plain and hearty: pale malt, often rough, protein-rich six-row barley and raw, unmalted wheat. Six-row, so named for the number of kernels lining its stalk, is meatier and coarser flavored than the two-row varieties most brewers use. Unmalted grain breaks down slowly and produces richer but harder-to-digest sugars when it finally does. You'll see it in the health-food aisle: rock-hard wheat berries that take hours to cook. In most beers that's bad news. Brewers want fast and clean fermentations, which require simple, quickly digestible sugars. But in lambics it works. Think of brewing yeast as a domesticated hound—strong and fast but raised on store-bought kibble. Wild bacteria are like wolves, and those long-chain starches and aminos in rougher grains like grisly hunks of raw caribou.

The brewing techniques those Pajottenland farmers developed made that simple foundation richer still. Lambic brewers steeped their grains long and hot in a kettle-filling gruel. Called a turbid mash, the unique practice developed in 1822 when the Belgian government started taxing beer by the size of the grain kettles—or, in brewers' lingo, mash tuns—used to make it. This law pushed brewers to stuff more grain into smaller pots. Instead of heating these kettles directly over a fire, which would scorch the tightly packed grains, brewers strained out some liquid through a sieve called a brewers basket, boiled it, and added it back to the thick soup, or *slijm*. It was tiresome but effective. The long, slow boiling coaxed out the complex sugars of unmalted grain and more thoroughly broke down the heavier barley's larger proteins than a quick cooking would.*

The hops they used were usually low-end leftovers, added for preservation only, to keep beers safe during their long fermentations from truly nasty bacteria, most notably lactobacillus, which would turn a pleasantly sour beer undrinkably rank. After their long aging, the bright citrus, pine, and flower notes we associate with fresh, high-grade hops would have vanished anyway; their volatile aromatic compounds are fragile and flighty. So lambic brewers didn't waste money on quality goods. The problem is, you get what you (don't) pay for. Cheap, old hops often smell like cheese or feet. Or both. Or worse. Some are described as cat piss on cardboard. But if boiled extra long the taste and smell will isomerize, disappearing into vapor. The old-school lambic brewer Lindemans was once infamous for an epic boil that lasted twelve hours.[†]

At this point, the hot, sweet wort is an untended picnic of sugars and other nutrients. Most brewers today use coolant-filled heat exchangers to chill their wort quickly, add their preferred yeast, and then squirrel it away in a clean and sanitary fermenter. Not lambic brewers. Those busy farmers let their beer cool naturally, overnight. But one night is all it takes to infect the wort with millions of cells of sugar-eating bacteria and yeast. (The organisms differ, incidentally, in their cell walls. Yeast, a fungus like mold and mushrooms, has hard walls fortified with the molecule

---

* The Mash Tun Act was repealed in 1885, but drinkers found the new beers thin and lifeless, and brewers kept the *slijm*.

† Belgium's "Special Traditional Guarantee" limits the pH of so-called true lambics to 3.8 and the bitterness to 20 IBUs—a barely registered blip on America's scale, which tops out past 100 for some IPAs.

chitin—the same tough stuff in crab shells. Bacteria cells are more flexible.)

After the *koelschip* it's into the barrel, where lambic's story really takes off. Other sour beers, Flemish browns or Oud Bruins, for example, host a similar bouquet of microorganisms as lambics do, but they aren't barrel aged. Fermented instead in stainless-steel tanks, they tend toward a balsamic sweetness not so present in sharp, dry lambics. That's partly because the airflow through porous wooden barrels encourages a different sort of bacterial growth—critters that prefer a breezy veranda to a cozily sealed-up space capsule. The practice began, of course, by necessity. In wine country, spare barrels are easy to come by. There, they're mostly European oak and, of that, mostly French. French oak is looser-grained and higher in tannins than spicy, vanilla-tinged American "white" oak—the kind bourbon distilleries use. Liquor and wine can stand up to American oak's spice, but not so a light beer like lambic. Some brewers say it makes their beer taste like a tree branch.

Once ensconced, the beer's resident bugs take over. Lambic fermentation is a profound, complicated process involving sprawling casts of dozens of types of yeasts and bacteria. It can sometimes last for years. One can divide the whole process into convenient stages, but the truth is much more complicated. Microorganisms grow and die symbiotically, and a beer's sourness fluctuates over time. A rich mix of bacteria, like a tightly knit ecosystem, is healthiest.

Once a fermentation is under way, a brewer can do little to control it, or to manipulate which organisms die, which ones thrive, and what specific flavors they contribute to the beer. Temperature plays a role, and timing their schedules with the weather gives brewers a useful if loose leash over the process. As barrels flex, stretch, and breathe through the changing seasons, the organisms inside them change too.* An old lambic maker's adage goes, "A beer must spend a summer and a winter in the barrel."

The cycle runs, more or less, like this. Brewers typically operate between October and April, when farm work is light. The first organisms to take root in a fresh-made lambic are bad ones indeed: *Enterobacter cloacae* (the bacterium responsible for urinary tract infections), *Klebsiella pneumoniae* (culprit of the eponymous sniffles), and *Escherichia coli*. They're dangerous but they're only temporary tenants, and, frightening as they are, they play an important role. Such bacteria produce vinegary acetic acid, which can linger with a pleasant tang in some lambics. More than that, though, they change the young beer's chemistry, breaking down glucose into smaller pieces easier for friendlier bacteria to digest.

Next, *Saccharomyces cerevisiae* moves in. This is the familiar brewer's yeast, a lazy single-cellular beach bum. It likes its home kept warm, around 70 degrees Fahrenheit, and its kitchen stocked with quick-to-digest sugary junk food. Come summer's warmth and following that bacterial scrubbing, it performs its usual job with aplomb. The cells munch away on the beer's most accessible simple sugars and produce alcohol and carbon dioxide, which bubbles foamy through the barrel staves. When they die, their corpses decompose in a process called autolysis to become food for the next wave of organisms.

---

* Some think the secret to lambics is as simple as finding the right temperature. One lambic-making guide I found recommends the nerdiest home brewers check daily weather in Brussels and adjust the temperature of their own barrels accordingly.

S. cerevisiae—even the uncultivated strains lambic brewers catch in the wild—works quickly, and this stage lasts only a few weeks. Then, things turn sour with *Pediococcus* and *Brettanomyces*, slow-moving but thorough. While *S. cerevisiae* claims the easy sugars, these strains eat the complex, longer chains that beer yeasts miss. *Pediococcus* bacteria produce lactic acid, lambic's dominant flavor note, but can also emit funkier flavors like buttery diacetyl and sometimes even a viscous slime on fermenting beer known as rope. *Pediococcus* sounds scary, but it's quite common in chorizo and salami, and you can thank that rope for the sour in your kraut and the buttery smoothness of your chardonnay.

Brettanomyces is beer's most common wild ingredient. The yeast occurs in lambics as well as most any beer (or wine, for that matter) left open to the elements in barrels or uncovered fermenters. It's so common, in fact, brewers know it by nickname: Bretta, Bret, or just B. Discovered in 1904 by a Carlsberg brewery lab tech named Niels Hjelte Claussen, *Brettanomyces* means "British brewing-industry fungus," named after the old, stale English beers in which he first found it. There are five main strains. Claussen's namesake, *claussenii*, is responsible for the winey notes in vintage barleywines. The two types most often found in lambics are *bruxellensis* (more common, for some reason, in beers brewed in cities) and its rural brother *lambicus*. Whatever the strain, *Brettanomyces* dries a beer out. No sugar is safe; it'll eat anything, even cellobiose carbohydrates in the barrel itself. *Brettanomyces* also alters the oxygen content of the beer. Its long, cylindrical cells branch into chains and bunch together on the surface of fermenting beer, forming a goopy film called a pellicle. This gives the floating cake of *Brettanomyces* access to fresh air while keeping the beer underneath relatively sealed off, oxygen free, and safe from infection by aerobic or oxygen-dependent bacteria like *aceto-bacter*. (Like *lactobaccillus*, *acetobacter* is a wild microbe even freewheeling lambic makers try to avoid. It feeds on alcohol and creates acetic acid, turning good beer into vinegar.) *Brettanomyces* also brings its own peculiar flavors to the party. Scientists call these chemical by-products caprylic acid and ethyl lactate. Brewers know them by smell: "goat" and "horse blanket." They're what make a farmhouse beer taste, well, like a farm.

Brewers can tweak a lambic's flavors to their tastes—more goat, less horse, say—by blending batches of finished beer or mixing in sugar and fruit. Framboise, for example, is flavored with raspberries; kriek with cherries. A sweeter brew called faro is blended with brown sugar or caramel. Straight, unmixed lambics are traditionally served flat, right from the barrel. Bubbly gueuzes (a name derived perhaps from the Old Norse word for geyser) are sparkling. They were originally made by blending young, slightly underfermented beer with older batches, then sealing the mixture tight to referment and carbonate in the bottle. (This *méthode champenoise* also gives sparkling wines their fizz.) Today, though, some gueuzes are cheap shortcuts: a wheat beer spiked with sour citric acid, and sweetened with saccharin and aspartame.

With lambic fermentation such a delicate and complicated dance, brewers can be notoriously protective of their methods. Cantillon, one of the most famous lambic producers, sneers at shortcuts like those used to make modern gueuzes—one reason its fourth-generation brewmaster Jean-Pierre Van Roy refuses to join Belgium's lambic brewers guild. When Van Roy adds fruit to his kriek, he uses only whole pieces, not purees or juice. This, despite the fact that the classic Belgian Schaarbeek cherry trees that grace the Cantillon label—known for dark black fruit and big pits that, some say, give the beers an amaretto-like hint—are few and far between in the brewery's urban digs, near the Gare du Midi. When Cantillon updated its 112-year-old brew house, Van Roy saved its old ceiling tiles and thus the magic—or at least the bacteria—therein.

Van Roy, and lambic's most obsessive devotees, would argue that this close guard on tradition preserves "true" lambic, a beer made the old-fashioned way in—and this is crucial—one narrowly defined place. *Brettanomyces* and *Pediococcus* exist everywhere. A beer will turn as sour on the Mississippi as it would on the Senne. But unless its bugs are Belgian, a sour beer, these sticklers say, is not a lambic. Or is it? Can you make lambic without sacred ceiling tiles, without a Belgian breeze? I went to two American breweries to find out.

I met Allagash's brewmaster Jason Perkins behind the brewery, next to an unassuming wooden shed tucked among the trees in the forested outskirts of Portland, Maine. Lit by a bright, Atlantic sun, the woods smelled clean and fresh and perpetually autumnal, even on an early spring day, even with I-95 humming in the near distance. The shed's heavy front door bore a stained-glass window made by one of the brewery's tour guides, marked with a calligraphic *A*. Through it, I could see a tight, sauna-like wood-paneled room, almost entirely filled by a shallow, stainless-steel—though not to say unstained—*koelschip*. "We don't use chemicals in here," Jason said, pointing out a film of grime around the tub. It's cleaned with hot water only.

For Allagash, that dirt ring is precious. It's the physical trace of the scores of site-specific microbes that make the brewery's sour beer its own. The hut is a shrine to localism. Its wood was reclaimed from trees cut down when the brewery expanded, its windows from an old church in town, its door from a nearby salvage yard. And its dirt was blown in from the forest outside. Jason and Allagash's other brewers are not trying to mimic Belgium, to make a simulated Senne here. Instead, they want to capture where they are: the crisp air, the faint sea breeze, the spirit of the Maine woods.

Although its mix of scientific diligence and monastic patience stays true, in spirit, to Belgian lambic brewing tradition, and while, yes, it *does* use a *koelschip*, unmated grain, and other hallmarks of "authentic" lambic brewing practice, Allagash's beer is its own. "One thing we're careful about, from a philosophical perspective, is not to call it lambic," Jason said. Allagash's *koelschip* works more or less identically to Cantillon's, but this brewery calls it, and the beers it makes, Coolship. Like Rogue's Chatoe, an irreverent twist on tradition.

On brew days, Jason runs a hose from the brewery to the shed and pumps beer over the cooling snow, through a basket to strain out any loose hops, and into the tub to chill overnight. "This room turns into a steam bath. We wouldn't be able to see each other," Jason said. "We model our brewing after lambic production—we don't hide that. But we were curious. If we do the same thing in a different part of the world, what would happen? And what does it taste like?"*

Before they began their work on the Coolship series—a sudden burst of inspiration that took years of research to come to full

---

* Despite Allagash's claims of uniqueness, a DNA analysis of its beers ("Brewhouse-Resident Microbiota Are Responsible for Multi-Stage Fermentation of American Coolship Ale," published in *PLoS ONE*) showed they have similar kinds and concentrations of species as Belgian beers.

fruition—Allagash's brewers studied the masters. The brewery's owner Rob Todd spent a week geeking out in Belgium, swooning over tastes of abbey-made Westmalle and sour Rodenbach, fresh from the barrel. ("I was totally that guy," he laughed. A typical beer nerd.) They talked to Jean Van Roy, whom Rob invariably calls Jean-from-Cantillon, in one breathless word. They learned his process and learned, also, that it wasn't so mystical after all. "Some of the methods they use—old hops, the turbid mash—were created out of necessity," Jason said. And, coincidentally, so are some of Allagash's. The Coolship room is as big as the local zoning rules would allow. The tub size was, Jason admitted, a guess.

A cramped, backwoods shed, beers made in a bathtub—can it get more small batch than this? Still, not far from the shack gleams Allagash's vast production brewery, all fresh white tiles and polished tanks. Inside, *Natty Dread* plays loud enough to hear over the chugging bottling line. The brewery just expanded from making 45,000 barrels a year to, with a clutch of new fermenters recently installed, close to 60,000. It's a success built, like that of many craft breweries Allagash's size, on one remarkably popular beer. Allagash's is called, simply, White. When it first released the bright lemony spritzer of a wheat beer in 1994, Allagash was one of the only breweries in the country making Belgian-style beers. Now, when I told the guys at the Boston Hertz, where I rented my ride to Portland, that I was headed to Allagash they smirked. "Oh yeah," one said. "Allagash White. Girls love it." I told Rob the story and he grinned. High-minded brewers like Jean-from-Cantillon might see an insult; Rob sees a sale. "You sell beer one pint at a time," he said with a shrug.

That's not entirely true, of course. Allagash sells White by the truck-full. But not Coolship. These beers are available only at the brewery, and each batch is precious. "People who live here in the neighborhood get first dibs," Jason said. The Coolship series isn't about scale; localism is a one-on-one game. Like Josh at Rogue, Jason and Rob try new things, they take risks, they make mistakes, and they share the fruits of their labors with a self-selecting group of kindred spirits. They tell their story to a keen audience: beer journalists, curious neighbors. "We've done thirteen batches so far, so we have thirteen experiments," Jason said. "Each beer is unique to itself."

Rob and Jason took me into the barrel room, a warm, dark sanctuary—a womb, really—inside their chilly, fluorescent-lit brewery. The room has two chambers. The first, where Allagash stores hundreds of casks of its bourbon-barrel-aged Curieux, has the sweet, caramelly musk of whiskey and wood. Through a little back door, like the reliquary of an old church, is the second. Smaller, warmer, funkier, and cheesier than the first, this is what Jason and Rob call the wild room. Like a country road with skunk on the breeze, it's perfumed with the faint sulfurous tang of the wicks burned in empty barrels to keep them from rotting. Rob set down his yellow plastic coffee mug on a keg and introduced the locals. "That's Jared's beer. That's Ryan's. That's Jared's too. That's Greg's," he said. "It's our personalities in these beers." Brewer-in-training Kate Dunleavy stopped by as we talked to check on hers, quietly, as if peeking in on a slumbering child. One barrel was crossed out with red tape reading, ominously, LAB USE ONLY. A giant, 2,700-gallon vat called a *foudre* had a bloody arm hanging out of it, a remnant of a Halloween-night brew session of a pumpkin beer called Ghoulship. "We haunted this room to get all the spirits into the beer," Rob joked. Do you clean the cobwebs? I asked. "Yeah, but we leave the bloody arm."

Rob set out little stemmed flutes on an upturned barrel and poured our first sample—Resurgam, a blend of one-, two-, and three-year-old beers. It foamed up as if possessed. "Lively," Jason laughed. The beer tasted bright and vibrant, alive with a clean fresh tartness and subtle, strawberry finish. Next we tried Balaton, flavored with cherries, syrupy and sour-sweet, like roadside-diner pie; Red, with raspberries, tasted like a Jolly Rancher, so raspberry-y it seemed artificial. The beer's sourness was sharp but quiet: a razor's edge, not a cleaver. They were incredibly, unbelievably *fresh*, their flavors crisp and bright. Like pickled cucumbers that keep their juicy crunch months, even years, after being jarred, lambics preserve the season's bounty with bacteria. "Preservation through acidification," Jason says. It's ironic. They won't go bad because, in a sense, they already have. "These are indestructible. I've had a fifteen-year-old gueuze that tasted like it was two."

To make a beer that tastes so young takes time. "You can make a sour beer easily and quickly," Rob said. "You can make vinegar quickly. You can make it by accident. Some of these beers, for their first six months or so, they don't taste good. They really don't. For years, people would ask, how's that Coolship project coming? We'd say, we don't know! It wasn't until two years in when I thought, you know, we can sell these. To make a sour beer that's gentle, balanced, and subtle takes time and patience."

If anyone knows about patience, it's Jolly Pumpkin's Ron Jeffries. Ron is gaunt, longhaired, tattooed, goateed—pirate-like. He's partial to Hawaiian shirts. He signs his notes "Cheers and mahalo plenty." Friends call him Captain Spooky. "I worked in the cellar at one brewery, and I'd finish cleaning up at around happy hour, so

I'd pop up the stairs to the bar for a pint before I went home," he told me. "There was a regular who would never see me come in. I'd just appear at the bar all of a sudden. He called me Spooky."

Ron's brewery sneaks up on visitors too. The low, whitewashed building sinks into an empty, suburban Michigan parking lot, windowless and unmarked. The only sign I was in the right place when I drove up was a trash can out front on which someone has spray-painted the brewery's leering pumpkin logo above the stenciled name "Jolly Pumpkin Artisan Ales."

Inside, Ron commands wall-to-wall rows of cobweb-covered barrels, some cryptically labeled in chalk ("C-Dog," "Dos Loco," "Beast"), some bubbling over with foam. These are his beers. No *koelschip* here, but the barrels are full of wild yeasts living in the wood, and so are the bare rafters above them. The room smells sweet and damp. Wooden stoppers pop in the darkness. It is indeed a little spooky.

"We don't throw salt over our shoulder," Ron said when I asked him my now standard question about cobwebs. "But I have a lot of superstitions." For one thing, he saves the torn-off tops of the fifty-pound sacks his grain comes in. Why? He threw them out once and suffered what brewers call a stuck mash—a tank-clogging glob of grain, impossible to strain into the boil kettle. And no, he doesn't clean the cobwebs down, but that's mostly because the brewery has high ceilings. "It's just tedious," he said.

Ron speaks quietly, but once he gets up steam he unfurls in waves of weirdness. Some farmers eat their dirt; Ron likes watching his yeast. The bugs have spirits and each barrel has its own personality. "We have one two-thousand-liter barrel, and every November it'll produce ethyl acetate [an intense, nail-polish-smelling compound]. I don't know if it's the nights getting colder, or the heater coming on in the brewery, or what, but we can't leave a beer in there for more than three weeks in November. We learned that the hard way. There are a lot of unpredictable aspects making these farmhouse beers, but once you're familiar with the wild yeasts you have, they follow similar patterns. We just try to create an environment that the yeast is happy with, and set it on its path to make great beer. You brew good-tasting sour beers the same way you brew any other good-tasting beer. It's not just thrown in a barrel and put in a bottle. It's about experimenting."

You try something new, cross your fingers, save your grain bags, and wait. But still, Ron admits, things go wrong. "We have barrels that just get bad with age. It kind of sucks to dump beer, but not in a heartbreaking way. If it's bad, good riddance. If you're not brutally honest with what's in the barrel . . ." He trails off, obviously sensitive to the issue. "Well," he admits. "I have mixed emotions. In a way, it's dumping money down the drain. But any brewer, if they say they don't dump beer, they've sold bad beer."

Ron's beer is sour, but it's a good kind of sour. Bam Noire, a dark ale, has the earthy fruit of good Napa pinot; woody brown Bière de Mars snaps with the crisp tannins of cranberry juice. The rich, golden Oro de Calabaza zips with spice and acid. Still, he gets his share of drunk dials from angry drinkers, slurring into his answering machine, "It went bad! It's sour!" Made in close quarters, barrels stave to stave with each other, one beer breathing and bubbling onto the next, all Jolly Pumpkin creations share the same pleasant tartness: a prickly dry finish that, even in an extra-strong brew like the nutty, 9-percent ABV Christmas ale, Noel de Calabaza, leaves you ready for another round. That unique micro-biological fingerprint is Ron's trademark, the thalweg running through all his work, as diverse as it is. And it can be confusing. As a slightly flat brown ale might not immediately seem "farmhouse," so you might not expect your cacao-nib-infused pumpkin ale, abbey-style strong golden, or light and cloudy wheat beer to be sour. But this is farmhouse beer. Not technically lambic nor, technically, saison—somewhere in between. Ron bends the rules, or ignores them entirely.

"There aren't really any rules," he said. "Luciernaga is half saison, half pale ale. IO is a red saison. That's a style I made up. We made it red with hibiscus. Bam Bière is lighter. A session beer, like a British bitter—a farmhouse beer you can have a couple glasses of." If farmhouse beer, for Ron, has a guiding thread, that's it: beers unique to themselves, perfect for their own moment. Allagash doesn't use the name *lambic*; Ron doesn't really use style names at all. As a Bière de Garde might work best for miners and a saison for farmhands; as lambics preserve a season's treats, its sun and rain reanimated when the cork is popped, so each Jolly Pumpkin beer is unique to where, when, and why it was made—and where, when, and why it's enjoyed.

"I think of myself as an artist. My vision is to create something beautiful and wonderful—the ever elusive, ever changing perfect beer. Perfect for that moment, right there, for what you're doing," Ron said. "The next day, things will be different. Every instant has its own perfect beer, then it's gone. That's the fleeting art of the brewmaster."

"How To: Capture Wild Yeast" is one of the most vibrant and—fair warning—time-consuming threads on Homebrew Talk, the online forum for home brewers. If home brewing has its own Warhol Factory, its Greenwich Village Gaslight café, it's this. On its dozens of pages (and counting) convene a gloriously goofy mix of nerds and poets, brewers and beer snobs. They have names like Mad Fermentationist and Saccharomyces. Their avatars are red-cheeked monks and foaming steins. And they're engaged in a seemingly endless game of one-upmanship: who can make the most natural, most spontaneous, most authentic sour beer, and who can describe it in the most florid prose. My yeast fell from my neighbor's apple tree, they brag. Mine was carried by a fly!

I began following the thread to learn if it was possible to make lambic-style beer at home. To an obsessive and adventurous few, yes, it was—and there were pictures of mold to prove it. Brewers show off Technicolor petri dishes and bulging yogurt tubs. Pellicle porn, I called it. Their wives weigh in, begging for their Tupperware back—or destroyed. "A shame," one brewer commiserated when another described a spouse-nixed batch. "Looked like a nice pellicle." Even amateurs—especially amateurs, thank god—dump. But when the beers work, out come the thesauruses. Such flavors! Such smells! Banana, honey, eucalyptus, egg, dill, cinnamon, pineapple, mango, pepper, bubble gum. "Feet with a hint of sour milk," "dank musty funkiness," "like a medium-stinky camembert," "savory, footy, almost cooked-corn," "rhino farts mixed with sour fruit."

Homemade lambic walks a line between devoted scrutiny and hands-off hope. The advice I found on Homebrew Talk ranged from "if you happen to own a dye-terminator capillary sequencer . . ." to "squash a pollen-laden honeybee on a plate." Vague warnings such as "When you're confident it's not mold" offered little reassurance.

The mix of poetry and nerddom reminded me of fly fishing. And, in its way, making wild farmhouse beer is similar. Both sports demand patience and obsession, wading into nature's chaos to pluck one glimmering bit of perfection from under its roiling surface; both are an attempt to tie oneself, however briefly, with one wild speck of the infinite universe.

The general idea is yes, you can catch a trophy trout from an untamed stream. Fill a jar with wort and a little bit of hops. Leave it out overnight to attract bacteria and yeast, then wait while the bugs go to work. When it starts bubbling in a week or two, slowly build it up—skim off the foam, add it to a fresh batch of wort, and repeat, each time increasing the overall volume until, eventually, you get a beer.

You can adjust the pH to encourage certain kinds of bacteria and fend off others, you can use agar to isolate individual colonies and pluck out the healthiest ones, you can use a stir plate and a warmer to incubate your strains. You can set your plates out in early spring when oak tree sap starts flowing, hoping to catch a particular strain of yeast. You can kick-start your fermentation with some fruit or honey. Or, as a more laid-back poster advised, you can just "let it ride" and leave taste to chance and *terroir*.

Whether it will taste like ripe plums or rhino farts depends on what bacteria you catch, which depends on where you live. Everywhere from the Nile to the Senne has Pedio, Bret, and the like, but Belgium's particular mix is, indeed, special. Neva Parker, a scientist at the White Labs brewing yeast company, confirmed this. White Labs is based in San Diego, and Neva wouldn't try to make a backyard sour beer there. "The problem is the environment," she said. "Around here, we just don't have the right type of microflora. We don't know why. In Belgium, their cultures are very unique. What we do is try to re-create that." White Labs concocts its own strains, based on what blows through lambic-producing regions like Pajottenland, with a few tweaks. "Obviously, we don't grow *E. coli* in the lab," Neva assured me.

I decided to make a lambic—or, as I'd call it, *san franambic*—but first I'd fish a stocked pond. I used some of Neva's yeast, Belgian Sour Mix 1, aka WLP655. But I aged my beer in a small, three-gallon barrel—unsure of what was in the wood or could get through its pores and cracks—for a little wild flair. With my sauerkraut on the shelf above and a sourdough starter in the fridge nearby, my kitchen was a bacterial zoo. Not Belgium, but distinct in its own way. I figured I might luck out and get a few wild interlopers into the mix. I stashed the barrel in the pantry, my own cobwebbed reliquary, and "let it ride" for a year and a half.

Brewing with wild bacteria is dangerous, but only if you're not careful. One of the most commonly cited reasons for drinking beer in the first place is that it's cleaner than water. This is somewhat true. A better explanation is that bad beer tastes bad, whereas contaminated water can fool anyone, especially if he's thirsty. Yes, homemade lambics could teem with *E. coli* and streptococcus but they'd smell like a sewer. If it doesn't seem drinkable, it's probably not. And my lambic did not.

This was liquid fire—it actually hurt to drink. The san franambic's sourness didn't blossom in layers of fruit and herbs—it stabbed. It didn't ripple into lingering furrows of flavor—it slapped. I tried to taste the seasons it spent in that barrel, the spring breeze through my kitchen windows, winter's chilly fog, sticky Bay Area Indian summers. I tried to let those flavors transport me, but all I could taste was a grating, alcoholic burn. One note, and not a good one. No poetry here. Rhino farts and sour milk? It was just bad.

If, as Ron Jeffries says, there's a perfect moment for this beer, I'd be hard pressed to think what it could be. I sipped, I scowled, I sighed, and I dumped it into the sink.

I had tried to be careful. I had used a proven, lab-tested bacteria culture. I was patient, I gave it time to develop, and still I came up empty. I felt like a kid taking swings at a tee ball and grounding out to first base. But I realized that the game I was playing went against the spirit of lambic. I was missing the essence of the beer. Maybe that's why poetry failed, why it tasted thin and empty. More than patience, maybe lambics required surrender.

I wouldn't call myself a Mad Fermentationist but I know my way around a crock of pickles. Maybe the hard part here was already done. I didn't live in Belgium, or even the Maine woods, but San Francisco has its own *terroir*. Belgium has lambic, San Francisco has bread.

As any home baker knows, compared to that packet of Fleischmann's RapidRise, sourdough is a different animal—or rather, like a lambic fermentation, animals. Instead of using dried cells of pure *Saccharomyces* that rehydrate in fresh bread dough, coming back to life to chew up starch and spit out dough-rising bubbles of CO_2, sourdough bakers deploy a living stew of wild-caught bacteria and yeast called a starter or, if you want to get French about it, *levain*. Each teaspoon of sourdough starter teems with some 50 million cells of yeast and 5 billion cells of bacteria. As with lambic cultures, the bugs themselves are all relatively identical starter to starter; what varies is their ratio. Each region has its own mix. Here in San Francisco the yeast side of the equation is mainly *Candida milleri* and the bacteria *Lactobacillus sanfranciscensis.* That strain of yeast is unique in its tolerance for acid. Sourdough can get down to a pH of 3.8—as sour as lambic and acidic enough that Yukon trappers used their starter for tanning hides. It's far too sour to support most life. But not *Candida*. The yeast, however, can't digest maltose, one of the major sugars in bread dough. *L. sanfranciscensis* can, though, and so the two work symbiotically. Like Jack Sprat and his wife, the pair licks clean all the sugars it can get.

Starters, like lambics, are born spontaneously. A wet dough left uncovered will catch (from the air, from the flour, from the baker's own hands—no one quite knows) enough wild yeast to ferment on its own. The infected dough is kept alive with regular feedings of flour and passed, loaf to loaf, baker to baker, generation to generation. As with lambics, superstition reigns. One French bakery claims its starter dates to the Napoleonic era. Mine, in any case, came from my friend Ryan Kelly, a biologist, who got it from an Oregon soil scientist. With the starter, Ryan handed over a pile of Xeroxed notes and recipes: "Ryan's Sourdough Book," with chapters called "Fun with Flour" and "Sodium's Story."

Ryan was serious about his bread. Or so I thought. "If I were *really* serious," he told me, "I'd be using Petri dishes, plating out bacteria, creating a pure mix." No—for Ryan, that was work. When we decided to make a sourdough beer he hung up his lab coat and we just brewed one. We let it ride: made a simple pale ale, replacing the usual vial of store-bought yeast with a spoonful of bubbly starter. The results were surprising. It tasted *good*. It tasted better, in fact, than the lambic I'd made with my vial of WLP655. The sourdough beer was bready and light, with the slight crunchy sour snap of a good loaf. It lacked the pop of Allagash's Resurgam, the deep, balsamic layers of Jolly Pumpkin's Bam Noire. It was more like the brown ale I had with Josh in Rogue's Oregon barn. A fine beer, enjoyable; stress-free to make, refreshing to drink. What's less farmhouse than a store-bought vial of yeast? What's more farmhouse than a slice of homemade bread? My sourdough beer was perfect for its time; Neva's vial felt out of place. I still don't have a farm. But give me a piece of toast and a glass of home brew after a long day and I feel right at home in my fourth-floor farmhouse in the sky.

5

THE INDUSTRIALIST

London's Blackfriar is a bar worth flying three thousand miles to sit at. A tiny corner building, dark inside with gilt-flecked vaulted ceilings, its patinaed wooden wall panels carved with dour-looking monks, the bar is a festering sliver of the past stuck in the thumb of the present. The hard edges of the Tate Modern a few hundred yards across the Thames feel centuries away. Clutching a *London A to Z* street map and the Campaign for Real Ale's guide to local beer, my jet lag momentarily stunted by a syrupy meatloaf-and-onion sandwich, I bellied up next to an old man in a threadbare blue suit. Judging by the slackness of his half windsor, he was nursing one of what surely would be, or already was, many pints. "I'm sixty-three years old," he told me when he saw me eye his glass of tawny ale. "And I've been drinking Fuller's London Pride since I was sixteen." He felt like a plant from the city's tourist bureau, picture-book British, from gnarled teeth to polished brogues.

The Blackfriar has been serving beer since the 1870s, when it was built on the site of a Dominican friary shuttered by Henry VIII in 1536.* Today's Blackfriar hasn't changed much, and neither have its wares. It serves what my CAMRA guidebook calls "real ale": beer kept in a basement-chilled cask instead of a pressurized, refrigerated keg. Real ale is, yes, warm and flat, at least compared to what American drinkers are used to. It's served at "cellar temperature" (55 degrees Fahrenheit or so) and lightly carbonated by the digestive action of living yeast. Pasteurized kegs are sterile but, in gently cared for casks, yeast survives to continue eating sugars and producing burps of carbon dioxide. Gooseneck spouts top the Blackfriar's marble bar, hooked to hand-powered levers called engines that suck beer up from the barrels below ground. The levers wear shields marked with the style and brand: nutty brown ales, crimson bitters, wood-hued milds, smoky stouts. An impressive array, I thought, looking forward to a long afternoon's journey through the myriad flavors of the past.

I ordered a basket of chips and a pint of porter and tucked in. My anticipation deflated with a sigh. The fries were stale; the beer was not much better. Musty, sweetish, warmish. In fact, "ish" seemed to sum it up—as limp and lifeless as my barmate's combover. I asked the bartender for his take. "It's an ale," he said, in a near impenetrable South African accent. "It's darkish. Eh, I don't know mate. They all taste the same to me."

Spend your life among relics like the Blackfriar and you're bound to grow indifferent to history. Still, I had come to London wide-eyed and ready to drink and was surprised to find the home-

---

* Henry closed those monasteries in the name of Protestant temperance, but he was no teetotaler. His court drained 4.8 million pints of beer a year. A French spy reported home that his countrymen needn't fear; the English king was "constantly intoxicated."

court opinion of British beer as lukewarm as it was. Bartenders seemed bored, drinkers set in their ways. My girlfriend was offered light lager at every turn or, worse, cider. "Like beer, for girls," one particularly pushy bartender advised.

Was the England of my fantasies gone? Had expertly cared for casks of flavorful, handmade brew, tapped by genial publicans and served with a wink and a "cheers mate," all vanished? Or, like the perfect Parisian café, was it all a romance, the product of one too many P. G. Wodehouse books? London's scenery was a cacophonous tapestry of story. The city's beer, though, and the locals' reaction to it, a mere shrug. *Ish.* Was this all there was?

British beer is a story of high class and low, purity and dreck, good beer and bad. My fantasy of British beer, of golden, sparkling, cask-conditioned ales, each one alive, unique, and of its time and place, is one part of the story. That old stale porter is the other.

It's a story told in two bars, and two beers. In London's trapped-in-tar Blackfriar and San Francisco's fresh-faced Magnolia, leagues apart but joined in spirit. And in lowbrow porter and upscale IPA. One, a healthy, rustic staple turned mass-market dross, the other hifalutin and as heavy with hype today as it was when it first appeared. It's a tale of history, authentic and artificial; of new worlds and old; of preservation and change; of empires lost and those just emerging. I'd eventually find the romance I was looking for but I'd have to sift through the dreck. The story of British beer is the story of moving out of the darkness and into the light.

London, October 17, 1814. Soot-choked and deafening, muddy and cramped, the city writhes into the industrial age. It had seen fires and factory accidents, plagues and riots, but nothing compared to this. A rumble, a shadow, then a towering wave: 323,000 gallons of beer burst the hoops on a twenty-two-foot-tall holding tank in Soho's Horse Shoe Brewery, exploded through its walls, and surged into the streets, carrying away four houses and the eight women and children inside. This was porter, the world's first industrially made beer. And that flood was one ripple of a truly global conquest.

The British empire floated on porter as Rome's had on wine. Captain Cook sipped porter on the *Endeavour*, bobbing in the South Pacific. Jailers tapped casks in Sydney Cove to toast the founding of the penal colony there in 1788. Settlers pined for porter on the American frontier. Even today, some of the best versions of the style are made in far-flung former colonies: Sri Lanka's Lion and Jamaica's Dragon. Porter is a beer of scope and scale. For millennia beer had been made at home, on the farm, or in the church. In the span of only a few decades at the end of the eighteenth century, porter turned brewing into heavy industry, ruled by fiercely competitive businessmen whose scientific approach—and dastardly cost-cutting tactics—would come to define beer in the modern age.

But first, beer had to crawl out of the henhouse.

British indifference to beer seems as old as British beer itself. For most of its history it was nothing to cheer about. Warm, murky beer is a centuries-old tradition. Horrible beer was once so common, in fact, that it spawned an entire genre of poetry called "good gossips" stories. John Skelton's *Tunnyng of Elynour Rummyng*, written around 1550 is one about a Leatherhead alewife so bad she let her chickens roost in her brewhouse. "And dung when it comes drops right in the ale," it read. That's not to say medieval British drinkers didn't know good beer when they found it. "Muste be freshes and clear," one book explained. "It muste not be ropy, nor smoky . . . and sowre ale, and dead ale is good for no man." Still, the odd bit of chicken shit didn't seem to stop drinkers. Spiced to some semblance of potability or just stiff-upper-lipped, the English drank their fill. In one year, the medieval manor of Humphrey Stafford, duke of Buckingham, went through 40,000 gallons of beer. That's a daily gallon for him and every member of his staff. As the centuries advanced beer changed little—if anything, it got only more intense. Unappetizingly potent Elizabethan ales had names like Mad Dog and Dragon's Milk. And those were the ones popular or potable enough to be sold. Homemade beer could be even worse.

The brew kettle was often the only source of hot water in the house, serving as brewery, washroom, and laundromat, and brewing was a housewife's daily chore, as it had been since Gilgamesh's day. "Our English housewife must not by any means be ignorant in the provision of bread and drink," a 1615 home owner's handbook read. And, indeed, few housewives lacked for instruction. Home brewing guidebooks abounded, including *A Treatise on Strong Beer* and *The Compleat Family Brewer*. But *more* guidance did not necessarily mean *better*. Even through the 1840s home brewing books dismissed thermometers as useful but unnecessary. Water temperature was judged by touch. Grains should be steeped in a pot "hot enough to bite smartly upon your finger," one guide read. The resulting wort should then be drained into a boil kettle slowly enough that its stream runs "as thick as a crow quill," explained another. This romantic tinge did not elude one Scottish lord describing his estate's brew house on a fall morning: "The primroses are basking in the morning rays; the dewdrops are sparkling the last upon the leaves; the blackbird trills his mellow notes in the thicket . . ."

As bucolic as brewing might have seemed, the beer itself was often less sunny. "Old women can brew, though when we meet with thousands, aye, millions of barrels of beer unfit for drinking, we do not immediately conclude that every old woman is fit to brew," sighed the beer writer William Littell Tizard. Tizard was more than just a snob, he was a historian, inventor, brewing instructor, and relentless self-promoter. His half dozen self-published books, including 1846's exhaustive *Theory and Practice of Brewing,* were packed with instructions, scientific analysis of ingredients and process, explanations of the latest brewing inventions (most of which, such as the "Octuple Fermenting, Attemperating, Cleansing, and Preserving Apparatus," were his own creations), and often hilarious riffs, asides, and personal observations on the nascent brewing industry. Tizard was a grump, but a well-meaning one, confident in the power of chemistry and science to uplift beer for all. "It is here as with other branches of the useful arts and sciences," Tizard wrote in the preface to *Theory and Practice,* "that the errors of each generation must submit to correction by future experience."

Tizard's day teemed with such errors. Bad batches came out tart or "pricking," "foxed" with furry red mold, or slicked with the gelatinous growth called rope from infection by beer-souring wild yeasts. After dispensing with needless science, brewing books seem compendiums of cures for spoiled batches. Some advised adding chalk, lime, or oatmeal. One, a mix of chopped mutton, egg shells, and potassium carbonate or potash. "Your liquor," it promised, "will soon be restored to its first perfection." Yet the margins of brewing logs kept by lords like that poetic Scot were filled with disappointed notes. "Something which should not be allowed to happen," one read. But as in Mesopotamia most home brew was drunk fresh, before it could turn too sour. "One thing in our favor with this brew," one lord sighed about a foxed batch, "is that it is likely to be disposed of quickly."

With the coming of the industrial revolution at the turn of the nineteenth century, most of the newly urbanized middle class gave up brewing. They didn't have the time or the space in cramped, modern cities. What few lords were left in the country switched to drinking trendy new imported Indian tea and, now that the War of the Spanish Succession was over and trade with France had resumed, Bordeaux wine.

Brewing didn't disappear, it just modernized. The shift appears in home brewing handbooks' updated tone—now, with science! "Perhaps there is no art which from the careful manipulation it exacts, and the application of science it demands, should receive a larger share of thought and attention," wrote William Robert Loftus in his 1856 manual *The Brewer: A Familiar Treatise on the Art of Brewing*. "Mere routine may suffice with most brewers, though the result in many instances may be doleful; but the intelligent brewer will extend his observations." The thermometer, once a nerdy frivolity, was "an instrument of such exquisite sensibility" to this new generation of brewers. Loftus's advice was neurotically specific, explaining everything from the proper arrangement of taps on a mashing tank to the size of the canvas flap on the boil kettle drain spout (exactly one foot wide). No crow quills here.

Science made brewers more observant, but even an observant brewer wasn't always in control. Loftus called the process of malting grain part of the "mysterious workshop of vegetable life," and that's exactly how it seemed to him and his cohorts: ordered but unknown. Now wielding thermometers, brewers learned a surprising amount. They discovered the volatile oils in hops by measuring how their flavor and aroma changed over time as they were boiled. They knew how grains naturally germinated and had a rough understanding of the heat and moisture necessary to activate their enzymes artificially. They could recognize the language of the workshop but they couldn't yet speak it.

Since the days of Ninkasi and her snarling dogs, malting was an art ruled by ritual not science. Even a stickler like Tizard wrote that good maltsters and kilners, the men who managed that artificial germination and ran the furnaces to dry out the sprouted grain afterward, could judge malt "with the eye, the teeth, and the palate." He told aspiring maltsters to pick grains "of a bright color" and germinate them "until they emit an agreeable scent." Maltsters sifted grains with a seventy-pound rake called a *wohlgemut*, German for "pleasant disposition."

Variations in flavor were out of brewers' hands; not matters of choice but dictated by location and method—what kind of wood kilners used or how hot their ovens got. Southern British beers took on the smoky tones of the region's straw-fueled kilns; western ones were slightly cleaner, made with barley cured over wood.

Still, kilners had a few tricks. One was to roast the grains wet. That let kilners use higher heat, which produced darker grains with richer flavor, without scorching the kernels. Sprinkled with water as cord after cord of beech or birchwood, bale after bale of straw, was loaded into the roaring fire, the grains piled above it on a perforated metal floor turned dark and shiny as burnished leather, sometimes even popping like popcorn. This was called brown malt, blown malt, or snap malt, both from the sound of the exploding kernels and from the distinctive sweet tang of the beer it made.

Brown malt's enzymes died, or denatured, in the high heat, disrupting the cellular machinery that would otherwise convert the grain's starches into fermentable sugars. With starches still too raw for yeast to digest, a beer made with brown malt stayed sweet, thick, rich, and relatively low in alcohol. And that was porter.

Ah, *porter*!

Nineteenth-century London, wrote Thomas De Quincey, was as filthy "as if the waters had but newly retired from the face of the earth. A duller spectacle this earth of ours has not to show than a rainy Sunday in London." De Quincey took to harder stuff, but most Londoners found their respite in porter. In what was now the largest city on earth, nutrition was scarce. Dark beers were a valuable source of carbohydrates, especially for the working class from whom the beer got its name. Porter, wrote one contemporary fan, is "a very hearty and nourishing liquor, very suitable for porters and other working men." (Those porters would often sneak tastes of the beer from the barrel as they moved it, a trick they called "sucking the monkey.")

Good enough for moving men—good enough, even, for nursing mothers, whose doctors prescribed them porters made extra rich with milk sugar. Branded Nourishing, Diatetic, Tonic, For Ladies, and For Invalids, the beers, wrote one doctor, were "destined to occupy an important place in alimentary hygiene." But what Loftus called porter's "ethereal character"—sweet, musty, and as comforting as a worn Chesterfield sofa—had a secret. The sweetness from brown malt was part of the story. But the beer's slight sour tinge "assumed through the agency of time, contact, or decay," was, Tizard wrote, "inexplicable." Where did it come from?

Tizard suspected the barrels in which porter was stored—a subject, he wrote, "darkly wrapped in obscurity." He wasn't far off.*

Beer back then was often served mixed. Instead of dumping unsold kegs of "low" or stale beer, bartenders would just top them off with new "high" beer. Joseph Bramah, madcap inventor of the hinged toilet bowl valve and an unpickable lock, patented a two-handled, single-spouted tap that made mixes of fresh and old beer right at the bar.

The best of the blends, bartenders discovered, was porter. The rich starches from brown malt, impervious to quick-acting brewing yeast, mellowed with time, becoming food for *Brettanomyces* and other strains of slow-moving bacteria that infected the beer as it sat in airy barrels. Stripped of what remained of brown malt's starches, the resulting old porter became especially dry. Mixed, the fresh beer enlivened the old, and the old added complexity to the young. The result: "an inviting brunette complexion and a mantling effervescence, with a spumous, cauliflower head," according to one fan. "A fullness on the palate, pure and moderate bitterness, with a mixture of sweetness, a certain sharpness or acerbity without sourness or burnt flavour, and a close creamy head instantly closing in when blown aside, and a tart and astringent flavour," Tizard wrote.

Brewers caught on and began selling premixed porters. Leg-

---

* Even Tizard made mistakes, though. One of his more crackpot theories was that electrical currents controlled fermentation. Instead of studying the barrels' porous wood, or the influence of oxygen or bacteria, Tizard was obsessed with their iron hoops and rivets. "Of this, however, we are pretty sure," he wrote. "That the preservation or destruction of beer depends upon electricity; and the most certain mode of preservation is to insulate, as much as possible . . . all utensils or vessels connected with the brewing or storing of beer."

end has it a Shoreditch brewer named Harwood was the first to do so, mixing up an "entire butt," or barrel, for local bar the Blue Last in 1722. It's likely apocryphal, a tale first told some eighty years after the fact by a writer named John Feltham. True or not, however, Harwood failed to cash in on the trend—he went bankrupt in 1747. The Blue Last was smarter. It used the porter myth in its ads, and the place is still around today.

Preblended porter revolutionized the industry. Brewers invested in bigger and bigger mixing vats until barrel size became an arms race. Breweries unveiled their newest and biggest with dances and dinner parties—held inside the barrels. At the height of the porter craze Huck's brewery had so much beer fermenting in its warehouse that a cellarman making his rounds asphyxiated from the carbon dioxide coming out of the open tanks. The rescuer sent to save him died too.

The biggest brewers won seats in parliament. Sir Humphrey Parsons's pair of 54,000-gallon vats earned him a knighthood and his beer the title "Parsons' Black Champagne." Giant barrels alone didn't guarantee success, though. Brewing porter required mountains of grain and the finished beer had to age for months before it could be sold. As brewers grew, they looked for shortcuts. In 1784 the Red Lion brew house in the East London district of Wapping installed a steam engine, the first in the city, which it used to grind malt and pump beer between its giant sheet-iron vats. Soon, ads for Tizard's "Mashing Attemperator" and other steam-powered gizmos filled the back pages of brewing journals.

As their tools advanced, the brewers' observations grew keener. Perhaps the most revolutionary change came with a device called the hydrometer. Popularized in John Richardson's 1786 book *Statistical Estimates*, a hydrometer is a delicate glass rod that, when floated upright in a liquid, reveals by how high it bobs the density of the sample compared to pure water. A hydrometer will tell you how much salt is in seawater or how much sugar is dissolved in beer. For the first time, brewers could judge the sweetness of their malt by more than its taste alone. By taking multiple readings of a beer over the course of its fermentation, they could also determine how efficiently it fermented, that is, how much of its sugar turned, eventually, into alcohol. The hydrometer revealed the root of porter's sweetness: brown malt itself. The grain's useless, denatured enzymes made it wildly inefficient. This also explained why porter was so expensive to make. Brewers had to use bushels of the weak malt to gather enough enzymes to convert even a portion of its starches into fermentable sugar.

Armed with this new data, Tizard fumed over the "slovenly and unscientific" state of malting. "Malt houses in general are badly lighted and ventilated," he wrote. And if the buildings were bad, the sight of the malted grain itself sent him spinning: "these maltreated cripples, swollen by putrefaction in shapeless mouldy masses," with "an unpleasant odour, like exhumed bodies of martyrs risen up to appall the assassins that sent them prematurely to their destiny."

Now fluent in the language of vegetable life, brewers tried speaking it—not just observing the workshop but seizing control of it. They hunted for a shortcut to a rich, dark beer. Could they design a more efficient grain? Could science succeed where straw bales and a "pleasant disposition" failed? With coke, they found their answer: pale malt, born in a cloud of soot.

London's skies had taken on a hacking porter-black hue over the decades. "A town of machinery and tall chimneys," Dickens wrote in *Hard Times*. "Out of which interminable serpents of smoke trailed themselves for ever and ever, and never got uncoiled."

This was Coketown, named after a powerful new fuel processed from tarry bitumen coal. Coke was first made successfully in the early 1700s and was used primarily for iron smelting and heavy industrial work. The first commercial breweries to adopt it were in northern English coal country: Derbyshire and Nottingham. Coke burned bright, hot, and, more important, consistently. The smoky constituents of coal get cooked off when it's refined into coke, making it much cleaner as compared to wood or straw. Malt kilned in coke-fired ovens could be roasted extra slow, which kept its enzymes intact, and it emerged without the smoky tinge that characterized brown malt.

No longer sniffing for "agreeable odors," kilners could adjust temperatures to the degree. They developed a new technique, drying malt slowly, over three or four days, at gradual increments of low temperatures: 80 degrees Fahrenheit the first day, in the 90s the second and third, finishing at a relatively balmy 120. Still full of healthy enzymes, this new pale malt provided the starch-converting power brown malt lacked. Brewers call this its diastatic power, or DP, measured in degrees Lintner. A malt with a DP of 35 degrees has enough enzymatic strength to convert all of its own starches to fermentable sugars. These malts are called "self-converting." In general, the lighter a malt is dried or kilned, the more enzymes are preserved in it, and the greater its DP. The palest malts can have DPs as high as 150 degrees, which means they'll not only self-convert but have enzymes left over. A dash of pale malt provides the boost of enzymatic fuel needed to handle brown malt's unconverted starches.

Lighter malt, of course, also made a lighter beer, in color and taste. Pale malt added enzymes but not much flavor. That was the gift of darker roasts and the Maillard reaction, which explains why the charred sugars in, say, a piece of toast give more flavor than those in a plain slice of bread. Brewers made up the difference with black malt. If pale came from a slow simmer, black malt was born in a blaze. A process based on coffee roasting, making black or "patent" malt (so called after the British engineer Daniel Wheeler secured official rights to the procedure in 1818) involved toasting grains in a coal-fired drum at temperatures edging past 400 degrees Farenheit. This was snap malt, amplified: sharp, astringent, and strong. Just a dash would give all the flavor and color porter brewers using pale malt were missing. Whitbread, the first purpose-built factory brewery in the UK, ordered a shipment of Wheeler's malt as soon as it hit the market; Truman's, one of London's largest porter breweries, and Barclay Perkins, in 1815 the largest brewery on earth, got hip soon after.

With pale malt's enzymes and black malt's roasty kick, this new breed of dark beers were turbo porters: drier, sharper, blacker, and, now that once unfermentable starches could be transformed into alcohol, stronger. Brewers called them, simply, stout and stamped barrels with crosses indicating their strength: XXX, XXXX. Simonds of Redding's Archangel Stout tipped the scales with a ludicrous XXXXXXX.* The most famous stout came from Southwark's Anchor, a beer especially popular in the Baltics that presaged today's Russian Imperial Stouts. The style hit big in Ireland, too. Guinness's Extra Superior Porter, introduced in 1821, was slow to catch on at home—imported English porter was still

---

* Today, that nomenclature is just confusing: A Wadworth 6X, for example, is light and bittersweet.

popular then. By the 1840s, though, the brewery would be export-
ing much of its output back the other way.

Some missed the humble tang of mellow, old-fashioned porter. In a midcentury guide to London life, one W. Weir described
the difference between brown malt–brewed porter and black
malt–brewed stout as "the strained and shallow efforts of a pro-
fessed joker compared with the unctuous, full-bodied wit of
Shakespeare." Tizard, naturally, was even harsher. He bemoaned
the loss of his beloved "nappy brown," writing that "in many houses
a black sulky beverage [is] substituted in its stead, on the taste of
which the stranger experiences a shake, as sudden and electrical as
that which seizes a spaniel when quitting water."

Strained and shallow was better than poisonous. Coke-fired
kilns were expensive, and cost-conscious brewers turned to dubious adjuncts to save a buck. Some were tame, like molasses, licorice (sometimes called "Spanish juice"), and "essentia bina"—sugar,
boiled, then set on fire. Others less so. Iron sulfate for a frothy
head. Gentian root or chile pepper for, one guidebook advised, "a
sensation of warmth." One adventurous recipe included beef
bouillon. Purists like Loftus denounced this "homicidal quackery," and petitioned the government to stem the tide. It tried. In
1824 fines included £100 for sugar, molasses, or honey; £20 for hop
substitutes; and £100 for outright drugs. But brewers fought back.
They formed the Free Mash Tun Association to lobby for a looser
approach to regulating beer. And the government relented, first by
allowing brewers to use sugar as a substitute for malt and then by
removing all taxes on ingredients altogether, taxing beer instead
by strength. Brewers could get their sugar—in fact, any flavor at
all—from whatever source they found best or, in other words,
cheapest. Strength declined and quackery flourished. In the mid-

1800s the Society for the Diffusion of Useful Knowledge, publishers of educational pamphlets for the working class, tested 215 beers and found chemical adjuncts in more than half.

Where brewing failed, chemistry tried to cure, with its chest of shiny new toys: salicylic acid and saltpeter for preservation, sulfate of lime for bitterness, hyposulfurous acid for clarity. Brewers led the charge, but the larger food industry soon followed. Shoppers saw their pickles colored green with iron sulfate crystals; their bread whitened with alum, chalk, and ammonium carbonate; their candy dyed red with arsenic; their Gloucester cheese rind made bright orange with lead; their milk laced with lime. This exuberant chemistry experiment finally led, in 1876, to Prime Minister Benjamin Disraeli passing the Sale of Food and Drugs Act and starting the modern practice of food inspection.

Beer hadn't improved much in the three hundred years since Elynour Rummyng's doleful wares, but it had surely moved out of the bathtub and into the factory. And I followed it.

At home, I warily eyed my greasy stove, my mismatched mason jars of grains, my bubbling fermentation jugs, labeled with masking tape and Sharpie and tucked into corners around the kitchen. No chickens but no steam-powered flywheels either. I was four floors above urban San Francisco, but this was still country-house brewing. To really make porter I'd have to upgrade. I needed some industrial-strength gear, and I also wanted a way to test my beer on a crowd. Until now, I'd been brewing tiny batches at home—a fine way to replicate rustic shamanic grog. But porter was mass made and massively popular. Part of its story was its scale. I wanted to see if it would be as big a hit today as it once was.

I sought out the only beer baron I knew. I called Jim Woods. Jim runs a small brewpub a few blocks from my apartment, and he agreed to let me turn its twenty-gallon system into a porter factory and his clientele into time travelers. His setup is cramped but a world apart from mine. In a tight back corner of the bar, big steel kettles are stacked over propane burners. Fermenters line the tiled wall, their silver inverted cones like an arsenal of stubby warheads. The stainless steel control panel shows digital temperature readouts, blinking colored status lights, a name badge—"created for brewmaster James Woods"—and dramatic-looking buttons and knobs. Firing it up, with the hiss of propane, woosh of catching flame, and brief puff of singed arm hair, I couldn't help but shout *Ignition!*

Tizard's tsk-tsking scowl hovered overhead as Jim flipped open his laptop and clicked on ProMash, the computer program he uses to calculate his recipes. In my brew logs, color is recorded mainly by splashed stains. Jim asked me for an SRM to plug in—a Standard Reference Method number corresponding to the beer's color (1 and 2 for the lightest pilsners, 40 for the darkest stouts). "An 'inviting brunette'?" I joked. What is the International Bitterness Unit grade for "mantling effervescence"?

We guessed, and we brewed. We had ordered some proper English brown malt from Thomas Fawcett and Sons, a seven-generations-old West Yorkshire malting company. It's no longer toasted over wood or straw-bale fires, but today's industrially kilned brown malt is still as flavorful—and as inefficient—as it was in centuries past, especially from a small-batch producer like Fawcett. Jim and I had to boost its diastatic power with pale malt, just as our predecessors had done. To make up for the loss of flavor we added a pinch of acidulated malt, laced with lactic acid to give the beer a slight sweet-sour tang, and some black patent malt for a roasty edge. The brown malt was gorgeous: shiny oaken nubbins cracked to reveal a creamy caramel heart, like tiny roasted chestnuts. The black patent had been furnace-blasted into bitter, sooty shards, smoky and dry. We used earthy, woody Fuggle hops, a classic strain, thanks more to its hardiness to disease and longevity when stored than to any remarkable bitter flavor. That was okay. Brown malt was the star of the show and we wanted its taste to shine undisturbed.

We steeped our grains and boiled our hops. As with lambics, a longer than normal boil not only concentrates the brew, making it sweeter and richer, but also evaporates many of subpar hops' more funky aromatics. Then we drained the raw wort into two ten-gallon fermenters. It smelled like coffee and poured dark and viscous (as thick as a crow's quill?). One thing Jim didn't have in his high-tech but tightly packed setup was a thousand-gallon barrel in which we could age the brew to give it the dry, slightly acidic tinge of classic stale porter. Lacking the wood, and the beer-souring microorganisms living within it, we provided our own: a plastic vial of *Brettanomyces,* labeled in frightening orange to warn brewers that despite its sterile packaging this was not a typical, mild-mannered domestic yeast. We carefully cracked the seal and added the creamy slurry to one of the fermenters. We let each bubble for a month, then we mixed the two, high and low, young and artificially aged, in a blend to serve at the bar.

Bostwick's Best Brown Porter, as we called it, was a little sweet, a little sour, with a creamy body and slight tannic bite, like milky coffee. With a scoop of vanilla it made a fair affogato. Perfect(*ish*), I thought, for San Francisco's damp and drizzly November. We charged six bucks and sold it all—no need to top off the keg with a fresh batch. But Bostwick's Best didn't get rave reviews. "It tastes old," one drinker said. "Dusty," sniffed another. And then he plunked down a crisp twenty bucks for a bottle of pale ale. Bitter and bright, his preferred drink was as far from my sweet, dark porter as he could get, as far from rainy London streets as sunny Calcutta. My porter was okay, but drinkers want IPAs.

Ninkasi and the gods of grain have been dethroned. In today's beer world, all hail the hop. Craft brewers outbitter one another with double, triple, imperial IPAs and fight pun for pun with their names: Hoptimator. Tricerahops. Hoptimus Prime. These beers can be as pricey as they are potent, but drinkers still lap them up. Their popularity is not a new phenomenon, though. IPA's hype, quality, and expense have been central to its story since the beginning.

Most beers have humble origins. Take saisons, a chore of running a farm, brewed with whatever was at hand. Or porter, the result of a working-class trick that eked a little extra life out of a stale keg. Not IPA. IPA was royal born, a drink of the effete, designed for princely palates. While porter lived in dank, dark cellars, IPA matured in the holds of India-bound clippers, jostling mahogany tables and pungent sacks of tea and saffron. Porter filled chipped tankards and IPA glittering glassware. Porter comforted with sweetness; IPA braced with astringent vigor. Bitter, all of a sudden, was better.

Today's bitterest beers confer badges of toughness on those who brave them, named Palate Wrecker or Arrogant Bastard (its motto, imprinted under a snarling gargoyle: "you're not worthy"). But the first IPAs were marketed as healthy, temperate alternatives to the rich, thick stouts and porters most drinkers were used to.

After the soot and sour beer of the factory age came an era of coffee and tea, bitter and bright. When a prosperous dawn punctured London's fog and Samuel Johnson's cutting wit sliced through the Romantic poets' misty-eyed histrionics, drinkers turned to kicks instead of comfort. Coffee shops buzzed, tea cups rattled nervously on their China dishes. "Coffee," wrote the historian Mark Pendergrast in his history of the drink, was "the sole, bitter companion of the lost soul," a symbol of—and balm for—the modern condition. Not all were pleased. "That newfangled, abominable, heathenish liquor called coffee," one critic noted at the time, has caused "a very sensible decay of that true old English vigor, our gallants being every way so Frenchified that they are become mere cock-sparrows." As tastes evolved to appreciate the bitter and bracing, drinking itself changed from necessity to choice. By the late 1800s British drinkers had more free time and more money to spend. They had options. Beer could be more than sustenance. As midday refreshment, or an after-dinner celebration, beer became a status symbol.

Porters, thick with "heavy mucilaginous matter," were "better for hardy and healthy constitutions, such as workers in metal, soil, or mortar," suggested doctors. "Fast young gents" were too delicate, too Frenchified. They allayed their "embittered existence," *Punch* magazine joked in the 1850s, with something lighter. Something new that sparkled in their glasses. Bitter, hoppy pales.

Pales, "carefully fermented, so as to be devoid of all sweetness, or, in other words, to be dry," were best for the delicate middle class, wrote Jonathan Pereira in his 1843 *Treatise on Food and Diet*. Physicians touted their favorite brands to medical journals. Writing in *The Chemist,* one doctor reported that, of all the alcohol he'd tried—"and I have paid some attention to the subject"—the pale from Edwin Abbott's Curtiss brewery in East London was supreme. "From the many examinations that I have made of it," he wrote, "we are convinced of its purity. A peculiar bitter and agreeable taste, found of much advantage to patients recovering from low febrile states, and during convalescence after various complaints, as it strengthens the body and gives vigor to the system." He signed his letter, authoritatively, "Medicus."

That dryness and agreeable taste—that vigor—came from hops. In vogue on the continent where the piney blossoms had become a preservative key to international trade and a symbol of Protestant resistance against ceremonially and medicinally herbaceous Catholic-brewed ales, hops were slow to catch on in England. There, they were scoffed at as fatteningly Dutch. Fifteenth-century Flemish refugees from the Hundred Years' War had brought with them a taste for hoppy beer. Hopped beer "is a naturall drynke for a doche man," physician Andrew Boorde wrote, and "doth make a man fatte and doth inflate the belly, as it doth appere by the doche mennes faces and belyes." But thanks to a newfound appreciation for life's bitter pleasures, hops eventually became not just popular among the English but a panacea.

Hops could do anything. "The spirit of the hop. . . has ascribed to it several valuable qualities," Loftus explained. "That is is cordial and warm, aperitive, digestive, diuretic, stomachic, and sudorific. It certainly acts as a tonic and anti-spasmodic; and its aromatic bitter restores the depraved appetite, corrects unwholesome nutriment, promotes digestion, and increases the nutritive quality [and] virtue of all food united with it."

That "aromatic bitter," though, was lost in old, sweet porter, boiled away or mellowed with age. Neither were the dark murky brews particularly attractive to the rich, who now drank, increasingly, from fancy glassware.* In response, brewers cut out the black malt, toned down the brown, and made a light, clear beer that put hops on display. Made in such huge quantities, and aged so long, porter brewers used the cheapest hops they could find. Now that drinkers could actually taste them, pale ale brewers wanted the best. And in England the hop of choice has stayed practically the same since it was first grown centuries ago: Kent Goldings, now, as then, the spring-green jewel in pale ale's crown.

Abbey brewers and their secular competition had already discovered hops' sedative and preservative qualities from the antimicrobial acid humulone. But hops' sticky little packets of resin tucked among the flowers' leaves contain more than medicine—they're packed with flavorful oils and acids too. Humulone and lupulone produce strong bitter flavors, while farnesene and myrcene oils contribute more ethereal notes of spice, citrus, and pine. The kinds of acids and oils in a given strain, and the ratio of acids

---

* Again, an age's drinking vessels hold more than its booze—they carry its culture. Auroch horns hid a shamanic brew's potent turbidity, but as glassmaking evolved to make clear mugs, tankards, and rummers possible in Britain and Bohemia, beer followed. For years, glassmaking was a highly secretive and rarified art, ensconced on the Venetian islands of Murano. But in the 1670s, the English glassmaker George Ravenscroft figured out how to make clear glass cheaper and more durable than the Venetians by mixing in lead oxide, kick-starting Britain's domination of the global glass trade. Industrial-scale glassmaking there took off in the 1880s with steam power and the repeal of a debilitating excise tax. Ravenscroft, though, abruptly shuttered his business just five years after revolutionizing the trade; today only about a dozen of his pieces, marked with a raven's head seal, remain.

to oils in general, determine that particular hop's contribution to a finished beer. These characteristics are determined by *terroir*: the soil and climate in which the hop grows. High-acid hops are more effective—it takes fewer of them to get the bittering, preservative actions brewers wanted. But their flavor proved too intense for lighter beers. Strains like Sussex, with what Tizard called its "intolerable smatch," or the dreaded Nottinghamshire North Clays, grown in rock-hard northern soil, "remarkable for a rankness of taste approaching to nauseousness," said Loftus. These hops, "fit only for porter-brewing, when mellowed by age," according to John Levesque's 1836 *Art of Brewing,* were relegated to beers whose dark toasty notes and sweet full body would counteract the hop's intensity.

Light-colored high-oil hops got the highest price, and some unscrupulous growers even took to bleaching their crop with sulfur to gain an edge. Hops from Kent were thought to be the best of all, mellowed by the cool kiss of North Sea breezes. And over all the strains grown there, Goldings reigned. Like Red Delicious apples, though ubiquitous today, Goldings began as a singular and serendipitous find. A lucky "Mr. Golding, of the Mailing quarter of the district," out hiking his moors, stumbled on a rogue plant "of extraordinary quality and productiveness." He snipped a few cones to plant back home and stepped into brewing history. Like Red Delicious, too, Goldings are remarkably tame. Bland even. Goldings are only about 3 to 4 percent acid (in some new high-octane American strains, the acid content edges past 15 percent) and boast high amounts of the flowery, herbal oils humulene and caryophyllene. British pale brewers and their clientele prized Goldings for their delicacy—grassy and mild, like a clover field in spring.

Hops, even delicate Kents, had another benefit. Brewers noticed that the more they used the longer their beer would last. The bitter aromatic oils in hops, as continental brewers in Germany and Belgium had by now discovered, are naturally antimicrobial, keeping at bay the bugs that, given free rein in sweeter, less-hopped beers like porter, turn them sour. Bitter hops weren't just good for the drinker; they kept the beer healthy too.

As hops took root in Kent, the British Indian army abroad was parched. Soaking through their khakis in the equatorial heat, clutching sticky pints of thick Crown-issue porter, they pined for a different kind of refreshment. One Bombay-bound ship was saved from wrecking in the shallows when its crew lightened it by dumping some of its cargo—no great loss, a newspaper reported, "as the goods consisted principally of some heavy lumbersome casks of Government porter."

Most of that porter came from George Hodgson's Bow brewery, just a few miles up the river Lea from the East India Company's headquarters. The EIC made all its profit on the return trip, when its clippers rode low in the water, holds weighed with skeins of Chinese silk and sacks of cloves. Outward bound, they carried supplies for the army, who paid well enough for a taste of home, and particularly for beer.

The trip to India took six months or more and crossed the equator twice. In these thousand-ton ships, called East Indiamen, the hold was a hellish cave, hazy with heat and packed gunwale to gunwale with crates and barrels that pitched and rolled and strained their ropes with every wave. While sailors sick from scurvy groaned above, the beer below fared just as poorly. It often arrived stale, infected, or, worse, not at all, the barrels having leaked or broken—or been drunk—en route.

Hodgson sold his beer on eighteen-month credit, which meant the EIC could wait to pay for it until its ships returned from India, emptied their holds, and refilled the company's purses. Still, the EIC was frustrated with the quality Hodgson was providing. The company tried unfermented beer, adding yeast once it arrived safely in port. It tried beer concentrate, diluting it on shore. Nothing worked. Nothing, that is, until Hodgson offered, instead of porter, a few casks of a strong, pale beer called barleywine, or "October beer." It got its names from its strength and its harvest-time brewing, made for wealthy country estates "to answer the like purpose of wine"—an unreliable luxury during years spent bickering with France. "Of a Vinous Nature"—that is, syrupy strong as good sherry—these beers were brewed especially rich and aged for years to mellow out. Some lords brewed a batch to honor a first son's birth and tapped it when the child turned eighteen. To keep them tasting fresh, they were loaded with just-picked hops. Barclay Perkins's KKKK ale used up to ten pounds per barrel. Hodgson figured a beer that sturdy could withstand the passage to India.

He was right. His first shipment arrived to fanfare. On a balmy January day in 1822, the *Calcutta Gazette* announced the unloading of "Hodgson's warranted prime picked ale of the genuine October brewing. Fully equal, if not superior, to any ever before received in the settlement." *Finally.* The army had been waiting for this— pale and bright and strong, those Kentish hops brought a taste of home (not to mention a scurvy-busting boost of antibiotics).

Hodgson's sons Mark and Fredrick took over the brewery from their father soon after, and the praise turned them ruthless. In the years to come, if they heard that another brewer was preparing a shipment, they'd flood the market to drive down prices and scare off the competition. They tightened their credit limits and hiked up their rates, eventually dumping the EIC altogether and shipping beer to India themselves. The suits downriver were not amused. By the late 1820s EIC director Campbell Marjoribanks, in particular, had had enough. He stormed into Bow's rival Allsopp with a bottle of Hodgson's October beer and asked for a replica.

Marjoribanks's challenge arrived just as Allsopp had lost its hold on the Russian market. Reopened after the end of the Napoleonic wars, the door there shut again in 1822 when the czar imposed new tariffs on British imports. The Russians had liked stouts, and most of the export market came from Allsopp and other Burton breweries. It was cheaper for them to send their wares downriver to the port in Hull and across the North Sea to continental Europe than it was overland to London. There was no direct rail service to town and drinkers there were already well stocked.

Allsopp was good at making porter—dark, sweet, and strong, the way the Russians liked it. When Sam Allsopp, only a few years shy of turning the business over to his sons, tried the sample of Hodgson's beer Marjoribanks had brought, he spit it out—too bitter for the old man's palate. Still, India was an open market. Allsopp agreed to try a pale. He tapped his maltster Job Goodhead, who steeped a test brew (legend has it) in a tea kettle. Good enough, they thought, and sent it out.

Allsopp's India pale ale wasn't an immediate success. Some thought it was too sweet, others too flat. Everyone agreed Goodhead's pale malt wasn't quite pale enough. He fired his coke kilns again, extra slow this time, and made an even lighter shade. He called it white malt, the finest grade yet produced. The beer it made was something special too: "a heavenly compound," one satisfied drinker reported. "Bright amber, crystal clear," he went on, with a "very peculiar fine flavor." Meanwhile, in its hubris, Hodgson's brewery had overextended itself and its quality slumped once more. The former champ was being called out for sending, according to an anonymous 1830s editorial in London's *New Monthly Magazine*, "very indifferent beer, sometimes very bad beer, and sometimes no beer at all." Bow lost its monopoly and sheepishly turned its ships toward less picky markets in Turkey, Syria, Greece, and Egypt.

Allsopp owed its success to more than malt. Deep underneath the brewery, forces beyond Goodhead and Marjoribanks's reach were at work. Calcium sulfate–rich gypsum deposits in the Permian-Triassic sandstone strata west of Burton leached sulfur into the water—drinkers called its eggy undertones the "Burton smatch"—which lowered the pH of the beer it made. A more acidic beer ferments especially dry, with fewer fruity esters and residual starches. Starches can turn a finished beer cloudy—not a nice look in fancy glassware. And esters are what give the fruity notes to porter, a beer made with the soft water bored from London's chalky soils. The result? Burton IPA, a strong, bitter, "clear, sparkling, Champagne-like" beer. Its water made Burton special; its beer would conquer the world.

The story of its rise begins, apocryphally, thus. In 1827 an India-bound clipper wrecked in the Irish Channel. Stuck with three hundred hogsheads of IPA five thousand miles from their target market, the ship's underwriters decided to unload the beer cheaply in Liverpool, giving working-class Brits their first taste of pale ale. A decade later, a new railway finally made it viable for

Burton brewers to ship by train and IPA hit London. The rail came in 1839—Burton's production spiked by half that year alone. From 1850 to 1880 the tiny town went from making 300,000 barrels to almost 3 million.

London's porter production slowed to a trickle. "The fickle public has got tired of the vinous-flavored vatted porter," Alfred Barnard, one of the day's best, and only, beer critics wrote at the turn of the century. (If anyone would tire of porter, it was he: the pince-nezzed beer and whiskey writer was known for having visited every working distillery in Great Britain and more than a hundred of its breweries.) Pales, according to William Ford, then secretary of the British maltsters association, were "of great and increasing estimation with the middle and higher classes of society." The last porter-only holdout in London added pale to its brewing schedule in 1872. By 1887 porter made up less than a third of all the beer brewed in town.

Brewers far from Burton chased the local flavor. Chemists began peddling "Burtonising" gypsum to mimic the town's hard water. Those companies with more means cut out the middleman and simply built a factory in Burton. The river Trent was soon crowded with satellite plants from the big-shot London breweries Ind Coope, Mann, Crossman, Truman, and Charrington. While Allsopp and the long-suffering Bow battled for market shares, Bass slipped into the cracks they left open and soon eclipsed both. Bass called its beer Champagne Ale and soon it was as celebrated as the wine. In 1853 Bass built its second brewery and, a decade later, its third. By the end of the century Bass was the largest brewery on earth, and the first ever to make a million barrels in a year. Its beer, branded with the world's first trademark, a bright red triangle, was recognized "in every country where an Englishman had set foot," said an ad at the time, from India to the South Pacific to the frozen north. The first Arctic explorers hauled sleds of pale through the ice. "As nourishing as beefsteak," one captain wrote. "The sustaining qualities of a beer such as this are far greater than those of wine or spirits."* For a time, IPA's domination was complete.

But even golden gods must fall. First marketed as the pure, invigorating alternative to porter's murky depths, IPA was a victim of its own success. Not every brewery could afford the best white malt and Golding hops. The famed Kent hop yards could produce only so much. As IPA's popularity grew, brewers began to look for alternatives. By 1860 Bass was supplementing homegrown hops with American strains, mostly Fuggles and Clusters from New York and Oregon. Drinkers rebelled, complaining that the new beer tasted like black currants. An editorial in the *Edinburgh Review* ran: "American hops may be dismissed in a few words: Like American grapes, they derive a coarse, rank flavor and smell from the soil in which they grow." This "American tang" is prized today; the musty intensity—cat piss, some call it—defines such Northwest-grown hops as Simcoe and Columbus.

---

* A beer so strong it could reportedly stick a pint glass to a table could stand a chill. Captain Edward Belcher, who sailed after the vanished John Franklin in 1852, set a glass of beer on deck one brisk, -42°F day, and reported that it took twelve hours "before affording any symptoms of coagulation." It was a special recipe so viscous, one brewer said, the wort wouldn't flow through the brewery's pipes but had to be carried tank to tank in buckets. Barnard wrote that a fourteen-year-old bottle of the 1875 brewing had "a nutty flavour" and "was as sound as the day it was brewed." More than a century later, the beer writers Ron Pattison and Martyn Cornell tried the same batch. "Liquid Christmas cake," they declared. "Pears, figs, charred raisins, stewed plums, mint, a hint of tobacco, a memory of cherries."

Despite complaints, Bass stayed the course, soon adding hops from Germany and California and barley from France, Turkey, and Algeria. It was a slippery slope: sneaky brewers first used foreign hops, then no hops at all. Some, taking cues from the porter brewers who came before them, used quinine as a replacement. Others were more nefarious. A niggling French professor named Poyen wrote into a British paper with his suspicion that brewers were recruiting French chemists to better bitter their IPAs—what became known as the Great Strychnine Libel of 1852. Bass's owner vehemently denied the charges, writing in the *Times*, "Why, Sir, India would long ago have been depopulated of its European inhabitants had there been anything pernicious in pale ale."

If not lethally strong, beers became middlingly weak. A new style called mild, or just plain bitter, emerged at home. Without the rough passage to India to brace for, brewers didn't need as much preservative antibiotic oils in their beer and could scrap the expensive hops altogether, avoiding spoilage by serving their delicate beer extra fresh, or "running." In 1857 Bass's bitter used three and a half pounds of hops per barrel; by the turn of the century the countrywide average was down under two pounds. By 1910 the AK Mild from London's Fuller's brewery used barely a pound and a half.

The mighty pale had fallen. I would bring it back.

There was nothing mild about IPA—there still isn't. Built to last, and to please the most discerning palates, these potent beers use the choicest ingredients available, the palest malt, the finest hops. IPAs were all class. To re-create them I'd need the best, and that meant Maris Otter malt and Cascade hops.

If your pint smells like a loaf of country bread, if you could almost eat your beer with a knife and fork and a slice of sharp Wensleydale, if one sip swims in anglicized visions of hearths and hay lofts, chances are these images are conjured by Maris Otter barley. Maris Otter is a touchstone for British and British-style beer. A hardy winter-harvested barley prized for its warm, full tones, its taste might be traditional, but its provenance is modern. Maris Otter was first developed in 1966 at the Plant Breeding Institute on Cambridge's Maris Lane.* Those were dark days for British beer. Cheap, lowbrow milds dominated the pubs, and an expensive grain like Maris Otter never quite caught on with big brewers. (Fuller's was an exception and Maris Otter is one reason its London Pride is so admired.) Maris Otter almost vanished. By the 1990s no one was growing the barley at all. What grain stores were left in the few old-timers' barns was all that remained, the last aromatic breath of a golden age. Then, in 2002, two companies bought the rights to the heirloom strain and Maris Otter started popping up again.

A passion for baking, or some deep-seated Anglophilia, draws me to the rich and grainy. When I see a beer on the menu that lists Maris Otter in its ingredients—what brewers call the grain bill—I order a pint, no question. When I saw the raw grain at my local home brew store, I grabbed a handful and munched away as if they were M&Ms. Heaped in a white plastic bucket in a row of identical white plastic buckets, Maris Otter was almost indistinguishable from the other pale malts—one shade given dozens of names, British, Belgian, German, Canadian; Golden Promise, Halcyon, Victory, Pearl.

---

* The PBI's other agricultural contributions include Maris Piper and Maris Peer potatoes and Maris Widgeon wheat.

I asked the guy at the counter if he could pick out Maris Otter by taste alone. He rolled up the sleeves of his ratty windbreaker and crossed burly, tattooed arms. "What matters is, can you?" he scowled. Sure, my perception was clouded by romance. Was I swayed by the story of a rescued heirloom? Of course. But that is what IPAs are all about. The status, the rarity, the tradition—in a word, the hype. I bought a bag.

Now, I needed hops—and I needed the best—so I went to the source. I met John the hops farmer a few years back over a plate of local duck at the Lagunitas Brewing Company's backyard beer garden in Petaluma, California. He was wearing a sterling silver, cowboy-style belt buckle emblazoned with a pair of twirling hop vines. Our conversation quickly turned to beer. John is John Segal Jr., a hops farmer in Washington's Yakima Valley, the hop world's Napa. The Segals are a dynasty there. John's dad wore a matching buckle. John's son wears one too.

Segal Ranch has been growing hops for decades, but things got rocky in 2008 when they lost their biggest client, Anheuser-Busch. The Belgian-Brazilian brewing conglomerate InBev had bought the company and changed Budweiser's recipe, passing over John's delicate Willamettes for cheaper, more robust strains. In classic American agricultural irony, to honor the last of its contract InBev paid John *not* to grow.

John downsized and started catering to the Northwest's then booming craft beer scene, planting classic strains—minty Northern Brewer and grassy Fuggle too delicate for most big brewers— alongside trendy, extra-bitter palate scrapers, resinous Nugget and CTZ. But I wanted Cascade.

What Maris Otter is to British beer Cascade hops are to American. Thanks to high-profile flagships like Sierra Nevada's Pale and

Anchor Brewing's Liberty, American pales are defined by the spritzy grapefruit blossom nose of Cascade hops. And John Segal grew them first. As influential as Cascades are, they're relatively new. Like Maris Otter, their roots go back to the late 1960s. The American hops industry had never fully recovered since the one-two of Prohibition and a plague of the hop-withering parasite downy mildew in the late 1920s wiped out the crop and many of its buyers. Farmers grew almost entirely Clusters, a workhorse bittering hop, leaving the specialty strains to Europe. Coors Light's image may have been all-American but its spicy-sweet nose was decidedly Teutonic, from aromatic German Hallertau Mittelfrühs.

But when a fungus-spread epidemic of verticillium wilt in the 1950s cut the Mittelfrüh harvest and inflated prices, American brewers—already wary of the Cluster monoculture's susceptibility to a similar outbreak—started pushing for homegrown diversity. Coors talked to the Department of Agriculture, which talked to some breeders, who talked to John Segal, who planted a few samples of a hybrid strain he called USDA56013 in 1968. Four years of test brewing (and a name change) later, Coors bought Segal Ranch's first commercially available crop of Cascades, paying one dollar a pound at a time when most growers were lucky to get half that. Two years later, a fledgling San Francisco start-up called Anchor bought some for a new beer it was making, Liberty Ale. Liberty shocked American palates, the Cascade's citrus bite too aggressive for most. But growers saw its quality, and corresponding price, and Cascades soon swept the valley. Today, Liberty is a craft beer common denominator and Cascades are an icon.

Victorian British brewers could taste the North Sea air in Kent Goldings, dank Nottinghamshire dirt in North Clays; John can tell the difference between his Cascades and those grown in

Moxee, fifty miles northwest of his farm. John's Cascades are especially high oil—less bitter and more flavorful than most, rich with citrusy myrcene. They smell like a slow-simmered reduction—not grapefruit but grapefruit sauce. I asked John for a taste and a few days later a zip-tied bag of bright green leaves landed on my stoop.

I'm an off-the-cuff home brewer. I use what I can find: a dash of whatever's in reach and a pinch of whatever seems interesting. I rarely follow recipes and I almost never write things down. It's about the process, not the product, I remind my long-suffering friends as they stare down the latest whim: a cranberry-and-honey smoked pale, say, or a chipotle-chocolate pumpkin stout. And so I work best on forgiving canvases, beers with room to play, like saisons, where long aging and a powerful yeast temper my elastic sense of time. The IPA was different, an exercise in taking something great and then trying my best to ruin it. I brewed carefully, watching my temperatures to the degree, lest my grains steep too hot and, like overbrewed tea, leech bitter tannins into the brew. I made sure not to boil my hops too vigorously or for too long, in order to keep as many of their fragile, volatile oils intact. I carefully cleaned and sanitized a fermenter and added an all-purpose, classic yeast strain—with none of abbey yeast's fruit or saison's pepper, called Whitbread Ale and described, lamb-like, as clean, mild, and delicate. I gave my beer time. I was gentle. I was patient. And then I sent my baby to India.

Symbolically, of course. First, safety. I buckled it in with an extra handful of hops, a preservative boost for the aging time ahead. Then—no room for barrels in my galley-size kitchen, and no hold belowdeck in my fourth-floor apartment—I simulated a wooden cask by sprinkling a handful of toasted oak chips into the fermenter. I banished the brew to the top of the fridge, the warmest, dustiest corner I could find.

Then I went out for a beer.

On a cold and blustery November day it was warm inside Dave McLean's Magnolia gastropub, the Grateful Dead softly noodling on the stereo. The skies felt British, but the only thing Anglo here was the beer, porters and pales, barleywines and bitters. Dave's an Anglophile but he's not a nut. "I have a deep distaste for anything that comes across as a period piece," he says of other British bars, with old-timey charms as stale as their fries. "Historical re-creation without any new energy and thought applied to it. It makes me think I'm at a Disney theme park." No Ye Olde mirrored signs here; no Union Jack fluttering out front. Just great British beers.

Dave, big bushy beard and big burly belly, was a Jerry Garcia–like presence on his bar stool throne this afternoon, quietly commanding, a gentle twinkle in his eyes. The waitress came over, asking if we were ready for another round. Dave hemmed and hawed a bit—"Yes. No. Yes, I am"—and settled on a pint of his own Billy Sunday Bitter. "I was really looking forward to this. Sitting down, having a couple pints, talking about British beer. It's a treat for me." Steeping Maris Otter steamed up from the basement brewery, filling the bar with bready perfume. "That's what the heart and soul of this place is all about."

Dave grew up in Pennsylvania, went to school at Boston University, but soon he followed beer—and the Dead—out west to California, where he enrolled in the UC Davis master brewers program. Others took their diplomas to the Budweiser brewery down the highway in Fairfield; Dave moved to San Francisco and, in 1997, opened a little neighborhood pub on the storied corner of

Haight and Masonic, just steps from the Dead's purple Victorian crash pad.

Dave fell in love with British beer on a pilgrimage to London in the late 1990s. "I remember the Lamb, on Lamb's Conduit Street, near the British Museum," he said. "And I remember standing at the bar there drinking my way through all the beers, and loving them. I had had bottled Fuller's in the States, even draft Fuller's. But there, they just tasted so lively. It was real ale: Unfiltered, fresh, vibrant, alive." But when he went to the source, he found a dried-up shell. "Burton was in ruins. We pulled up to Bass, and they had a whole rack of barrels just rotting in the parking lot. Fifteen or twenty barrels, dragged out of the brewery and left to rust. It was a pilgrimage to a place that wasn't appreciated even by the people there," he said. "The brewers didn't know what to do with us. These odd American fellows here for their beer tour."

In these dismal days for British beer, Dave got lucky at bars like Lambs. Consumption in Britain was plummeting, breweries were shutting down or consolidating into massive international conglomerates. By the late 1990s the Japanese bank Nomura owned more pubs in England than anyone else. Meanwhile, in the United States, what British beer made it over was likely skunky and stale, shipped too warm by clueless distributors, served too cold by bars, and local brewers were keen on the bolder styles from Belgium and Germany.

Dave would have to re-create tradition back home. At first, he tried to make the exact beers he had had in London. "When I started, I was aiming at a target. The first beers I made were clones. You gotta start somewhere," he admits. At brewing school, he was annoyed there was no "IPA Week," no "Porter Syllabus." Then he realized: "There's no IPA that's the model of an IPA. There's no one thing. It's always just a snapshot in time, like particles that only exist when you look at them. A clone is the opposite of beer with life and vitality. Beer is of a moment, of a time. There are a million ways to answer the question *What is good beer?*"

Dave answers with ingredients. Good beer means good material: Maris Otter from the tiny, family-run Branthill farm in East Anglia. Hops from growers like the Segals. "It comes down to a personal philosophy of how things are made, and who makes them," Dave explains. His manifesto: "Small is beautiful, hands on is better, slow is the way to go. The people and the methods that are gloriously inefficient make things I like the taste of the best. That's how we approach our craft."

Dave rethought his approach to beer at a time when similar stirrings were reinvigorating the dreary scene he left in London. There, a new breed of craft brewers is keeping the traditional alive by giving it new blood. Leaving the Blackfriar, I needed a taste of something fresh, so I headed north. Following the sounds of Bob Marley—the soundtrack to practically every American brewery I've been to, from Maine's Allagash to California's Russian River—I found Camden Town, under the train tracks on the northwest edge of town. Started by a winemaking Australian named Jasper Cuppaidge, Camden Town epitomizes the UK's new-school brewing scene. I asked about inspiration, and brewer Mark Dredge opened the walk-in fridge and showed off his private stash. It's all American: cases of beers from Colorado's barrel-aging specialists Odell and the hop-mad California stalwarts Lagunitas and Bear Republic. The tap handle for Camden's IPA is green—an admitted nod to Sierra Nevada's verdantly labeled flagship. Dredge brews a hoppy pale, along with an Irish stout, a Czech pils, a Bavarian hefe, and other international styles, on a gleaming German brew system.

Elsewhere, I'd see the same mix of new and old. At a little alley bar called Gunmakers, I found hoppy California-style IPAs from Kernel, based on the southeast edge of the city, on the banks of the Thames. "Kernel? Oh yeah," owner and UK beer writer Jeff Bell said. "They're basically an American brewery." At Euston Tap, another tiny bar, this one tucked into a nineteenth-century railway station entrance, I had Redemption's Trinity: citrus and bread notes, as fresh as jam on toast. At Craft Beer Co., under a vintage sign for "Charrington's Celebrated Burton Ales" and a baroque chandelier hanging from the mirrored ceiling, a pair of drinkers sat in front of a half dozen half empty pints, arguing over hops. Herbaceous, lip-smacking Targets, one says, "are the worst hop in the world. They taste like toothpaste!" Here, I drank a Dark Star Hophead—pineapples and almond—and a Magic Rock West Coast PA, as dank as NorCal's, er, *other* famous export.

Even the old-timers are getting hip. At the Fuller's brewery complex in Chiswick on London's north end, the oldest wisteria in Britain still slowly inches up the two-hundred-year-old walls of the brewer's house, but there are no moldering barrels in the parking lot. Unlike Dave's visit to Bass, the Fuller's people are used to tourists. They expected me. Brewmaster John Keeling greeted me in the parking lot with a handshake and a neon green safety vest.

"Thirty years ago we were the smallest brewery in Britain," John said, proudly. "Now we're the largest." Like London itself, the brewery is a palimpsest—not a corpse like what Dave found in Burton but an exquisite one. Tucked among the modern tanks is a 150-year-old copper kettle and similarly ancient mash tun, a big, black, cast-iron monster, bristling with rivets and copper pipes, adorned with leather-belted flywheels, enameled red, blue, and maroon. "We refurbish them every thirty years," John said.

The glass-walled computerized control pod looks across a pair of shining boil vats into the servant quarters and dining room of the original brewer's house, a gulf some twenty feet and two centuries wide.

Up and over gangways, through the ages we walked, past lines of earmuffed workers filling casks dented and dinged, some thirty years old or more, slamming in bungs with heavy mallets, as they always have. No Bob Marley here, just the classic, mechanized din of wood on metal.

Peering into an ancient square-shaped fermenter, its copper-lined walls pocked with age, I asked about tradition. Some say these open squares, into which young beer is poured or "dropped," are the only way to get the creamy butterscotch flavor that marks the best old-fashioned pales; others say they're a bitch to clean and their temperature is impossible to control. What do you lose when you drain the squares for the last time? "Some brewers swear the square makes the best beer, but it also makes the worst," John told me. "Once in a blue moon you'll hit a peak and it's sensational. But you don't know why." He's not traditional for tradition's sake. "Some people think that the best way is the traditional way. No. Making consistent beer is about making small adjustments." And that means changing with the times. Using newer machines, and better—not just older—ingredients. "The best way to do it is how we do it."

We went down to the cellar for a beer. Here, under the brewery's stone and wood and iron and copper—the material weight of time—we breathed the musty air of antiquity. John waxed historical. "We have all the old records. We're still keeping them. We brewed a Double Stout from 1893, with the same exact recipe." They tracked down the same sugar, the same hops. They found a vintage strain of nineteenth-century barley called Plumage Archer—grown by Prince Charles himself. But Keeling remains a London Pride man. He beckoned me behind the bar and let me try my skill at pulling the perfect pint. "Pour it gently," he told me. "It's a living thing."

A bright January day felt equatorial enough to announce my IPA's arrival and dust off the jug for a taste. The beer-logged hops had settled to the bottom. A few wood chips remained afloat. In between, the beer was clear, pale, and sparkled through the dust. I thought that months steeping with sodden leaves and lumber would stain the flavor of pure-bred hops and malt. I anticipated old and stale; traditional IPAs could not have been as great as the fantasy. Those thirsty soldiers would have relished any taste of home, their palates primed by want. Instead, the beer I made was fresh and flowery, finishing with just a touch of caramel sweetness, like a dusting of toasted coconut. Quenching and bright, a taste of spring in the dead of winter, a glimpse of the southern Asian sun. What I thought would be flat tasted alive. Exactly as good beer should, no matter how old.

IPA's success suddenly made sense. It wasn't just an antidote to porter, it was new approach to beer itself, a symbol of what was possible if it were treated as a luxury, not as sustenance or medicine and not a factory-made product. This may explain why IPAs are craft beer's darlings, why the style has endured as a showcase for new ingredients and creative craftsmanship (Dogfish Head's continuous-dosing Randall, Sierra's French-press-like Torpedo). The style wears its age with grace, changed by time but made stronger, more vital by the journey.

Dave sets down his fifth or sixth pint, wipes his beard of spindrift. "I'm becoming more reflective after brewing for half my life," he says. The afternoon beers surely have helped. "Beer is a living document of history. You can get stuck in your ways, which is the same as dying. Or you can stay as fluid as you can." And with that we order another round of the same.

6
THE PATRIOT

Thanksgiving was on its way and I was almost ready. I had my local yams and my organic cranberries. I was reading up on quinoa stuffing. In San Francisco, November might be an incongruously balmy Indian summer but the food scene here is all tradition: heritage this, heirloom that. Thanksgiving demanded an artisanal, homestyle feast. The food would be classic—that, I was sure of. I just didn't know what to drink.

By this point in my research I was deep into beer. Every meal presented a chance to explore one or another of history's forgotten corners. Every drink was, much to my friends' dismay, work. Bar tabs I could write off as necessary sensory training, but what was the cost of a bored-to-death drinking buddy? Few were the pints that didn't provoke a stoolside lecture on the history of the grain therein, the noble provenance of the hops. "And Hallertau begat Mount Hood and Mount Hood begat Sterling and its brethren..." For me, though, my work hadn't spoiled the pleasure of a good beer. In some ways it had actually enhanced it.

Drinking had become a game of free association. Each glass,

each flavor, would trigger a revelation about the past, remind me of a curious anecdote or an arcane bit of trivia, a "did you know that you're drinking a . . ." (and a chorus of sighs in response). On good days, at least. On bad, drinking was a puzzle of translation and interpretation. What was the beer trying to say? Why these flavors? Where—*when*—were they taking me? My drinks were either rich with story or empty canvases on which to paint a history I had yet to discover. So with Thanksgiving approaching I hit the books. *What* to drink? That, I didn't know. But at least I knew *when*.

I had heard that the Pilgrims put in at Plymouth Rock, making an earlier stop than they'd planned, because the *Mayflower*'s stores of beer ran dry. A myth, surely, I figured. Like Franklin's famous aphorism about beer and God and love and happiness, tacked above bars and stretched over bellies from Missoula to Miami, most of what we think about our forefathers' relationship to beer is hopeful, romantic justification of our own enthusiasms. Franklin, it turns out, was actually talking about wine.* The Pilgrims on a beer run? I doubted it. Still, they must have been sipping something. What had they been drinking or, if the stories were true, wishing they were?

---

* The quote in question comes from a 1779 letter Franklin wrote to his buddy the French economist André Morellet: "We hear of the conversion of water into wine at the marriage in Cana, as of a miracle. But this conversion is, through the goodness of God, made every day before our eyes. Behold the rain which descends from heaven upon our vineyards, and which incorporates itself with the grapes to be changed into wine; a constant proof that God loves us, and loves to see us happy!" It first took on its mutated form, with beer as the "living proof," in a 1996 article in *Beverage World* by Anchor Brewing's founder, Fritz Maytag. Maytag admitted to making an edit, "but I am sure [Franklin] would have agreed to my modification."

My early research into Pilgrim beer turned up dry. It's hard to parse the truth from the buckle-hatted legend. No one kept a bar tab at the first Thanksgiving. But digging through books on early colonial food I stumbled on something with more historical weight: a beer recipe from another American icon, George Washington. Not quite as foundational as the Pilgrims but a founding father nonetheless. (Besides, the first official Thanksgiving holiday was Washington's idea.) The spirit was there, I thought. At least I had a recipe.

Washington has always walked a compelling line between high brow and low. Gilbert Stuart's famous portrait of him is a case in point. The first president's giant, uniformed shoulders look ready for the weighty responsibility of helming a new nation; his disproportionately puny head sits atop them, with a sheepish "who, me?" stare. He's the kind of founding father, like Franklin, with whom you can actually imagine sharing a beer.

Washington entertained his high-society guests at Mount Vernon with good Madeira and other imported wines—he knew how to play the cultured host. But when the guests left, the Virginia boy dropped the act. "Ordinarily," reported the George Washington Bicentennial Commission in a paper on the president's weekly Thursday dinners, "a silver mug of beer stood beside the President's plate." And when it came to pleasing the populi, Washington—like centuries of presidents since—knew that beer spoke to the masses more effectively than wine. When he ran for the Virginia House of Burgesses in 1758, he rolled out the kegs on election night, hoping for a favorable turn. He knew his constituents well. In those days, the average American over fifteen drank thirty-some gallons of beer a year.

Ale-swilling George was even a home brewer. Or at least he

had a brewery at home—whether he had time between running a plantation, and a country, to stir a mash himself is another story. But he took enough of an interest in the brewing process to record a basic beer recipe in the back of one of his notebooks. Jotted in 1757, its scratchy lines have been intriguing and confounding home brewers for 250 years. It reads, in full:

To make Small Beer:
Take a large Siffer full of Bran
Hops to your Taste.—Boil these
3 hours then strain out 30 Gall
into a cooler. Put in 3 Gall
Molasses while the Beer is
Scalding hot or rather draw the
Molasses into the cooler & St[r]ain
the Beer on it while boiling Hot.
Let this stand till it is little more
than Blood warm then put in
a quart of Yeast. If the Weather is
very Cold cover it over with a Blank[et]
& let it Work in the Cooler 24 hours
then put it into the Cask—leave
the bung open till it is almost done
Working—Bottle it that day Week
it was Brewed.

This, then, was what I would serve with the turkey and fixings. A humble, homegrown beer, with a historic endorsement to boot—perfect, I thought, for a holiday so steeped in Americana. I was satisfied, though not at all confident. If I've learned anything from this project, it's that it is one thing to read about a beer and another entirely to make it. Remembering Ninkasi's similarly poetic—and equally vague—recipe, I was downright nervous. A lot was riding on this Thanksgiving. It wasn't just a meal anymore. It had become work. A *Project*, with a capital *P*. And I would be judged. My editor, my readers, the first president would be joining me—in spirit—at the table. And in person, of course, there was my family. This might have made me the most nervous of all. This particular Thanksgiving was all about reinvention. Reinventing Washington's recipe and the historic age it represented but also, for my family and me, bringing back the tradition of Thanksgiving itself.

We love the holiday, but not for the usual reasons. Years ago, our Thanksgiving was as traditional as they came—straight out of a Currier and Ives print. We'd gather the brood at a house my grandparents built in the Vermont woods. Perched in the birch and pine above a mucky pond, its giant porch—"the cabin," as we call it, is really more deck than house—looks out over the mountains. "On a clear day," my grandfather was fond of bragging, "you can see Mount McKinley." (He's optimistic: the deck looks east, toward New Hampshire's Presidential Range; Mount McKinley is in Alaska.) Heated by a heavy stone hearth and with wool-blanketed beds enough to sleep the whole clan, this was our family encampment. Cousins would drive in from Maine, grandparents from Ohio, aunts and uncles from Chicago, New York, and, if we were lucky, as far afield as Alaska (Uncle David's visits were as rare and miraculous as his once-yearly haircuts). And my parents, brother, sister, and I would pile into the family Volvo, toss the dog in "the way-back," as we dubbed the wagon's roomy trunk, and head out on I-95 for the four-hour ride north from New Haven.

Dinner was Rockwellian: turkey, stuffing, potatoes, and pie.

Grandma's homemade cranberry sauce for the adults (with little bitter shrapnels of orange peel and *real* cranberries) and, for the kids' table in dining-room Siberia over by the kitchen, a jiggling can-shaped blob. Maybe not San Francisco–style artisanal but classic in its own way. Memories of the meal itself, though, have faded. The ones that linger are from that drive. The wheeze of spinning tires stuck in the snow, Dad putting on chains in his penny loafers, a sick dog and sicker kids, all set to the drone of mom's endless books on tape. After a journey like that we'd have eaten anything. Forget the familial fuss, the premeal grace, the postmeal cleanup—all we wanted, like the Pilgrims after their own harrowing crossing, was a nice, cold beer. And so, as soon as we could, we moved our feast to New York City. We found an uptown Italian place with great pumpkin gnocchi (without the rigors of travel, this was a meal we could actually savor) and launched a new tradition. We'd meet there every year. I'd take Amtrak in from college in Providence, or ride the Q from Brooklyn. We'd rendezvous at Penn Station and spend a long weekend shopping for sweaters, touring museums, humoring my sister with a Broadway show, and breathing the crisp, roast-chestnut-scented air of November in New York. This version of Thanksgiving became our favorite holiday. Minimal travel, minimal family, and no cooking—the Thanksgiving we loved was the anti-Thanksgiving.

This time was different. This would be the first Thanksgiving in years not in New York, not at a restaurant, and my first ever doing the cooking. We had bucked tradition, and now it was back in full: not just a home-cooked meal but, with my plan for the beer, one drenched in the gravy of Americana. One problem. My setup was as slapdash as the Pilgrims' first settlement. Recent transplants to the west coast, my girlfriend and I weren't prepared to host any visitors, least of all to a formal family meal. We were living in the second apartment (so far) of our San Francisco life, a thrift-store-furnished, CraigsListed third-floor sublet with a finicky stove, dull knives, and not nearly enough chairs. We had just finished writing a book together—a process that shook but strengthened our relationship and, ultimately, brought us out here to San Francisco. We hadn't planned on staying but one book led to another, one sublet to a second and now here we were. We felt transient, unmoored as the *Mayflower* afloat. A successful meal would give us confidence and show a skeptical family we could, from these scraps, build a tradition; that we could, like the Pilgrims, hack out a home from wilderness. And so this beer seemed perfect, a symbol of the new country, of making do on the frontier. Its tastes, I hoped, would conjure a rich past, deep history, a warm wool blanket of tradition. Classic. Artisanal. Don't fail me, George, I thought. And I started to brew.

All recipes are like games of telephone: they change each time they're made. No matter how precise or how well-worn, they always need a tweak or two and they never work out the same way twice. Sometimes the more vague a recipe is, the better—it acknowledges that variability, makes it okay to cut corners as needed. Take my mom's recipe for apple pie. I'd made it hundreds of times but still consult, like a security blanket, the torn and stained index card on which I'd sketched it out so many years ago: "½ to ¾ C shortening," "scant 2 C flour," "bake 375° / 350°." To the uninitiated a Hymn to Ninkasi–esque puzzle. I thought of Tom Waits: "If you want a recipe for banana bread, I'll leave three things out," he once said in a characteristically cryptic interview. If family recipes are bad, historical recipes are even worse. Making sense of notes like Washington's can feel like trying to nail cranberry sauce to the wall. I made it four words in. What the hell is a "siffer"? And, more to the point, did I really want thirty gallons of this stuff?

No, I decided. I did not. I would scale down. Whatever a siffer was, I aimed for a thirtieth of it. Adding hops "to my taste"—like that "scant" cup of flour in mom's pie crust—seemed like an invitation to bring my own flair. After all, I wasn't trying to please George alone; I had the family to think of. I didn't want to subject them to anything too terrible. I knew from unfortunate experience (an ill-fated attempt at a ginger-mocha porter) that the molasses would impart a thinning, slightly cidery tang, so I included some seasonal spices for a little balance—nutmeg, cinnamon, and cloves. I added some malt extract syrup—a brewer's shortcut, liquid grain sugar that eliminates the need to steep raw malt to extract its fermentable starches—and a handful of darkly roasted grains for extra depth of flavor. I even tossed in a few pieces of roasted pumpkin. 'Twas the season, after all.

Had I gone too far? Was my interpretation too loose? With mom's pie, an hour or so's bake will reveal, with a crust either nimbus light and brittle as eggshell or deadened and toothsome as old gum, if my two cups were scant enough. Here, I had a week or so of nerves ahead. ("That day Week," I figured, was a typical fermentation of about seven days, plus a few more in the bottle to carbonate.) To ease my fears I called Jeremy Cowan, the owner of Brooklyn's Schmaltz Brewing. Jeremy knew Washington's recipe well. He'd found it, like I did, referenced again and again in old-time brewing books and beer histories and had been just as curious. But running a full-scale brewery and not, like me, a home brewer with a pet project, Jeremy wasn't quite curious enough to stake his paycheck on verisimilitude. When the New York Public

Library called, though, to ask him to supply the booze for the iconic Forty-second Street building's hundredth birthday gala, he knew just what to make.

I was happy to learn that Jeremy took some liberties too. His beer had to be historical but, more than that, it had to be *good*. I had my family to please; he had "the glitterati," as he called them. And the museum's wealthy donors and arts patrons had limited patience for historical accuracy. Library party or not, the beer had better be tasty. So Jeremy added some toasted malt for flavor and skipped, as I did, the potentially unsanitary barrel fermentation brewers in Washington's day had to risk. Especially with, as Washington recommends, "the bung open"—that is, with the barrel unsealed—brewing in porous wooden vats extends an open invitation for wild yeasts or airborne bacteria to crash the party, turning the beer sour or aggressively foamy. (Excessive carbonation is a telltale symptom of infection; some bacteria can ferment even weak beers with exceptional vigor.) Some brewers, and a few drinkers, cherish that fizzy farmhouse funk but not Jeremy. "We didn't want any bottles exploding on ball gowns," Jeremy said.

I missed the party, but by all reports Jeremy's beer was a success. Gowns stayed dry and the library got plenty of press in the beer rags and mainstream papers alike. Jeremy pleased the glitterati, but what of ole wooden teeth? Would Washington have minded Jeremy's edits? Of course not. Washington understood the importance of being a good host—remember his Madeira wine. He likely intended the recipe to be used more as a guide than a hard-and-fast rule. In 1757, when he kept that journal, George was a swinging twenty-five-year-old, a decorated commander fresh from the French and Indian War, living it up at his Mount Vernon bachelor pad. Jeremy imagined him dashing off the recipe as a note to himself and his buddies. "He wasn't going out of his way to make the best, most innovative beer he could," Jeremy said. Instead, the recipe—if you could call it that—"was shorthand for his pals. They were probably home brewers too. They'd come over for a drink. 'George,' they'd say, 'we love your porter. How do you make it?' And he scribbled this down in his beautiful hand. I love the personal flair, like 'blood warm.' It's like when you ask your grandma for a recipe, and she'll say, 'oh, add a pinch of this,' or she'll forget to include the cumin." The recipe left room for personality. In fact, Washington likely expected it. Viewing the recipe in a more liberal light, I felt better. That took care of one guest, I thought.

And then the rest of them arrived. Thanksgiving came. Squanto style, I spread the dining table. (Well, not a dining table but a table and a desk pushed together, their seam hidden by a tablecloth. Well, not a tablecloth, a bedsheet.) See the bounty of this new land, I said. See! We won't starve this winter! (No, don't ask about the rent. Yes, it's a safe neighborhood . . .) The food was abundant and, surprisingly, not half bad. The Brussels sprouts were browned, the bird was moist. Even without ravioli the family was happy. Better yet, the beer didn't explode. But it tasted horrible. Thin and cidery, sour and overspiced, like a piece of fruitcake. Worse, in fact—like stale fruitcake. We toasted, we politely sipped, and then we switched to wine. A ten-buck local pinot at that. Not even Madeira. Sorry, George.

I needed some expert advice, so I took my questions straight to the top. I called Mount Vernon. Some curious docents there had made the beer years ago, and they had taken a hard-line approach. They were the authorities, after all. Keepers of the presidential flame. Jeremy wanted accessibility, they wanted accuracy. If their

THE BREWER'S TALE

version of Washington's beer had worked—that is, if it had tasted any better than my lackadaisical take—I'd take another, more obedient shot.

I spoke first to Mary Thompson, a taciturn, bookish-seeming research specialist. She hadn't actually brewed the beer, not personally, but she knew all about the recipe, and she had dutifully tried the results. I asked her straight: Any good? "Well, I'm not really a beer drinker," she said, and then she took a long pause. I'd become familiar with these stallings, sharing and talking about old beers like this one, as drinkers racked their brains for appropriate adjectives—usually just another word for "bad." "There's a very strong molasses flavor," Mary admitted finally. "It takes two or three sips to get past the shock."

Strike one, I thought. Mary transferred me to Dennis Pogue, who runs Mount Vernon's replica distillery. Farmer, soldier, politician, brewer—Washington, it turns out, also made whiskey. And it's pretty damn good, Dennis says. "Fruity, spicy. It's a cool thing." He keeps a flask in his desk drawer. The beer, on the other hand, wasn't worth saving. When I asked for his tasting notes, Dennis didn't hesitate: "God, that stuff sucks." Like Mary, he blames the molasses. And, like Mary, he does it delicately. "A real *different* flavor," he called it.

Such flavor surely was not lost on Washington and his drinking pals. But why use molasses if it was so awful? Simply put, American brewers—even those of Washington's means—had little choice. Barley was tough to grow in rocky eastern seaboard soil, and imported malt fit for brewing was as rare a delicacy as Washington's Madeira wine. "I make use of no barley in my distillery," Washington wrote. His whiskey was distilled from local rye and native corn—hardier grains than barley but, with fewer and less

accessible starches, more challenging to make into beer. Thanks to
a booming West Indies sugar trade, though, molasses made a
cheap alternative.*

Molasses is scraps. When sugarcane juice (or beet juice, or
corn juice, for that matter, though in Washington's day it was
mostly cane) is boiled, pure sucrose crystallizes, leaving behind a
rough, viscous syrup of salts, iron, other minerals, and complex
long-chain sugars. Those sugars will eventually ferment, especially
if fed to wild microbes like those in sour farmhouse beers, but the
other trace materials remain. They're what give molasses beer its
"different" taste.

In a pinch, though, molasses works. And, Dennis said, "Washington had a lot of hands on his farm." This wasn't just a beer, it
was a ration. Washington called it "small beer," which, Dennis
explained, was one of "a whole category of lesser, cheaper beers,
requiring less skill to make" and using more affordable ingredients. Table beer, in other words. Washington actually made some
money off of his whiskey. His distillery was, for a time, the largest
in the country, producing 11,000 gallons a year. The beer, though,
was fit for home consumption only. Those workers got a daily beer
allotment and, as I had learned drinking my kitchen-sink saisons,
thirsty farmhands weren't picky. But Washington must have been.
What filled that silver pint of his, if not this scrapped-together
home brew?

Dennis offered one hint: What Washington didn't brew himself,

---

* The trade paused during the Revolutionary War—the Indies being British
land—but picked up again soon after in a big way as the fledgling nation
developed a taste for rum. The first distillery opened in Boston in 1700; by the
1770s there were almost one hundred fifty, and estimates put postwar consumption at three pints per man, weekly.

he bought, and bought locally. Dennis read me part of a letter Washington sent to his friend the Marquis de Lafayette. "I use no porter or cheese in my family," Washington wrote, "but such as is made in America; both these articles may now be purchased of an excellent quality." His favorite beer was from Philadelphia, made by the British-trained brewers Robert Hare and J. Warren. In 1788, Washington wrote to his importer Clement Biddle, "I beg you will send me a gross of Mr. Hare's best bottled porter if the price is not much enhanced by the copious draughts you took of it." It must have been a good beer, if you'd steal from the future president's stash. In fact, Washington liked the porter so much he made Hare a delegate at the Constitutional Convention and, in 1795, a speaker of the senate.

This seemed a beer worth trying. The following Thanksgiving, while the rest of my family returned to New York (and who could blame them?), I went to Philadelphia.

Talking over my project with other brewers, a few names kept coming up, and I learned to triangulate them like blips on a radar screen. Pat McGovern was one. "You have to talk to Dr. Pat about that," brewers would shrug whenever I brought up some esoteric piece of Sumerian lore. Stephen Buhner was another. The weirder the recipe, the more likely I'd be told it came from him. "What *is* this?" I'd ask. "Well . . . have you read Buhner?" brewers would reply with a grin. And then there was Rich Wagner. If a fellow brewer knew about Washington's recipe, chances are he also knew about Rich, dropping his name with little more than a knowing smirk, as if to say, Don't take my word for it, you gotta see this one for yourself.

I arranged to meet him in Philadelphia at Yards, a brewery a few blocks up the Delaware River from where Hare and Warren's once stood. The scenery had changed. Instead of merchant clippers and riverside taverns, the Delaware's banks were now home to the SugarHouse Casino and Roxxy dance club. Rich, though, was stuck in time. Hefting a Franklinesque gut, his long hair, the color of weathered slate, bound into a ponytail, Rich squinted at me from across the bar through wire-frame bifocals. A pair of leather gloves sat folded in front of him and a leather mail satchel was slung over his chair back, as if he'd just ridden in on the post road from Boston. He looked downright colonial. A feat, I thought, as he looked up from a chili cheeseburger, considering the circumstances. If anyone could make a cheeseburger seem eighteenth century it was Rich. The knowing smirks were starting to make sense.

Rich is a reenactor. A former high school science teacher, he has the same kind of twinkling grin—wise, patient, wearily bemused—I remember from Mr. McCloud's tenth-grade bio class. He's been teaching and writing about colonial brewing since the early 1990s, when he built a period-correct brew house at Pennsbury Manor, William Penn's Delaware River estate. A copper kettle hung over a brick oven or "firebox," a wooden fermenter carved from cypress logs and coated in a mixture of wax and pitch called mammut—Rich trucked it all in on a wooden wagon. He writes books (that satchel was stuffed with signed copies of *Philadelphia Beer: A Heady History*), he leads tavern tours, he lectures. He brews in buckled shoes and a tricorn hat. He single-handedly convinced the Pennsylvania Historical Commission to honor the country's first lager brewer, John Wagner (no relation), with a staid blue and gold marker on the otherwise forgotten corner of Poplar and American Street. Surely, he's been asked it all. Before I can get out my long list of questions, Rich holds up his dripping burger and stops me with a disclaimer.

Don't be fooled by the retro hairstyle. Rich is a reenactor but he's not exact. If I was looking for specifics, or for a straight-from-the-archives replica, I came to the wrong guy. He's not an academic historian, and he's not trying to please any partygoers or family members (his wife, it sounded like, was happy to play along—she uses his leftover brewing grain for bread). He brews what he likes, and he likes history. "I'm trying to make good beer with the methods of the day," he said.

The process is what counts; it's foolish to worry about specifics like ingredients. I'd never be able to taste Hare's porter, or even the true—call it "authentic"—flavor of Washington's home brew, Rich explained. "They used varieties of hops and grain that we don't know about, like extinct heirloom tomatoes. And the yeast"—he throws up his hands in resignation—"back then you had breweries next to bakeries, all sharing yeast and bacteria." To authentically re-create eighteenth-century beer, in other words, you'd have to re-create the eighteenth century. To start from scratch, as Carl Sagan said, "first, invent the universe."

Once, at a brewing demonstration, Rich unloaded his wagon of gear next to another, more modern-minded home brewer. "He had this fancy stainless-steel setup and an app on his phone that told him things like temperature, and I'm going, 'Oh yeah, that's neat.' He says to me, 'What temperature do you strike your mash?' How hot do I steep my grains, he means. I said, 'When the water bites my finger smartly.'" Rich winks, referencing an eighteenth-century British brewing guidebook I happened to know. "I don't know! I've never put a thermometer in there. So the other guy uses his app on my beer and he goes, 'That's a hundred and seventy-three degrees! That's exactly what mine is!' That validated my methods." I remembered Brian Hunt sniffing at iPhone-wielding foragers as he stops and chews the tree. Good beer without modern equipment is possible. "I'm flying without instruments," Rich said. "I'm just out there making beer. Beer in the field."

With Rich as my guide there would be no recipe. I was okay with that. I just wanted to try something worth drinking, some proof that the past wasn't all bad. I wanted to taste the richness of history. I wanted a story! I wanted romance! Rich wiped the chili from his stubble, dug into his satchel, and pulled out a Gatorade bottle with the label peeled off, about three quarters full of pale yellow, slightly fizzy liquid. I'd seen similar bottles, similarly filled, dotting highwayside weeds, castoffs from truckers who just . . . had to go. So much for romance. "That's a stoneware jug," Rich said, winking again behind his spectacles. "Use your imagination." He poured out tastes and added another disclaimer. "One of the last batches I made, an expert tasted it, and he goes, 'It tastes sour!'" he said with a wave, snorting out the word *expert* derisively. "Well, you're missing the point. This isn't world-class beer here. That's how it tasted. With our modern palate, you would find any number of things they ate and drank back then to be abhorrent." And with that thin encouragement we sipped. Sour, yes, but in a crisp, bright, lemony way, with a whiff of flowers and the chewy, fluffy body of a buttermilk biscuit. Rich but refreshing. Not bad at all. "I don't make bad beer on purpose," Rich said. "I'm trying to make a good batch of home brew with the obstacle of a wooden mash tun over an open fire." He grew the hops himself, dried them in a brick oven, strained the beer through burlap. The taste—its sourness, the slight phenolic tinge of smoke—"I'm not concerned about it," Rich said. If anything, its flaws "help people's imagination go back to that place. My house flavor, some say it's smoky. Well, they see me cooking over an open fire. It's all psychological." The romance was there, if I used my imagination.

Rich's beer wasn't world class but, then again, it wouldn't kill you. In Washington's day, this was no small praise.

Early America was a scary place, and beer helped. But it wasn't just a luxury or a comforting sign of civilization. Beer was, to the first settlers, up there with food, shelter, and a family Bible: necessary. What else were they supposed to drink, *water*? Few would dare.

When the first settlements on the new continent struggled for footholds or, like the legendary lost colony of Roanoke, failed outright, the British back home blamed the foreign water. "To plant a Colony by water drinkers was an inexcusable error," wrote the Virginia governor Francis Wyatt about Roanoke's fate. (The colony's stores of beer wrecked off the coast when the island was settled in 1585.) No one trusted the water. Plain old water had been suspect even to the Greeks, who thought it was dangerously sobering. Eschewing liquor's loosening effects, tight-laced water drinkers, or *hydropoteo*, clearly had something to hide. To the English, used to London's fetid Thames, water wasn't taboo, it was silt slicked, brackish, and unhealthy, for animals only. Water was even worse when it came from a land as frighteningly strange as America. How better to explain the savage natives than their diet? No, settlers wouldn't risk a drink from its sandy, fish-filled streams. They needed beer, and fast. Scared and alone in the wilderness, the colonizers saw beer as more than good etiquette—it was a matter of life and death.

The *Mayflower* had a few kegs left, but the sailors were saving it for their return trip. Not a drop went to the settlers, who spent their first winter ashore drinking water, dying, and pining for the stores on board. Not even the captain was allowed a drop. When William Bradford got sick, he was denied even "a small can of beer," and was told by the sailors that "if he was their own father he should have none." (The next Massachusetts Bay Company ship to arrive, in 1630, the *Arabella*, came better prepared, with 10,000 gallons of beer and 120 barrels of brewing grains.)

When those stores ran dry, what were the settlers to do? Thomas Studly complained from Jamestown that "there remained neither taverne, beer house, nor place of relief." Another Virginia Company official wrote home that "there are 300 men there, more or less, and the majority sick and badly treated, because they have nothing but bread of maize with fish; nor to drink anything but water." Of the twenty thousand settlers who landed in Virginia during the colony's first decades, three-quarters died—a death rate as disastrous as Europe's at the height of the plague. Send brewers, the survivors begged. *Fast.*

But the settlers hadn't painted their new home in the rosiest light. Few brewers answered the call, so the lonely locals soon changed their tune. After making it through a year or two drinking the stuff, some reported that, never fear, New England water was "as pleasant as any wine or beer."

The strongest praise came from Plymouth resident William Wood, the country's foremost—if not its only—water critic. In his travel brochure to the new land, *New England's Prospect,* Wood wrote that the colonies were "as well watered as any land under the sun, every family or every two families having a spring of sweet waters betwixt them." The water, he went on, "is far different from the waters of England, being not so sharp but of a fatter substance and of a more jetty color. It is thought there can be no better water in the world." But even Wood had to admit that it wasn't great. "New England water drinkers are as healthful, fresh, and lusty as they that drink beer," he said, "Yet dare I not prefer it before *good* beer as some have done. But any man will choose it before bad beer, whey, or buttermilk."

The Massachusetts General Court eventually passed a law requiring every new town to build an inn—and for every inn to serve beer. As the Roman empire stretched on grape vines, the British flowed on beer. Settlers judged their remoteness by how far they were from the nearest bar. The Massachusetts law was a brilliant move, requiring, as it did, not just beer but "some inoffensive sign obvious for direction to strangers." Nothing would draw more settlers than the promise of a pint when they stumbled ashore. Roadside bars like Joseph Armitage's Blue Anchor between Boston and Salem became welcome signs for new arrivals, like a Burger King glowing on the side of a desolate highway: *Ah, civilization!*

Perhaps more than anything else the malty smell of brewing marked the new land as British. We drank beer, the settlers said, and so we belonged. Captain Thomas Walduck, a traveler and military man stationed in British Barbados, wrote in a letter to his nephew that while the Spanish tame the wilderness with religion, and the Dutch with force, building churches and forts, "the first thing ye English do, be it in the most remote part of ye world, or amongst the most barbarous Indians, is to set up a tavern or drinking house." Indeed, another *Mayflower* legend has Samoset, the first native the Pilgrims met, greeting the awestruck arrivals by asking for a glass of beer—their reputation, apparently, had preceded them.

Inns brought more settlers, and with more settlers the inns grew. One, on the road from New York to Boston, had a barn big enough for a hundred horses, and even a pasture where ranchers bringing their stock to market could graze their cattle. More inns meant more glasses to fill, and brewing or importing beer became lucrative businesses. Brewers made the country's first fortunes, and their names echo still today: Vassar, Lispenard, Rutgers, Van Cortlandt. These weren't humble alewives, they were ruthless capitalists. During the Revolutionary War, brewer William D. Faulkner supplied beer to all sides—the Continental, British, and Hessian armies.

The best beer, for now at least, was imported, and American brewers mimicked British classics. Washington may have bought locally but he drank to British tastes. John Noble & Co. advertised "excellent-flavoured Porter, warranted to stand the warmest climate." George Appelby & Co. bragged it didn't just make British-style beer, but used "the best English malt and hops." Most brewers, though, weren't that lucky—they had good intentions but made do, like Wagner, with limited resources. The porter recipe from Coppinger's *American Practical Brewer and Tanner,* the first American publication on beer making, required a shortcut: twelve gallons of "sugar coloring"—the dreaded molasses.

Faced with half-baked attempts at homemade British beer or pricey imports of the real thing,* thirsty Americans took it upon themselves. "Almost any householder may brew," one popular homesteading book advised, "without putting himself to much, if any, charge for an apparatus." Most families arrived with a private

---

* The "real thing," though authentic, wasn't always top quality. British goods often arrived in the colonies worse for wear. One merchant, a Mr. Dupper, was rumored to have killed two hundred souls with the spoiled brew he delivered.

stock of malted grain, and most houses had a brew pot perpetually bubbling over the hearth, or a barrel of beer for farmhands and passing travelers on the porch. As early as the middle of the seventeenth century, property records of Massachusetts homes show 60 percent of households having some kind of brewing equipment in their stores.

And what filled those pots? Barley and wheat barely grew. Even hops were a hassle. The sticky vines need trellised gardens and fleets of pickers at harvest time. America wasn't yet a bucolic field of grain, and pioneer home brewers used whatever they could find. Not the "finest imported hops and malt" but corn, pumpkins, spruce, maple sap, and lots of molasses.

In one of the first reports of homegrown American beer, Thomas Hariot wrote from Virginia that his thirsty crew malted some Indian corn, "whereof was brued as good ale as was to be desired." In other words, at least it works. Or as Sam Calagione more poetically put it to me, explaining the free-for-all attitude that led Norse brewers to augment their beer with berries, or Sumerians theirs with dates: "Did it ferment? Did it get me closer to the gods?" Good enough.

Hariot's crew set the tone for an American-grown style. Frontier-living how-to books from Mackenzie's *Five Thousand Receipts* to the *New England Farrier and Family Physician* had recipes for bay-leaf-and-molasses "treacle beer," for beer made from spruce tips and maple sap. For beer from pea shells, beer from bran, beer flavored with sage and chicory. Molasses-and-ginger "Brattleboro Beer," fermented "at the temperature of new milk, is reported to be wholesome and agreeable," one book half-heartedly promised. A recipe from Providence, Rhode Island, called for senna, chicory, a mildly analgesic flower called celandine, and a handful of red sage boiled with wheat bran, molasses, and malt. This slop was, the recipe claimed, "famous throughout the countryside."

Pumpkins were a popular choice, mainly because they grew like weeds. "When people had no apples for pies, barley for beer, or meat for supper, they could substitute the prolific pumpkin," wrote Cindy Ott in her history of the plant. One settler recounted a legend of a single seed, "without any Care of Cultivation," sprouting an eight-inch-thick vine on which grew 260 gourds.

"We have pumpkin at morning and pumpkin at noon," a 1630s ditty ran. "If it was not for pumpkin we should be undone." Settlers practically lived on the things: pumpkin pie, pumpkin bread, pumpkin soup ("very windy," one recipe warned), and, of course, pumpkin beer, made from gourds "beaten in a Trough as Apples" and mixed with whatever was on hand. The Pilgrims added persimmons and maple syrup. Landon Carter, Virginia planter and buddy of Thomas Jefferson, liked his personal brew extra sour—kind of a pumpkin shrub. He called it "pumperkin."

Trees, too. The Boston minister Jeremy Belknap was so proud of his spruce beer recipe that he sent it to physician to the stars Benjamin Rush (the doctor famously mediated the peace between rivals Thomas Jefferson and John Adams). "The most superlatively excellent beer in the world," Belknap wrote. "I know of no other liquor in the universe that can match it."* Ben Franklin also tried

---

* Belknap and Rush bonded over their shared skepticism—the minister's moral, the doctor's scientific—of hard liquor, advocating beers like Belknap's to replace "ardent spirits." Beer, Rush wrote, "abounds with nourishment," while "spirituous liquors destroy more lives than the sword." They formed a prominent tag team in America's early temperance movement, though Rush's dream of having every distillery turned into a milk house by 1915 and

his hand at spruce beer, after tasting a French version, *bière d'épinette*, while stationed in Paris, flavored with spruce oil. In his American re-creation, Franklin had to resort to using twigs and, of course, molasses. (Yards makes a version of this beer, with real branches, like Franklin did. When I met Rich Wagner at the Yards tap room, the brewers there had just made a batch, and the piney scent beckoned us back into the brewery for an impromptu post-burger tour. Rich slugged a taste of the fresh wort from a plastic pitcher. "A good summer quencher," he declared.)

Recipes? No need, said Thomas Jefferson. "I have no receipt for brewing," he wrote, "and I doubt if the operations of malting and brewing can be successfully performed from a receipt." The beer he made and advocated for was closer to Nordic grog, those mixed fermentations of cloudberries, honey, and grain, than to the pure pales and porters his former countrymen were enjoying in England.

A seventeenth-century poem captured the prevailing attitude: "If barley be wanting to make into malt / we must be content and think it no fault / for we can make liquor to sweeten our lips / of pumpkins, and parsnips, and walnut-tree chips."

For my next take on American beer, then, I switched horses. I took Jefferson's and Rich's advice this time, and instead of following a recipe I followed the land.

A trip to a San Francisco farmers' market conjures the same awe as a paddle up the Hudson must have four hundred years ago. Star-

---

"the use of spirits as uncommon in families as a drink made of a solution of arsenic" fell a bit short.

ing agape from their skiffs, the first European explorers of the new world saw oysters the size of dinner plates, streams running black with shad. Weaving through the white pop-up tents in the plaza behind City Hall on Sunday mornings, I find squash the size of well-fed toddlers, towering crimson mountains of Early Girl tomatoes. The first settlers fit their discoveries into the framework they knew. Corn was "turkey wheat," pumpkins were a sort of melon, bison like particularly hirsute Jersey cows. I nicknamed my go-to growers: the Farmstand of the Unknown Citrus, the Farmstand of Nameless Roots. I'd elbow through a mass of stooping shoppers, point to a pile, and raise an eyebrow. "Obo," the farmer would say. Or "wild yam," or "sticky corn," or just shrug and giggle. Sticky corn, I learned (the hard way) takes an hour or more of boiling before its starchy kernels fuse into a sweet, gelatinous mass you can scrape off the cob with your incisors. Bitter melon is more like bitter cucumber. Peel luffa before you cook it. Avocados should be soft—but not too soft. Pomegranates should be hard—but not too hard. And then there are persimmons.

John Smith coughed up his first bite of the strange new fruit. He thought it was a kind of plum. "If it be not ripe it will drawe a man's mouth awrie with much torment," he wrote. He had met the infamous Hachiya. Creamsicle orange, hard as a rock, and full of astringent pectin when fresh; fleshy red and translucent, like skin over a flashlight, when finally ripe. It takes forever, of course, though you can help it along by freezing. It's worth it. "As delicious as an apricot," Smith wrote. No—even better. I love persimmons. They flood the markets every winter, and by now I've tried them all. My first season in San Francisco, I learned about fuyus, eaten crisp, like apples. About the accurately named giant or *hana* fuyus and the less accurately named, though still delicious, chocolate or *maru* fuyus. The season progressed, the farmstands overflowed, the prices dropped. "Two-dollar pound, mix and match," "dollar bag, dollar bag," the vendors shouted. And one day, an unmissable deal, fuyus at a dollar a pound or six pounds for five bucks. I loaded up two bags. Like an early settler staring at a pile of past-their-prime apples or a particularly overproductive pumpkin patch, I thought: when life gives you persimmons, make beer.

As early American beer went, persimmon brew wasn't that bad. Finnish scientist and explorer Peter Kalm "reckoned [it] much preferable to other beer" in 1750. British traveler Samuel Morewood called it "a beer preferable to most others." Even President William H. Taft liked it—he served a hundred gallons at a 1909 Atlanta rally, all made, the *New York Times* reported, by a tireless "Mrs. Watson of Richardson Street." How Mrs. Watson did it, I don't know. From Kalm and Moorewood, though, I learned that colonists made their persimmons beer not, as I would have assumed, like cider, pressing the fruit and fermenting the juice, but more like Sumerian bappir. They mashed up the fruit, mixed it with bran, and baked it into cakes, then dissolved these in water and fermented the slop. George Washington's cousin and estate manager Lund Washington made his persimmon beer this way too.

So would I. Two bags of persimmons went into the blender— beaten in a trough, I thought—then into a bowl. I mixed in a few handfuls of bran to make a wet, gritty dough and slapped out some patties. Then I baked them low and slow for a few hours to firm them into hard, brown cakes. The next morning, I crumbled the cakes into a bucket and topped it off with boiling water, a sprinkling of baker's yeast, and a few scoops of leftover persimmon pulp for good measure. After a relatively quick, three-day fermentation (persimmons, not as sugar-packed as barley or even apples, make short work for high-powered bread yeast) it emerged sour, cidery, and very light. As Hariot wrote, "as good ale as was to be desired." Did it bring me closer to the gods? Not exactly. But I was proud. I had tamed Bradford's "howling wilderness." I had taken a mystery fruit, learned its secrets, and transformed it into something if not delicious at least drinkable.

In early America, too, locally made beer eventually turned from a necessity to a point of pride. As Americans dug in, for one thing, they drank more. In the 1790s the average American over fifteen drained thirty-four gallons of beer a year, not to mention wine, liquor, and cider. In *Drinking in America*, the historians Mark Edward Lender and James Kirby Martin called this sodden age, from the late colonial period up until the 1830s, "probably the heaviest drinking era in the nation's history." And the more beer we drank, the more it became political, its homegrown, warts-and-all, git-'er-done attitude a mark of American identity. When the colonists started boycotting British goods, imported malt was high on the list—keep your barley, colonists scoffed; leave us our pompions. When the *Charming Polly* out of Yarmouth docked in Philadelphia in 1769, floating low with grain, the city's brewers, Hare and Warren included, turned up their noses, pledging "they will not purchase any part of it, nor will they brew the same, or any part thereof for any person whatsoever."

Stick it to the Crown: buy local, like Washington. Or, better yet, make it yourself. After some failed attempts at creating an American wine out of the sour local grape strains Catawba and Scuppernong ("more of an embarrassment than a credit to us," wrote one Virginian), Jefferson switched to beer. He read *The London and Country Brewer* and Michael Combrune's *Theory and Practice of Brewing* and built a brewery at Monticello. In beer making, Jefferson saw the perfect embodiment of his mythic yeoman farmer: self-sufficiency and homegrown creativity. He brewed with wheat from his field, honey from his hives, and hops from his garden. (More than for their taste in beer, he liked hops because their antimicrobial oils kept bugs off of his 250 varieties of vegetables, from Mexican peppers to his favorite English peas.) Localism became a point of pride—our beer might not be great but at least it's ours. Other politicians soon followed Jefferson's lead.

"It is to be hoped," wrote Samuel Adams, "that the Gentlemen of the Town will endeavor to bring our own October Beer into Fashion again, by that most prevailing motive, Example, so that we may no longer be beholden to Foreigners for a Credible Liquor, which may be as successfully manufactured in this Country." Alexander Hamilton lobbied for a brewery in the capital. "It is desirable, and in all likelihood attainable," he wrote, "that the whole consumption [of beer] should be supplied by ourselves." At Philadelphia's Constitution Day celebration in 1787, the city's brewers, barley stalks tucked in their tricorns, led a parade through town under garlands of hops and a banner proclaiming HOME BREWED IS BEST. Beer now bubbled with revolutionary fervor, and the act of drinking itself turned political.

Going back to mead-hall toasts, kingly funerary feasts, and even the first Mesopotamian *bît sabîti,* which King Hammurabi feared as hotbeds of antigovernmental plotting, drinking has often carried with it a stain of politics. But in the fledgling nation it took on extra color. The tavern soon became not just a warm sign of civilization or, as in England, a social hub for enlightened gossip, but something even more influential.

When Virginia's royal governor dissolved the local House of Burgesses in 1774, it reconvened on the sly in Anthony Hay's Raleigh

Tavern, where its members drafted a boycott of British imports, including "beer, ale, porter, [and] malt." When the boycott back-fired into a tea tax, the Sons of Liberty plotted their revenge, natu-rally, at a bar, gathering at the Green Dragon and toasting their defiance with sips from Paul Revere's silver Liberty punch bowl. Jefferson had an open tab at City Tavern in Philadelphia, where he scribbled the Declaration of Independence over pints of porter.

The tavern became an American staple, romanticized by the country's early bards Thoreau, Whitman, and Hawthorne. In "The Landlord," Thoreau's ode to the tavern owner, the humble barman "possesses a spirit of hospitality which is its own reward, and feeds and shelters men from pure love of the creatures." Through such rosy glasses, bars were civilized outposts from the chaos of the world, a place to build a more perfect union. Whitman's favorite, Pfaff's beer cellar on Broadway and Bleecker, was a safe haven where "the drinkers and laughers meet to eat and drink and carouse" while "myriad rushing Broadway" rolls overhead. Haw-thorne's Concord local, Parker's, had a screen to hide "the interior from the outside barbarian." "Nothing is so remarkable in these barrooms and drinking places as the perfect order that prevails," he wrote. "If a man gets drunk, it is no otherwise perceptible than by his going to sleep, or his inability to walk." (To Dr. Alexander Hamilton—no relation to the treasurer—it was a little more obvi-ous. He described the crowd at one Maryland bar in 1744 as "seated in an oblique situation, deviating much from a perpendicular to the horizontal plane. Their discourse was as oblique as their posi-tion . . . interlaced with hiccupings and belchings.")

Send us your tired, your poor, your weaving drunks, these tip-pling poets said. America itself is a warm, welcoming tavern and Uncle Sam the barman.

After my meeting with Rich I too stumbled buzzed, tired, and hungry into the Philadelphia dusk. I needed a beer and a meal. I needed a bar. Hare and Warren's was gone—a Dave and Busters loomed in its place, a sea of blinking neon, flashing screens, trays of pigs-in-blankets, and hypervibrant cocktails packed with crushed ice in giant glasses no amount of imagination could transform into stoneware. The Penny Pot on Vine Street—"a well-favored inn," wrote Fitzpatrick Stevens, where he breakfasted on "minced collops, or eggs with bacon, or a pasty of pigeon pie, with bread and cheese and a quart of proper ale, and so to the day's business"—was gone. Now a riverside venue served "a refined foodie picnic menu" of "veggie dishes and sammies." I'd prefer pigeon. After a quick game of Guitar Hero I hunted the past farther afield, venturing downtown to City Tavern. "Myriad rushing Broadway" was a narrow brick lane, the "outside barbarians" writhing packs of texting schoolkids ignoring their field trip. I walked the steps to the flat brick entrance and the scrim of the present slowly dissolved. John Adams called this "the most genteel tavern in America," and I was welcomed in by a bonnet-clad hostess carrying a candle. She led me into a cozy back room, lined with chipped wooden benches and lit with chandeliers. The walls were hung in replica old-timey maps of the city; the tables might have been strewn with digital cameras and Lonely Planet guides but flickered, at least, with real, honest-to-goodness candles, stuck in cast-iron holders. Tourists tucked into heaping skillets of stew. This was more like it.

A nonplussed waiter checked my ID. "I never know where to look for the birthday," he said, confused by the out-of-state license.

"No one ever comes here from here." As it once was, so it will always be—the tavern, the original tourist trap, welcoming tired strangers looking for a drink and some company in a strange and wild land, looking for beer in the field.

In 1744, City Tavern served beer from the brewer Robert Smith, who ran a brewery nearby on Market Street. In the British style, "friend Smith's brew hath the right Burton Smack," one pleased patron wrote. Now, City Tavern offers a line of beers made by Yards and inspired by colonial-era recipes. Yards takes, I have to admit, a dedicated approach. It uses real pine boughs to flavor Poor Richard's Tavern Spruce and real molasses in General Washington's Tavern Porter. And, yes, you can tell. If colonial America has a flavor, this is it: the bloody, iron-like bite of molasses. Knowing its story, I didn't grimace this time at the tang. In fact, I found it almost comforting. My molasses beer had it, and Jeremy's and Rich's did too. As Rich said, "That's just how it tasted." It didn't necessarily take me closer to the gods but, on a cold night in a dark city, closer perhaps to the comfort of some shared past. It's not perfect but it's tradition. Sometimes that's enough.

And so we travelers raised a glass to each other, and to Washington's ghost. We sipped, we savored, and then we followed the barbarians down the street for more video games and a late-night chili dog.

7

THE IMMIGRANT

I went to Boston to talk to Jim Koch, CEO of the Boston Beer Company, better known as Sam Adams. The biggest craft brewery in the country, in 2012 Boston Beer made more than 2.5 million barrels. The next largest, Sierra Nevada, made just under a million. Jim's a PR-savvy guy. Most small brewers today draw the line at a Facebook page, maybe a monthly newsletter—think Comic Sans, low-res photos. The message being, they have better things to do than worry about branding. Making beer, for one thing. But Sam Adams is different. Branding matters to Boston Beer, and the brewery works hard to keep its image small, even as it spreads around the world. In 2011 the company lobbied the Brewers Association—the American beer industry's governing body—to change the official definition of "craft" beer by bumping the production limit from 2 million barrels to 6 million in order to make sure it'd still make the cut. It uses the profits from its massively popular flagship beer Boston Lager to play with less lucrative side projects. The Utopias series, a liqueur-like blend of barrel-aged beers, is one of the strongest, most expensive, and most interesting beers in the world. If, at almost 30 percent ABV, you can even call it beer. Utopias brought me here in spirit but Boston Lager's sales paid my plane fare.

I thought about this on a bright, brisk New England spring day as Jim and I drove to lunch. Street signs swooshing past the car's windows told the neighborhood's story: Bismarck Street, Beethoven Street, Germania Street. This sleepy, south-side enclave of low-slung brick homes and old, cracked pavement has been Boston Beer's home for twenty-five years, but beer's history here runs much deeper. This is Germantown. Under its potholes flows a crystal-clear aquifer; over them, scores of work-hungry Germans and Irish built an immigrant community in the early nineteenth century. Workers and water: ingredients for beer. In 1870 the Haffenreffer brewery laid the first bricks of what would grow into a five-acre cluster of warehouses, crowned with a 118-foot-tall chimney, and hired most of the able-bodied locals. A century or so later Jim hoisted a home-brew system into one of the then empty buildings and started brewing.

The chimney still stands, the neighborhood is still working class. "This is the neighborhood where Mark Wahlberg used to get arrested," Jim told me as we pulled into Doyle's Café. It's a classic Irish bar, preserved in pickle brine, grease, and cobwebs. We walk sticky floors past peeling murals of Beantown bigwigs: Ted Kennedy drinking with Michael Dukakis, Paul Revere high-fiving a minuteman. "A good schoolboy, a dynamite ballplayer," Jim says of one figure I didn't recognize—mob boss or mayor, I couldn't say. Standard décor, in other words, right down to the bullet hole over the bar, a relic of a robbery gone awry. On tap, I tally the usual suspects: Guinness, Smitty's, Bud Light. And Boston Lager. Some things about this neighborhood have changed after all. Doyle's opened in 1882; it started serving Sam Adams in 1986—Jim's first account. He wheeled over the kegs himself. A local boy made good, Jim's a celebrity here. On our way in, we were waylaid by a couple of flushed Ohio tourists, stopping in for a post-brewery-tour burger. They recognized Jim from his commercials, they said, gushing. "We love your ginger porter!"

Hugs and handshakes over, Jim and I slumped into a corner booth in the Michael Collins room and ordered a round of Boston Lagers and a couple Reubens. Meat for me, tofu for Jim. "But let me do the onion rings," he added. "A little grease is good."

Boston Lager is an old Koch family recipe. Jim's dad was a brewer, his great-granddad too. The brewery's lobby has its own hero wall, of sorts, and the family portraits hang there in mustachioed glory, next to a framed copy of the recipe itself, swiped by Jim's great-grandmother from her husband's record books. Back in her day, back when Doyle ran Doyle's, serving mugs of lager and plates of kraut and potatoes to hungry Haffenreffer line workers, lagers like the Koch's family brew reigned. Haffenreffer, Hamm's, Schlitz, and hundreds of other German-run breweries churned out a flood of the pale, refreshing brew, and their workers slugged it back by the barrel. But when Jim got his start a century later, in the 1980s, lager was the last thing a young brewer, German name or not, wanted to make. The craft beer movement was just beginning and, as one of those upstart brewers printed on its label, under a crudely drawn portrait of a sneering gargoyle, "fizzy yellow beer is for wussies."

But for Jim tradition mattered, not trends. "My family's German. This is what we've done. That recipe had stood the test of time," he said. Unfortunately, its ingredients hadn't. Jim's great-grandmother's notes called for a particular strain of old-school German hops, Hallertau Mittelfrüh, a variety as revered for its delicate, floral aroma as it was notoriously challenging to grow. When Jim went supply shopping for his first batch of Boston Lager, he found Europe's Hallertau crop laid low by a one-two punch of verticillium wilt and, worse, no one willing to tend the drooping bines. Breweries that once bought those hops had gotten tired of their finicky yields and moved on to cheaper, more reliable—if less flavorful—strains. With no buyers in sight growers were giving up.

"The Germans were developing other varieties to replace them," Jim said as we sipped our beers—Hallertaus were going extinct. "But I said, I don't think it's a lost cause. We found some really good old-time growers," he remembered, and worked out a strategy with them. Saving the strain meant getting obsessive. As New York State growers discovered when the parasitic fungus broke out there in the 1920s, there is no surefire cure for verticillium wilt. The only way to treat it is to avoid it in the first place, quarantining susceptible bines from potentially infectious sources and neurotically sanitizing farm equipment, down to cleaning off tractor tires before driving from one field to another. Why'd these generations-old farms let a fast-talking Boston kid tell them how to hose down their John Deeres? Why not just sign up for a Budweiser contract, rip up the dead and dying bines, and plant some hearty Clusters instead? Because, Jim said, smaller is better. "We took the time to go there, to personally select the hops. Everyone else just bought off a spec sheet," phoning in orders from soulless pamphlets of facts and figures, crop yields and acid content— maybe a picture, definitely a price. Breweries like Budweiser cared about their bottom lines, not preserving great-granddad's recipe.

"I'm sure Dole buys a lot of grapes," Jim explained. "But they don't affect how cabernets are harvested." When it comes to quality ingredients, "people like us are driving the bus."

Jim is something of a paradox. Like his brewery—big on paper, small in image—he's a chatty, quick-grinning, wiry dude with serious big business chops. Part beer snob, part executive. When he says "people like him," he means the small, the reckless, the obsessive, the hungry. Brewers who'd fly to Germany to hand-select an order of hops. Who'd pass up the trendy for the traditional. Who'd name their brewery after a guy who told his countrymen to shun imported European beer for home brew. Before lunch, Jim and I had tasted some of Boston Beer's newest releases: one beer made with salt and coriander, another with juniper branches. After our Reubens, we'd try the latest Utopias blend. "Most of these have been commercial failures," he told me proudly of his one-offs and experiments, from a sage-spiced rye to a cardamom-pod-infused blonde. "We have the honor of brewing one of the absolute lowest-ranked beers on BeerAdvocate." Called WTF, it was a barrel-aged beer infused with flower petals. Average rating: 1.18 out of 5. "That doesn't mean the beer was a bad idea," Jim said. "We're still a tiny company."

Boston Beer's tiny, true, compared to, say, Anheuser-Busch. But Jim's no rubber-booted naïf with a home-brew kit. He came to brewing from the business world. When I met him, his denim button-down, tucked neatly into a pair of khakis, sported a Harvard shield next to the Sam Adams logo. Jim knows his bottom lines as well as any other executive. He spent six years working for Boston Consulting Group, straightening out million-dollar companies from his thirty-third-floor office in Boston's Hancock Tower. Even over beers at a greasy Irish bar Jim talks the talk. He leans in, far over the table, waggling his fingers, eyes flashing, brandishing an onion ring to emphasize a point, dropping references to forestry management and the Japanese auto industry. I thought of the German hop growers, nodding along—sure boss, I'll wash those tires. His obsession is infectious. When he broke midsentence to eye the bubbles in his glass, I stopped chewing and stared along.

This wasn't a typical glass. Jim had it designed especially for Boston Lager. The bottom of the glass is pockmarked with tiny "nucleation sites" where bubbles can form and tornado up into a frothy head. The top is bowed out like a lightbulb to support the aromatic foam. Jim had put in the effort to save those hops. He figured he'd better make sure they shone in the finished beer. He puffed out his cheeks, slurped in air like a wine taster, and, after a thoughtful, lip-smacking pause, offered a verdict: the glass works. Businessman turned poet, running those precious Hallertaus over his tongue. More tangerine-flavored than orangey Tettnangs, he said. A little less grassy than Saaz. Was this all marketing gibberish? I thought of cold-activated, color-changing Coors cans, of Miller Lite "vortex" bottles with necks etched to swirl up mountains of tasteless foam. But Jim shook his head. He did the research, asked the experts, put in the time and the money. He worked with the German glass specialists at Rastal and the TIAX tech labs in Cambridge, who told him how good glassware could enhance the flavor of wine. They had the three-hundred-page report to prove it. "If you're going to drink a good wine, you're going to drink it out of the proper glass, you're not going to drink it out of a juice glass," he said. It's not snobbery, it's business. And yet the glass does send a message. A classy drink deserves a classy vessel. This is a good beer, it's packaging says.

And that was when I asked him, Okay then, what's the *best* beer? This time, he doesn't hesitate. "Budweiser."

Sure, Jim's proud of his German heritage; he wears his B-school ties on his actual sleeve. I could see him appreciating Bud's historical roots or its business-world success. It's old, it's rich, it's the kind of company BCG swoons over. Still, a little grease might be good, but no amount of nucleation sites could change the taste of Bud. After all that talk of tangerine and orange, of the sherry notes in Utopias, the apricot in a new IPA Jim was working on, how could he like the blandest, the cheapest, the most common-as-water beer there is?

Jim waved an onion ring. "Hang on," he said. First of all, it's not about the taste. "Taste is heterogeneous." Jim's a numbers guy, and you can't put a number on what people like. Taste, in other words, is for wussies. I asked, he reminded me, about *quality*, not flavor. "McDonald's may be the best food in the country, if that's what you like. But quality isn't some metaphysical thing—it's a manufacturing question. Conformance to specifications and intentions. Did you make what you were supposed to make? So, yeah, Budweiser is a quality product. Everybody jumps on them, but they're great brewers. They care just as much about their product as you do [he points his onion ring squarely at other craft brewers] and they have better brewing skills."

Shocking as the pro-Bud argument sounds, I've heard it in even more unexpected settings. Whispered sheepishly by a bearded, Carhartt-clad brewer at Dogfish Head, grumbled by one of Anchor Brewing's white-jump-suited, curmudgeonly old-timers. In a barn, in the hills of upstate New York, with sunlight filtering through the malt dust—the whole bucolic scene seemingly airlifted straight from Belgium—yes, even there, Bud ain't all bad. At Ommegang, brewmaster Phil Leinhart makes fiery saisons, rich raisiny abbey ales, dainty and delicate spiced wheats, all corked and caged in big heavy bottles with big, heavy price tags to match. And yet "Anheuser-Busch people are smart," he said while showing off his bottling line (a Robino e Galandrino, "the Mercedes of wire hooders"). He should know. He worked there for twelve years. "I learned more there than anywhere. I learned about consistency. That was invaluable."

The craft beer scene loves a one-off: rare, temperamental heirlooms like Jim's prized Hallertaus, limited-edition bottles like Utopias. Drinkers who would happily wait in line for a taste of rarity scoff at beers like Budweiser. Where's the fun in drinking something anyone can get? In a sense, the essence of craft is its inconsistency, the *wabi-sabi* mark of the creator's hand. The essence of Budweiser is the opposite. No corks or foil wrapping necessary, no nucleation sites needed; from a can or a bottle, tin cup or chalice, Bud's factory-made purity is the same. I remembered what Andy Warhol famously said about Coca-Cola: "A Coke is a Coke and no amount of money can get you a better Coke than the one the bum on the corner is drinking. All the Cokes are the same and all the Cokes are good." Craft beer's essence is its nuance, Bud's is its blandness.

Since the beginning, brewers and drinkers both have chased lighter and cleaner brews, praying in ancient Egypt for "beer that never goes sour," pining in Calcutta's haze for a bright, clear IPA. The craft beer world's obsession with nuance may seem artisanally retro but it's really a dream of a past age that most have been more than ready to escape. The story of Budweiser—of modern, American lager, from the Koch family recipe to Coors Light—is that quest for clarity completed, the story of beer crawling free of the flame-lit cave into the fluorescent age, out of the home and into the factory.

America grew up fast. At the 1876 Philadelphia Centennial Exhibition, the birthday girl, just a short century old, was crowned with a forty-foot-tall, six-hundred-ton, 1,400-horsepower Corliss steam engine. The country's young, fiery heart was the factory, and its arteries a steel web of train tracks. They stretched continentwide: three thousand miles of rail by 1840, another six thousand the next decade, a hundred and fifty thousand by the end of the century. Where British settlers found a barren wilderness, nineteenth-century immigrants encountered a land of plenty. In fact, the homes they left seemed far worse. In Jamestown and Plymouth, in the Virginia swamps and the Massachusetts hinterland, British settlers missed the comforts of home. But in Milwaukee and New York, Chicago and Philadelphia, Germans found a paradise.

The land they left was in shambles. Germany in the first half of the nineteenth century was a warring jumble of states, a pan-Germany, really, of Bavarians, Württembergers, Saxons, and others, rocked by revolution, much closer to its tribal past than to the sleek, polished machine we think of today. The land was largely agrarian, and most Germans were farmers—or, rather, they had been before a devastating series of failed harvests and property grabs by a government grasping for control forced them off of their land.

Millions left, packing what little remained of their lives in Germany to look for something better. They found it in America. Here, the land wasn't just fertile—it produced on command. Machines swung the scythes while men worked in factories. Chicago's McCormick grain harvester plant—the largest of its kind in the country—had jobs for hundreds of workers. Food seemed *made*, not grown: Uneeda biscuits, canned Underwood oysters, Vienna wieners from Libby and Hormel topped with Heinz condiments. Here, the good life was for sale. And by the millions Germans cashed out and bought in: 600,000 in 1830; 1,700,000 in 1840; 2,600,000 by 1850.

"One cannot describe how good it is in America," Michael W. Winkels wrote home from Chicago in 1844. "We no longer long for Germany. Every day we thank dear God that he has brought us out of slavery into Paradise." America was a land of freedom and low taxes. Come with ambition, the immigrant waves believed, and you'll never go hungry. "Here," Winkels wrote, "a man works for himself."

One of those men was Phillip Best. In 1844 Milwaukee, Best was just another German among thousands crowding that city's sidewalks and trolly cars. A year shy of thirty, with $200 in savings, Best bought a little plot of land on Chestnut Street and spent the change on a stumpy, four-foot-tall brew kettle. His father, Jacob, was a brewer, his brothers too. Beer was all he knew. But how could young Phillip have predicted his success? Ten years after landing in town he was leading a parade of local dignitaries through Milwaukee's streets, prince of the city's Lenten carnival. By the end of his life Best was running the largest brewery in the world.

To Best and his countrymen, this was like turning lead into gold. To them, beer was sustenance, not a ticket to glory. Brewing was a respectable business but nothing world conquering. Indeed, in Germany's impoverished kitchens, beer was—as in Sumeria millennia before—a source of scarce nutrition. Many Germans started their days with a bowl of beer soup: beer, butter, a couple eggs, a crust of bread, maybe some sugar if they were lucky. Beer was a dietary staple. "My people must drink beer," proclaimed Frederick the Great in 1777. Trying to unify his country around a common heritage—and against the troubling, diluting influence of outsiders like the French with their high-class coffees and budding culture of gourmandise—Frederick proclaimed in his Coffee and Beer Manifesto: "His majesty was brought up on beer and so were his ancestors and his officers. The king does not believe that coffee-drinking soldiers can be depended on to endure hardships or to beat his enemies." In France, tea, coffee, and chocolate were status symbols, sipped in fancy china and mixed with pricey sugar and spices. In England, coffee had even unseated IPA as the tipple of the chattering class, now the new favorite drink of a buzzing, frantically modernizing nation, fueling Samuel Johnson and his philosophical sparring partners. But in Germany, from Frederick down to Der Deutsche Michel, the people lived on sausages and beer. "In coffeehouses, the *I* is central," historian Wolfgang Schivelbusch wrote. But "all rituals in pubs and bars issue from a collectivity, a *we*." Beer, as in Saxon times, was an equalizer.

A telling example of Germany's relationship to food, and especially to beer, is Princess Elisabeth Charlotte von der Pfalz, Duchess of Orléans. Born in Württemberg, but ensconced in Versailles after marrying Louis XIV's younger brother Philippe, she missed her southern German home—the breezy castle, the mountain air, and especially the food. Draped in finery, poor Liselotte, as she was known, pined for humbler fare: "Tea makes me think of hay and dung, coffee of soot and lupine-seed, and chocolate is too sweet for me—it gives me a stomachache—I can't stand any of them. How much I would prefer a good *Kaltschale* [a cold, fruit-flavored beer pudding] or a good beer soup."

In America, thirsty Germans found plenty of drinking buddies. The French effetely sipped; Americans *drank*. With such enthusiasm, in fact, that it had become something of a problem. Drinking hadn't just increased in scale as the country grew—its nature had fundamentally changed. Modern Americans didn't bask in the warm glow and welcoming gentility of bars like City Tavern anymore. Once a beacon of civility, by the nineteenth century the bar in America had deteriorated into muck and chaos.

With America's hearth now a factory furnace, bars were a refuge from its flames. "The worker must have something that compensates for his toil and makes the prospect of the next day tolerable," Friedrich Engels wrote. They found it in a shot glass. "A respite, a deliverance," Upton Sinclair called it in *The Jungle.* "He could drink!" Bars sprouted like mushrooms: from a hundred thousand in 1870 to three times that many nationwide by the century's end. Milwaukee had one bar for every 130 of its citizens; San Francisco had one for every 96 (21 packed a single downtown block). In 1890 Manhattan, Jacob Riis counted 4,065, all south of Fourteenth Street. Compare that to the scant 111 churches in the same area. Founded Christian, we now worshipped a new altar, bowing under "the saloon's colossal shadow," Riis said. At bars, he went on, "the congregations are larger by a good deal; certainly the attendance is steadier and the contributions more liberal the week round, Sunday included."

Saloons were dark and reeking, their floors caked with matted sawdust and lined with overflowing "pissing troughs." Gone were communal tables and warm, central kitchens. Gone, too, the beer. Now, tired workers rested their boots on the bar's brass rail, slapped down their pay, and knocked back shots of hard liquor. A new architectural element, the bar split patron from proprietor and divided drinkers among themselves, shoulder to shoulder, not face to face. From Heorot Hall to City Tavern, bars were closer to living rooms. Often, they actually were. Now they were business establishments. The bar, wrote Schivelbusch, had become "a nodal point at which business is transacted." He compared them to Haussmann's Place Charles de Gaulle in Paris, swarming with traffic, or to a bustling Woolworth's: built to move masses, a symbol of the modern age, a machine for consumption. "A traffic island," he wrote, the bar "sped up drinking just as the railroad sped up travel and the mechanical loom sped up textile production."

Immigrants gawked at the new American drinkers' efficiency. They drank "like an animal," one German wrote. Taverns had "neither bench nor chair, just drink your schnapps and then go." Some of the better-stocked establishments had snacks to wolf down between shots. One late-century Chicago bar boasted an impressive spread of "frankfurters, clams, egg sandwiches, potatoes, vegetables, cheeses, bread and several varieties of hot and cold meats." But at most saloons "the trimmins," as they were called, were slimmer: a dish of oysters, maybe, or a barrel of pickles in cloudy, months-old brine. Bartenders set out anything salty, the better to keep patrons drinking.

Lucy Adams, a Portland, Oregon, schoolmarm, described the sorry scene in that late-nineteenth-century frontier town: "The stench of whiskey often mixed with the nauseating smell of vomit on the sidewalks, and drunken staggering men blocking my way almost turned my stomach." You have to admire her gastric fortitude. At these bars, if the smell and stale oysters didn't get you, the drinks surely would. Barflies weren't washing down those trimmins with beer anymore. Drinking was fast and furious, and the drinks were too. Canal Street's five-cent shots were said to taste "like a combination of kerosene oil, soft soap, alcohol, and the chemicals used in fire extinguishers." Visit one of those twenty-one bars crowding Frisco's sleazy Howard Street and your liquor might be spiked with opium or tobacco juice, to give the back-room whores a hand—with pure alcohol, if you were lucky or, if you weren't, with blistering, poisonous cantharidin.

Out of this muck bubbled the first ferments of the modern temperance movement. Looking for a scapegoat, teetotalers passed by the pushers and instead blamed their patrons. This was a land of opportunity, after all, and saloons were making money, their owners often moonlighting as powerful local politicians. Those working-class drinkers, on the other hand—especially the immigrants—were a bad influence. Maine passed the country's first prohibition law in 1851, designed, said Portland's mayor Neal Dow, to protect "the working people." Everyone knew, though, whom he meant: jolly Deutsche Michel.

Other efforts were less euphemistic. The nationalist Know-Nothing Party pushed a dual temperance/anti-immigration stance through the political channels, electing nativist voices like Chicago mayor Levi Boone, who barred all immigrants from hold-ing city jobs. It was a striking achievement in a town by now almost half German. Where politics failed, citizens turned violent. When the Cincinnati Know-Nothings' mayoral candidate lost that city's 1855 election, his supporters attacked the German enclave Over-the-Rhine. The Germans set up barricades along Vine Street and defended their turf with cannon fire.

Tensions were high; salvation came with a beer. Not hearty beer soup, not poison liquor, but something entirely new. The Know-Nothings had it wrong: on the whole, Germans were genteel tipplers, drinking not cantharidin-laced swill but bright, refreshing lager. As British pales were to "heavy, mucilaginous" porter and the soot-stained laboring class it represented, so lager might be a sane—safe, even—antidote to the dreaded saloon. If we can't stop the drinking, Americans began to think, let's change what we drink.

My parents humor me. They'll dutifully read my beer reviews and they'll try—at least a sip—what I recommend. They've learned to talk the craft beer talk. Drinking out, Dad always asks for something local; Mom lugs a growler to the grocery store. (Yes, even their Ohio chain fills growlers.) They'll nod along as I explain dry hopping or barrel aging, they'll cautiously taste sours and imperial stouts. But peek in their refrigerator: in front of that dusty bottle of mystery home brew, and next to the growler of double IPA they can't quite finish, the fridge is stocked with Rolling Rock. Mom's a Pennsylvania gal. Plus, she says, "I just like how fizzy it is."

Lagers like Rolling Rock have conquered the world. Antidotes today, if not to opium-spiked whiskey, then perhaps to the ever stronger flavors of craft beer. Craft brewing's presence seems large, thanks to the shadows cast by the beers themselves—bigger and boozier, bitterer and sourer each year. Yet most people still drink mass-made lagers, light and Lite-er. All ten best-selling beers on earth are pale lagers, from Brazil's Brahma to, at number one, China's aptly named Snow.

Pale lagers like these, in one sense, represent beer's crowning achievement, the summit of a mountain up which brewers have been clawing for thousands of years. From the first Sumerian prayers for bright, sparkling beer to the British yen for IPAs, drinkers through the ages have wanted their beer as light in color and body as they could get. And with pale lager they found it: a straw-gold body and snow-white head. Pale purity.

When bar goers shout, "Gimme a lager" they're asking not for a specific beer but for a concept: something light, something easy. Attributes given to lagers by a unique brewing technique and a particular variety of yeast. "Lager" isn't even really a beer, it's a process. The word comes from the German "to store," and that's what sets these beers apart—a long, slow, cool aging time. Today it's perfected in lab-calibrated, chemical-cooled holding tanks, but lagering began, as most things in beer do, in response to climate and location. Lagers were first brewed in Bavaria, around the town of Einbeck. Brewers there worked in the fall, with freshly harvested hops and grain, then stored their barrels through the winter in the region's network of chilly limestone caves. When tapped months later to celebrate the springtime thaw, the beers emerged strong and crisp, brightened with age, not dulled by it. They called it bock beer, named for the town and, because *bock* is German for goat, perhaps also for the beer's peppy kick.

Whence its remarkable brightness no one yet knew. Fermentation—the life of the yeast—was still a mystery, a process ruled by luck and superstition. Einbeck brewers unknowingly discovered what others had been searching for for centuries, a way to ferment beer cleanly. Fermentation is controlled rot, and making beer is a delicate dance between cultivating the right kind of bacteria and keeping the wrong kind at bay. In other words, letting good wort go bad safely. Cold temperatures help. Most bad bacteria—the stuff that turns beer sour—prefer the heat. Most good bacteria do, too, which makes warm fermentations effective but dangerous. Then there's *Saccharomyces pastorianus,* a curious strain of brewing yeast that not only likes a chill, fermenting happily at 40 degrees Fahrenheit or so instead of at 70 degrees, but produces fewer esters, acids, and phenolic compounds—less flavor, that is—than *Saccharomyces cerevisiae. S. cerevisiae* is called ale yeast, or top fermenting. *S. pastorianus* is bottom-fermenting. Diesel-powered *S. cerevisiae* throws off a bubbly white head as it ferments—sometimes so vigorous it burst its barrels in what early brewers thought was a sign of devilish possession—but *S. pastorianus* does its slow work out of sight, like the quiet hum of an electric generator.* Ale brewers could easily harvest yeast from that foam and add it to future batches. Lager brewers had to scoop theirs from the bottom of previous batches, or add a bit of still-fermenting beer to a newly brewed one, in a process called *kräusening.*

S. *pastorianus* thrived in Bavaria's and Saxony's chilly caves, and its delicate touch became the trademark of all that region's beers. From bocks to dunkels, schwarzbiers to dortmunders, *S. pastorianus*'s crisp, clean finish kissed them all. Clean, yes, but not, alas, clear—yet. Without the esters of its ale-making cousin, and with a better flocculation, or tendency to drop out of solution when done working instead of floating like a cloudy haze, lager yeast can make even an ebony brew like schwarzbier (German for "black beer") sparkle and snap like good Champagne—but it can't

---

* Though Pasteur documented its effects in the 1860s, and gave his name to the strain, it wasn't until recently that researchers found *S. pastorianus*'s wild origins: the forests of Argentina, where the strain's ancestor *Saccharomyces eubayanus* grew up feasting on the sugary growths called galls that form on bug-infested beech trees. How the yeast got across the Atlantic to those Bavarian caves is still a mystery.

change its color. And for centuries lagers were, on the whole, quite dark. In Germany, the medieval mind-set still held sway, and beer was brewed mainly for sustenance, dark and strong, with lots of heavily roasted hearty grain. Brewers gave extra-potent *doppel* or double bocks names like Salvator, in tribute to their welcome warmth. But as Europe modernized, the monks' influence waned. To the new leisure class, drinking was a pastime—something fun—and drinkers wanted their beers light.

First to crack the code were the Brits, with their immensely popular pale ales. Even the best IPAs, though, were full-flavored brews, light in color, perhaps, but heavy on taste, fortified with extra alcohol and hops and fermented with fruity ale yeast. Still, on the continent, palate-fatigued drinkers gazed on Burton's sparkling gold wares, drooling.

One such salivating soul was Anton Dreher. An ambitious Viennese brewer's son, Dreher set off in 1840 on a grand tour, traveling Europe's beer routes with a notebook, a suitcase, and a curious hollowed-out cane. Dreher stopped in Munich, swung up through Scotland, then made his way down to London and, fatefully, Burton-on-Trent. Touring a brewery there—Bass maybe, or Allsopp—he snooped around the bubbling vats and, the legend goes, sucked up a caneful of beer to sneak home to Austria.

Back at his family's brewery, Dreher took some of his own homegrown barley, kilned it as light as he could, and, harnessing the power of lager yeast and a winter's rest, brewed what he called Vienna Lager or Märzen, after the month its barrels were tapped— in the spring, like the bocks made famous by his German neighbors. It was not quite as pale as the British version he aimed at. Austrian barley, even from Dreher's private reserve, was darker and richer than the British grain Goodhead used in his white malt. Still, the beer was a hit. At the 1867 International Exposition in Paris, "the amber-colored beverage with a white frothy head was much appreciated by visitors," remembered the food writer E. H. Fournier five years later. Dreher's Vienna Lager took home the gold medal. In Austria, it won Dreher the nickname the Beer King and, to top it off, a seat in the Austro-Hungarian parliament.

His countrymen were grateful,* but things could have been worse. A lot worse. Pity poor Pilsen. When it came to beer, the scruffy trading post in western Bohemia had it especially bad. Fed up with the local specialty, a dark, malty ale called *Oberhefenbier*, an angry mob in 1838 dumped three dozen barrels of it on the steps of city hall. (An ale, the beer likely got its name from its crowning foam of yeast, or *hefe*, in German.) The town brass got the message and put out a call for help. A cantankerous German brewer named Josef Groll answered—and changed beer history.

Swarthy, slack-jowled, and sideburned, Groll was not a friendly guy. His own father called him "the coarsest man in Bavaria." But he knew his beer. Groll understood that the secret to British pale ales was their barley, kilned in clean-burning, coal-fired furnaces. He knew as well the secret to bright, frothy Märzen was its yeast and cold, winter lagering. Groll married the techniques and added a pinch of local luck that, like Burton's water or Kent's hops, made

---

* Even some Brits were jealous of Dreher's lager and the good Gemütlichkeit vibes it embodied. Describing a Märzen-fueled evening in Vienna's Volks-garten, a writer in London's *Cornhill Magazine* swooned: "To sip from a glass of Lager, puffing wreaths from a cigarette of choice Latakia, while you gaze vaguely up to a sky flaming with the gold and crimson of a Danubian sunset, and catch the rhythm of waltzes and mazurkas—this is the perfection of ignorant and mechanical bliss. And nowhere else is such blessedness so surely to be found. For here is material luxury enough to lap the being into a Sybaris of indolence and delight."

all the difference. The light, fertile soil of Bohemia's bread basket, the Haná Plain, and the sandy yellow clay of the hop fields around Žatec produced some of the most delicate brewing ingredients on earth: pale, dainty Moravian barley and zesty Saaz hops. Then there was Pilsen's remarkably soft, limestone-filtered ground-water, stripped of harsh minerals that would otherwise overpower those prime ingredients. With these three elements—fine barley, light hops, and soft water—Groll had the makings of a perfect beer. He bought a British kiln, stoked its coal furnace, filled his kettles, and brewed. Months later, with a hopeful smack of his mallet and cry of *"O'zapft is"*—it's tapped!—he cracked a barrel. What emerged was brilliant white gold, kissed with honey and the herbal spice of freshly cut grass. It could only come from Pilsen, and so it was named: pilsner. From its humble origins pilsner con-quered Europe, then the world. This copy of British pale got so popular it supplanted even the real thing as the beer of choice for drinkers abroad: In 1900 Pilsen's Kaiser brewery exported more beer to India than Bass.*

But pilsner's special gift was also its Achilles' heel. Pilsner was unique by dint of place, and the delicate flavors of its region were impossible to copy elsewhere. As much as pales needed East Kent's ocean breezes, or bocks Einbeck's chilly caves, pilsner needed Pilsen.

When American drinkers pegged light lager as their ticket out of the murk and sin of the saloon, they faced a conundrum: how to

---

* Groll's contract with Pilsen lasted three years. When it expired, the city— pleased with the beer but hardly the brewer—chose not to renew. Groll went home to Bavaria and took over his dad's brewery. He died, stein in hand, drinking at his favorite bar. One hopes poor Groll had company.

transplant flavor, how to make one beer, so tied to its place, in a new home.

America didn't have Moravian barley, it had rough midwestern six-row, the same protein-rich strains lambic brewers were stuck with. American hops fields had no Saaz either. The loamy, glacial New York soil produced bitter, tannic strains. And hard, mineral-rich Great Lakes water did nothing to soften those edges. How would American brewers cope?

Unlike Groll and Dreher, the continent's first European settlers weren't aiming at a specific beer—any beer would do, anything but water—and they struggled with local ingredients. They made do, translating the local dialect, as best they could, into the Queen's English—molasses stood in for malt, spruce needles for Kentish hops. A century later, when German immigrants started brewing, matters had improved. They didn't have to resort to pumpkins—barley was available, just the wrong kind for pilsner. But the same native garden that produced pumpkins and persimmons held the answer. A weed once reviled became the secret to homemade pilsner: corn. From "heathan graine" to "luxuriant stalk," the story of corn is, in a kernel, the story of American beer.

The discovery of America coincided with a boom in scientific thought. As Europeans uncovered more of the world, they scrambled to box up and label what they found. In France, "naturalists"—some of whom had never set a slippered foot on American soil—explained away the new land's mystery. Guillaume-Thomas-François de Raynal and Georges-Louis Leclerc, Comte de Buffon, noticed America's curious lack of elephants and proffered a theory of "degeneration." America's lush forests, they said—in contrast to

Britain's and France's manicured pasture and Africa's rolling savannah—worked like an environmental shrink ray, their "heavy and noxious vapours" stunting the land's plants and animals. Native American species—bears, deer, wild pigs—were smaller than their European brothers; transplanted oats and barley didn't grow in colonial soil. It's "a very barren country," Buffon wrote, "in which all the plants of Europe have degenerated."

Crackpot though it was, frightened early settlers ate up the theory, worrying that if they breathed American air, ate American food, drank American water, they too would shrink. If British gardens withered and died in American soil, wouldn't the same fate befall the gardeners?

British grain, it's true, was fickle and stubborn—hence the first beer makers' experiments with pumpkins and parsnips—yet even to the most skeptical settler the native plants seemed impossibly lush. Perhaps, some speculated, America wasn't too barren, it was too fertile. Nature's "furious growth of vegetation," its "extensive marshes, crowded forests," left unchecked, pushed out the megafauna that would otherwise roam pastoral plains, explained William Robertson in his 1777 *History of America*. (When the first frontiersmen finally broke past the eastern forests onto the prairie, roiling with buffalo herds, the argument made even more sense—here, at last, were American behemoths.) Settler Francis Hiddinson went so far as to say the land's fertility "is to be admired at, as appeareth in the abundance of grass that groweth everywhere." And yet, he went on, "it growth very wildly . . . because it never had been eaten with cattle, nor mowed with a scythe." America wasn't barren, it was just a mess.

The naturalists got their lust for taxonomy from the Greeks, and from them as well a Cartesian, linear understanding of the order of things: heaven above, hell below, and the goal of all humanity a one-way striving from sin to godliness. In America, that system appeared in shambles. Aztecs sacrificed blood-soaked tamales to their corn gods in rituals spiraling around a circular calendar of birth, death, and rebirth. Eastern tribes gorged during harvest time and suffered starving through the winter, planting their crops on land cleared from the forests in periodic, cleansing burns. The new earth and its people played by different rules, embracing a seasonal cycle of boom and bust, feast and famine. The natives saw it as living in harmony; to the British, they were victims of their environment, ignoring the divine mandate to "replenish the earth, and subdue it," as writ in Genesis. They didn't "have dominion" over the land, as the Europeans saw it, and the land was, therefore, up for grabs. America would be Europe's pantry, its shelves stocked with spices and gold. Its fecund land would be put to use.

Just not, God forbid, for growing corn. The grain the natives prized—worshipped, even, in some cases—was, to the British botanist Thomas Dudley, "salvage trash, devoid of nutritive vertue" and "inferior in goodness to our reed and sedge in England." "A heathan graine," wrote the British herbalist John Gerard, author of one of the most popular—though not to say accurate—botanical compendiums of the seventeenth and eighteenth centuries. He disparagingly called it Turkie Wheat.* "It is of hard digestion," he wrote, "and yiel-

---

* While wondrous, fragrant cloves and grains of paradise were imagined to come from Eden itself, this indigestible corn had baser origins, thought Gerard: the dark, mysterious Orient. Incidentally, the bird turkey gets it name from a similarly mistaken provenance. Native to America, it reminded settlers of bald-headed guinea fowl (themselves actually from Madagascar), imported to England by Turkish traders.

deth to the body little or no nourishment. We have as yet no certaine proofe or experience concerning the virtues of the kinde of Corne. [It is] a more convenient food for swine than for man."

Gerard wasn't entirely off base. In its natural state, dried corn is as indigestible as any raw grain—more convenient, indeed, for a hungry hog. Unlike the rye and barley the British were used to, corn demands a special cooking process to unlock its starches and turn them into fermentable sugars. Malting as usual won't suffice. Corn needs to be mixed with an alkali in a process called nixtamalization to help soften its hard cell walls. Natives adapted in dozens of ways. The nineteenth-century anthropologist Frank Hamilton Cushing cataloged hundreds of different Zuni corn dishes, using cracked kernels or skinned, kernels left on the cob or stripped off, corn fermented, boiled, ground into meal. Some tribes mixed their corn dough with wood ash (the word *nixtamalization* comes from the Aztec for ash, *nextli*, and corn dough, or *tamal*). Some just chewed—and chewed and chewed. The amylase enzyme in human spit works too, if you can bear the sore jaw. Sam Calagione once tried making a beer from corn processed this way—the Inca call it *chicha*—but he couldn't get nearly enough for a production batch. "We bit off more than we could chew," he said.

A diet of pumpkin soup and corn meal didn't degenerate the new arrivals but it did alter their behavior—specifically, how they worked in the kitchen. Corn demanded a different kind of cooking and, for now, settlers couldn't change their ingredients. They had to change themselves.

Take John Winthrop Jr., son of the first governor of Massachusetts and, himself, governor of Connecticut. The state's motto—"he who is transplanted sustains"—in his case is particularly apt. Born in England to hearty Puritan stock, Winthrop was a budding naturalist and proud of his adopted home. In 1662, he found himself back in Europe, sweating before the newly formed Royal Society arguing, of all things, the merits of corn—what he called in an enthusiastic report, one of New England's "natural curiosities." Don't fear the ear, he said. One can "make very good bread of the meale" if only he adopted a bit of local know-how. "There is a different way of ordering it," he explained, "from what is used about the bread of other grain." Boil the ear whole "till it swell, and break, and become tender," he advised, then add your alkali and mix it into a thinner than usual batter.

Settlers might have cooked corn like the locals but they still farmed it like good Brits. Native tribes planted their corn in mounds, part of a famous trio with beans and squash. The settlers, though, cleared stumps, plowed furrows, and beat down the soil into monocultured cropland. Their efforts paid off. While wheat, rye, and oats "came to no good," one settler complained, corn "answers for all." James Claypole, a merchant to the Middle Colonies, wrote home in awe: "I have never seen brighter and better corn than in these parts." A Carolina farmer claimed he planted four acres with a bushel's worth of seeds and reaped one hundred times as much at the end of the year (one bushel of barley seeds brought only eight bushels of grain in return). By the late eighteenth century one Massachusetts town was reaping eleven thousand bushels a year. Some farmers got as much as two hundred bushels each. "Our barn, porch, and shed are full of Corn," the Quaker minister James Harrison complained.

What to do with those mountains of grain? Before most dared to dig in themselves, they first tested corn on their slaves. To their surprise, it "nourishes laborers better" than wheat. One farmer wrote that when he tried switching his hands' per diem back from corn to wheat bread, the workers "found themselves so weak that they begged [him] to allow them Indian Corn again." Corn wasn't so bad after all. At first, wrote one New England housewife, "I could not eat the bread made from ye maise, but now I find it very good." Even the most high-class cookbooks began to include recipes for "Indian Meal Pudding" alongside the roast mutton and chicken fricassee.

To some, these homespun, corn-based dishes were even a point of pride. In a precursor to Burns's ode to Scotland's humble fare and her "rustic, haggis-fed" inhabitants, and an echo of homesick Liselotte's beer-soup dreams, the popular American poem "Hasty Pudding" made a dish of cornmeal downright rebellious.

For thee through Paris, that corrupted town,
How long in vain I wandered up and down,
Where shameless Bacchus, with his drenching hoard,
Cold from his cave usurps the morning board.
London is lost in smoke and steeped in tea;
No Yankee there can lisp the name of thee;
The uncouth word, a libel on the town,
Would call a proclamation from the crown.

Corn also, of course, became beer. Once merely "as good as to be desired," according to Thomas Hariot, corn beer was, by 1775, when Landon Carter published his corn-stalk home brew recipe in the *Virginia Gazette*, not just convenient but "luxuriant." Corn, he wrote, was sweeter than candy, with "as saccharine a quality as almost anything can be."

From vile weed to dietary staple to political symbol, corn became America's champion crop. "Decade after decade, begin-

ning in 1780, the progress of American civilization was measured by the western expansion of the corn acreage," wrote
Henry Wallace, a farmer and seed developer, in his 1956 history
of the grain. By the turn of the twentieth century corn was truly
king. At the 1904 St. Louis World's Fair, Indiana's delegation
stood proud under a totemic ear, symbolizing "the Agricultural
Conquest of the Earth." The official guide to the fair's Agricultural Pavilion reads like Comte de Buffon's fever dream: "corn
overflows the whole centre of the building, yellow and white
and black and red, its products put to a hundred uses. There are
great pillars in the shape of ears of corn; King Corn surmounts
a lofty pedestal; corn is used in unheard-of structural and deco-
rative designs. . . . It is a very riot of corn, which makes one
catch one's breath at the thought of the boundless fecundity of
American soil."

As the country entered the modern age, corn became not a
plant but pure, man-made material: a widget. The most common strain, No. 2 Yellow, or "Commodity Corn," could not self-
pollinate; it was entirely dependent on the farmer's guiding
hand. At first, corn had transformed us. Finally, we transformed
it. "Anything made from a barrel of petroleum can be made
from corn," the National Corn Growers Association crowed in
the 1980s. This symbol of modern American might was just the
thing to bring us out of the saloon's shadow. Corn would be the
key to lager's sparkle.

Credit for the idea of using corn to lighten beer usually goes to
Anton Schwartz, a Bohemian who came to New York in 1868 to
edit *American Brewer*, a fledgling journal of the by now booming

beer industry. Just one year later he'd change the face of that industry forever, with an article called "Brewing with Raw Cereals," in which he proposed that the way to make light, European lagers in America was with corn. With more starches than barley and, because the kernels had no husk, less tannic afterbite—that is, less flavor—the "luxuriant stalk" was ideal. It simply required a different touch, as early experimenters like John Winthrop had discovered. Schwartz recommended boiling corn with a little barley malt, to borrow some of the more efficient grain's softening, starch-digesting enzymes, then adding the barley-corn mixture into the full mash. Later, brewers would make the system even easier once they learned how to further process corn into quick-cooking, oatmeal-like flakes that broke down without the need for extra enzymes or nixtamalization.

Corn's sugar ferments cleaner than barley's, resulting in a beer with all the same carbonation and alcohol but none of the rich, grainy taste. So even with that extra, premashing step involved, Adolphus Busch and his contemporaries took notice—if lighter beer was possible, they'd do anything to get it. In fact, with the right marketing spin, that extra processing, extra expense, and corn's humble, homegrown roots would only add to this new beer's appeal. Light lager wasn't just healthier, it was classier—more American, even. Busch was so proud of his St. Louis Lager (later renamed Budweiser) that on its first release in the 1840s he packaged the bright sparkling brew in corked champagne bottles. "America's first Thanksgiving was for corn," an early ad for the beer read, under a Rockwellian pile of speckled ears and a woman hunched over her grinding stone. "How the red man would marvel to see the part his native grain plays in the nutrition and industrial prosperity of modern America!"

No longer degenerate, corn was now health food, especially when corn-brewed beer was compared to the liquor poisoning American bars. A Buffalo, New York, paper reported corn-based lager as more "a kindly sedative than a stimulus." These beers were mild enough even to drink on the Sabbath. At the 1858 trial of Brooklyn beer seller George Straats, arrested for serving alcohol on a Sunday, the judge eventually declared lager "not intoxicating." At another trial, a testifying German drinker offered, as evidence of lager's harmlessness, himself: he had drunk twenty-two glasses of lager that morning, he said, and there he stood, no worse for it. Doctors took the stand as well, arguing lager's merits for women and invalids. Brewers went a step further—what was good for mom was fine for baby too. "Lager's amber fluid mild," ran an ad for Detroit's George H. Gies beer, "gives health and strength to wife and child." Another featured a tippling tyke: "the youngster ruddy with good cheer serenely sips his lager beer." For starving Civil War soldiers, a Union Army doctor wrote, lager "regulates the bowels, prevents constipation, and becomes in this way a valuable substitute for vegetables." For vegetables but, more importantly, for hard liquor.

A Cincinnati paper declared, happily, that lager "is driving out the consumption of whiskey." The *New York Sun* followed: "Beer Drives Out Hard Drink." Lager was sweeping away the murk and vices of the saloon. As Americans' drinking habits changed, so too their attitude toward German drinkers. To some, in fact, the lager-loving immigrant was a model citizen. The *St. Louis Republican* reported that, even though the city was awash in lager, lager drinkers—that is, Germans—"contributed the smallest ratio to the sick list and the smallest number of convicts or criminals." Germans, it went on, "prosper in health, worldly goods, and hap-

piness." In Richmond, Virginia, Germans were the "gayest citizens
... enjoy[ing] their hours of relaxation" with lager. "They maintain
a constant babble as they sit around the tables in the open air,
consuming the beer in unbelievable quantity." Even the English,
the inventors of pale beer, succumbed to lager's sparkle. A British
visitor to the Midwest wrote home a-gush over the "wholesome,
palatable, and invigorating drinks, which people could drink and
talk over."

Lager's most substantial gift was gab. It was light and refreshing enough to drink all day, a session beer, we call it now, not a shot
in the arm. Lager drinkers didn't knock 'em back; they sipped and
savored, and they did it outside in the light of day. Enter the age of
the beer garden.

Picture them: rolling lawns swarmed with thousands of revelers,
the tinkling din of steins raised in toasts, the men joining arms in
performance groups called *Turnverein* to sing throaty choruses of
the homeland or put on impromptu shows of acrobatic skill. Dangerous surely, even under lager's more lighthearted spell, but nothing like the marksmanship competitions held at some of the
breweries' backyard firing ranges—true tests of the drink's intoxicating properties. While the men danced, sang, and shot, women
in their Sunday best twirled their parasols, strolling among the
flower beds sipping mocha coffees—a new drink, made popular at
the Miller garden—and nibbling cakes plucked from passing waiters' silver trays. This was the warm, bright Gemütlichkeit the Germans brought, and Americans took to it with a passion.

German tradition, transplanted here, didn't just sustain. It
flourished into spectacle, sprouting boozy Shangri-las. Brewers

one-upped one another with bigger and bigger gardens. At Miller's, high on a bluff above the Menominee River, drinkers could hike a thirty-five-foot observation tower for "a striking view of the then unsettled river valley," a midcentury ode to the park in the *St. Louis Sentinel* recalled. At Schlitz's—built in 1896 for a whopping $75,000—the tower was sixty feet. Frederick Miller let visitors sneak around a state-run toll road by detouring their buggies through his private grounds; Pabst set up a direct trolly line to shuttle drinkers from downtown Milwaukee to his seven-acre Bielefeld Garden on Whitefish Bay. George Ehret's $220,000 garden in Weehawken, New Jersey, had its own ferry service from Manhattan.

Drinkers turned out by the thousands, whole families in tow. "A more liberal spirit pervades the mind of the public of the present day," one reporter observed of the crowds. A man is "neither a heathen nor a turk if he takes a few hours of innocent and instructive amusement on Sunday," the article went on. Rivers of lager poured through the gardens, faster and more roaring than the darker beers of days past. The *New York Times* reported in 1877 that Budweiser drinkers typically drained three times as much beer as those who drank the darker bocks and malty dortmunders of previous generations. On a good day, guests at the Miller garden emptied nearly two thousand gallons.

As fast as drinkers drained them, Miller and his fellow brewers refilled them. In 1810 the country's 129 breweries made just under 6 million gallons of beer; by midcentury those numbers had more than tripled. Between 1850 and 1890, while the nation's population doubled, beer consumption rose from 36 million gallons to 855 million. Beer was a runaway steam train, churning into the dawn of a modern age. Washington, cash-strapped and reeling after the Civil War, grabbed on for a ride. Brewing, like much of American industry, had been largely unregulated; now the government began taxing it, starting at a dollar a barrel. It was a smart move. By 1875 beer provided about a quarter of the government's revenue. Brewers, by now vastly wealthy men controlling serious industrial operations, didn't mind. They made up for the tax by making beer faster and cheaper still, tapping into the country's modernizing transportation network, hauling in raw materials and spitting out barrel after barrel, a constant ebb and flow of product and money. New York brewers carted in clean Adirondack water on the Croton Aqueduct, ice from upstate lakes, and midwestern barley via the Erie Canal—"a river of grain," Anthony Trollope called it. Beer, like corn, was a widget now, a product to make and ship, refine and tax. And Miller and Ehret weren't just brewers—they were barons. At his death in 1927, Ehret was New York's second largest landowner, after only the Astors. The small brewers stayed that way, stuck in the shadows, while the big only got bigger. At the turn of the century, most of the country's 2,271 breweries were still craft-scale operations, trickling out a thousand barrels or fewer a year. Meanwhile, Best Brewing—soon to be renamed when sea captain Frederick Pabst married Phillip Best's daughter Maria and took over the business—regularly brewed two hundred thousand a year. In 1893 Pabst became the first brewery on earth to produce a million barrels.

Observation towers wouldn't cut it anymore. Brewers now competed with smokestacks and grain elevators. These were factories, not gardens. At the 1893 World's Fair in Chicago, Anheuser-Busch proudly displayed a twenty-five-square-foot model of its seven-acre plant. Pabst's, though only thirteen square feet, was gold-plated, as glistening as its beer. Pabst bought its own power company to run its massive machinery, including a four-story kiln and a set of 1,000-horsepower engines spinning ten-foot-wide pulleys and sixteen-foot flywheels. Pabst had its own cooperage and its own timber holdings in Mississippi to supply it with lumber. Tired of filling its refrigerated storage houses with ice chipped from Lake Superior, Anheuser-Busch bought its own ice plant. Then, two railroads, a smattering of hotels, a coal mine, and a glass factory.

This last was a telling investment. Beer's future would be bottled. Brewers had been packaging beer in glass for decades, but the heavy, clamshell-molded bottles, sealed with corks and wax, were used more for their style—think of Budweiser's champagne bottle or, today, Ommegang's Robino e Galandrino machine—than their efficiency. There were no industry standards and bottles were rarely reused, let alone recycled. Each brewery's bottling line was different. Popped from imprecise molds, the bottles themselves could be as unique as fingerprints. It was a costly, inefficient mess.

In 1892 the crown cap changed all that. Instead of messing with those inefficient and unsanitary corks (who knew what bacterial baddies lurked in their porous wood?), brewers could line up a fleet of bottles and fill and slam them shut in no time. Anheuser-Busch was first to put the crown cap to use in a massive, two-story machine that, with an eighty-man crew at the helm, could fill forty thousand bottles a day. But technology advanced. Within a few years, Pabst was filling twice that amount in an hour. Bottling lines clanked into action at breweries nationwide, and their output flowed a river of glass west, following the stretching nation, swirling into eddies as the population settled. Warehouses, shipping depots, and outpost breweries popped up in Houston and Salt Lake City, Galveston and San Antonio and Arkansas. Phoenix city planners paved some of that city's first streets in beer bottles buried neck-down in the sand.

Whiskey was more durable to ship but it was a hard sell among the western territories' more parched or, in the case of Utah's Mormons, more prude settlers. On a trip through the American West in the late nineteenth century, the peripatetic British geographer and translator Sir Richard Burton noted that "the atmosphere is too fine and dry to require or even to permit the free use of spirituous liquors." No booze, and, God forbid, nothing dark either. Western Americans, more than anyone, wanted light beer, and they wanted it cold, and brewers worked hard to oblige. The trip west was arduous, this new, light beer more fragile than its heartier ancestors, and competition was cutthroat. A tainted shipment could lose a brewery's hold on a whole territory.*

Reputations were built on purity. And so brewers turned to science. Science, in turn, was examining beer. Louis Pasteur's *Studies on Beer* came out in 1876; four years later Emil Christian Hansen fermented a beer with yeast isolated and cultured from a single cell. Adolphus Busch had an especially tinkering mind. He bred chickens and founded the Chicago Crop Improvement Bureau. He read scientific journals in English, German, and French. As Pasteur started publishing his discoveries of yeast, bac-

---

* To this day, the most commonly heard complaint about bad lager is "skunky," a catchall term for any number of stale, cardboardy, sulfurous off-flavors. Overheating beer will ruin its aromatics, but the particular rotten-egg whiff of bad brew is actually caused by light. Blue and ultraviolet lightwaves vibrate hop oil's flavor molecules, breaking them apart into *thiol*-containing compounds—the same aromatics that give a skunk its stink. Today, Miller uses a specially modified hop extract called Tetrahop, treated to stabilize the flavor compounds against light waves. But the best cure is still the simplest: brown glass.

teria, and the science of contamination, Busch was one of the first to hear about it. Pure beer needed pure, healthy yeast, and big brewers like Busch soon began investing in new technologies to keep their factories not just efficient but cool and clean, white-washed models of modern production. Pabst, for instance, started carbonating its beer with pure CO_2, instead of mixing in a dose of fresh wort and letting the beer referment in the bottle. Europeans had been experimenting with chemical refrigeration for years, shipping perishable goods to and from their colonies—sheep from England's ranches in Australia and New Zealand, for example—but brewers were the first to fully embrace the new technology on a large scale in sterile, glass-lined fermentation tanks.

Where their beer went their brands followed. Frontier bars were bedecked in trays and murals, bottle openers and calendars, all proudly featuring pictures of breweries—the bigger, the more modern, the better. Early ads of ruddy German farmers and "marveling red men" de-peopled into images of thundering smokestacks and gleaming factory floors. Brewers took to calling themselves "manufacturers." In a fawning biography of Adolphus Busch published in the *American Mercury* in 1929, Gerald Holland wrote that "This king of brewers, curiously enough, was not really a brewer at all: he was a super-salesman, and perhaps the greatest ever heard of in America. Granted that he knew good beer and ever sought it, the fact remains that he did not know how to make it." Even Busch himself admitted he wasn't "a practical brewer." He got into the business through the supply side, opening a brewing store in Milwaukee and inheriting his brewery through a marriage to Eberhard Anheuser's sister Lilly. Instead, he said, he "keeps a general superintendence of the brewing process." He paid particular attention to his hops, for example, demanding his cones be stem free—not for flavor's sake, but because the stem is useless shipping weight.

As brewing modernized, though, a small but vocal "pure food" movement arose, stoked by industrial-age nightmares from tenement housing to Sinclair's tales of lopped-off fingers in cans of hot dogs. Some drinkers grew wary of the beer industry's modern methods. Lorax-like George T. Angell, one of the first animal-rights activists and editor of the Boston journal *Our Dumb Animals* (founded "to speak for those who cannot speak for themselves"), took on a pet project slinging mud at modern breweries. The glucose syrup they used in place of malt, he said, was nothing more than boiled-up cleaning rags, chemicals and all. In a series of articles published in 1878, echoing Buffon's anti-corn screeds, the *Milwaukee Daily News* revealed the amount of rice and corn bought by area breweries with the warning that beer from such industrial-grade cereals would cause "temporary insanity," and might even kill your children. Just look at those rice-munching Orientals, the paper warned, "dwarfed in features, body, morals, and intellect."*

More troubling was growing opposition to drinking itself. Though once seen as healthy refreshment, industrially made beer, some now said, caused deafness, dropsy, even death. Turn-of-the-century schoolchildren studied beer-poisoned livers in their textbooks, and families lined up for William W. Pratt's hit play *Ten Nights in a Bar Room*. Newspapers padded their pages with sensa-

---

* Even Nietzsche weighed in: "Wherever a deep discontent with existence becomes prevalent, it is the aftereffects of some great dietary mistake," he wrote in *The Gay Science*. "Thus the spread of Buddhism depends heavily on the excessive and almost exclusive reliance on rice which led to a general loss of vigor."

tionalist temperance stories. Walt Whitman even wrote one, *Franklin Evans, or The Inebriate.* "Within that cup there lies a curse!" it preached, though Whitman admitted he wrote it "in three days for money under the influence of alcohol."

As the twentieth century dawned, brewers took defensive action with euphemistically named propaganda organizations—the Personal Liberty League, the Farmers Educational and Cooperative Union—that retaliated with their own fabricated articles—anti-suffrage reports (women were likely to vote dry) like one in a Texas paper that featured this so-called farmer's testimony: "God pity our country when the handshake of the politician is more gratifying to woman's heart than the patter of children's feet." When propaganda failed, brewers simply bought out papers. In 1917 a coalition of fifteen brewers, including Miller, Hamm, Pabst, and Busch, took over the *Washington Times.* Other practices, Busch's political agent in Texas said, "are best not written about."

For the most part, brewers thought they were safe. They paid their taxes. Phillip Best even held political office. They were organized too—the Brewers Association was the country's first lobbying organization, founded in 1862. Plus, now packaged in bottles and wreathed in advertising, beer had left the genteel garden and drinkers had shuffled back into bars. The saloon had returned, in its horrid glory, and brewers hoped that it, not they, would take the brunt of the dry movement's rage. "Headquarters for Murderers!" cried the dries. "The Saloon Must Go!" The friendly neighborhood bartender devolved from workingman's confidant to, said infamous dry spokeswoman Carrie A. Nation, a "white-aproned priest of debauchery and licentiousness." Nation (her real name) was a scowling, six-foot-tall warrior queen, known for raiding bars with paper-wrapped bricks, pots, and pans she called her "smashers."

Broken glass could be fixed; laws, though, were something else. In 1913 the Taft Congress passed the Sixteenth Amendment—the first smasher hurled not at saloons but at the brewers themselves. This started the income tax, which gave the government a new source of revenue. No longer as reliant on beer taxes, Washington lawmakers could start treating brewers with a heavier hand. And they soon did, with the Webb-Kenyon Act. Passed later that year, Webb-Kenyon prohibited interstate sales of alcohol, meaning brewers in dry states—there were twenty-three by now—couldn't skirt local rules by shipping their beer across the border to be sold in wet ones.

Worse than bricks, worse even than the law, was war. Tensions with the kaiser in Europe rekindled anti-immigrant sentiment here, and Americans once willing to forgive them their foreignness over a shared pint now looked askance at German brewers. The nationalist rag *American Issue* called drinkers to action: "every bushel of grain that is destroyed" by brewers—that is, made into beer and kept from hungry American soldiers—"serves the Kaiser just as well as a bushel sunk by a submarine at sea." Dry politician John Strange (also his real name) wrote in the *Milwaukee Journal* in 1918, "We have German enemies across the water. We have German enemies in this country too. And the worst of all our German enemies, the most treacherous, the most menacing, are Pabst, Schlitz, Blatz, and Miller."

Wayne Wheeler, whose Anti-Saloon League started as a grassroots temperance group in Ohio and then spread over the country like cleansing fire, wrote to Washington, begging action: "Anheuser-Busch is largely controlled by alien Germans. Have you made any investigation?" The government hadn't, but it would. A Senate inquiry uncovered some shady dealings, such as the *Wash-*

ington Times buyout, but nothing too nefarious—Busch's shipments of cash overseas went to his family in their Rhine Valley estate, not to the kaiser's coffers. Wheeler's muckraking nonetheless stoked the public's fears. Iowa governor William Lloyd Harding's "Babel Proclamation" of 1918 made speaking German illegal. Beethoven was banned in Boston. Sauerkraut was renamed "liberty cabbage."* And brewers got nervous. With Prohibition on the horizon, Busch ran an ad in a St. Louis paper offering up his factory to make munitions: "We consider it a privilege to co-operate with the Government in making its war program effective." The government passed on the offer. By 1920 Prohibition was law.

Beer had been breakfast and business opportunity, poison and panacea. Now it was illegal. But beer, the immigrant brewer's transplanted American pilsner, would return, paler and purer than ever.

---

* "A food of such unmitigated German origin," an April 1918 *New York Times* story reported, was in danger of going to waste—consumption had fallen by 75 percent since the country had entered the war in the previous year.

8

THE ADVERTISER

The story of lager began in a cave but it ends in the laboratory. Born rough, lagers have been refined to industrial perfection, honed down not even to beer but to a symbol, an avatar, bright and flickering as the glow of a TV set. Prohibition turned breweries into multipurpose factories, and that spirit defined beer and its business as it moved into and out of the twentieth century. As the influence of advertising grew, and drinkers' tastes changed—or even disappeared—what brewers said about their beer became as important, if not more so, as the product itself. Beer was just an object, its brewer a disembodied voice. This tale becomes the story of beer not just made but manufactured, not just light but empty. It's the story of beer losing its brewer.

During Prohibition's thirteen long years the biggest brewers couldn't make beer, and they didn't make bombs, but some still survived. Their factory-scale machinery, like the corn it transformed into beer, could be used for anything. Refrigeration systems proved especially adaptable. Some brewers made ice cream or eggnog. Anheuser-Busch peddled their chocolate-dipped

Smack bar. Pabst filled its refrigerated warehouses with bricks of cheese and its bottles with soda. Schlitz made chocolate. Some made malt extract syrup for home brewers—Anheuser-Busch sold 6 million pounds of it in 1926. "We were the biggest bootlegging supply house in the United States," Adolphus Busch Jr. joked later. Or they brewed beer without the booze. Malt-and-hops "tonics" like Vita-B, Bevo (after *pivo*, Bavarian for beer), and all the iterations thereof: Pabst's Pablo, Miller's Vivo, Schlitz's Famo. Invigorating, bitter hops were still viewed by most as relatively healthy. Alcohol instead was the killer. These so-called near-beers boasted a "real prewar taste" and, in fact, didn't do so poorly. Anheuser-Busch was selling 5 million cases of Bevo a year by 1918—the brewery even had a dedicated bottling line for it. But drinkers eventually got hip to the more potent kicks of cocktails and sugar-packed sodas. Coca-Cola was based on a French variety of tonic that, instead of hops, used much more stimulating coca leaves. Near-beer sales flattened by the late 1920s.

Drinking, naturally, boomed after Prohibition's repeal but relief was brief. The night the hammer finally fell, and the first kegs were ceremoniously tapped, twenty-five thousand thirsty fans swarmed the Anheuser-Busch brewery; another ten thousand packed the streets around Schlitz. Having spent the intervening dry years keeping their flywheels greased and moving making ice cream and chocolate, those venerable breweries were up in no time. Beer, it seemed, was back, and hundreds of eager entrepreneurs opened their own breweries hoping to cash in on the trend. The bubble grew and, finally, burst. The start-ups couldn't match the more established brewers' quantity, or quality—in the first months after repeal, bad batches of beer caused outbreaks of food poisoning in Los Angeles and Dallas. The drinkers who weren't already skipping over beer in favor of soda and hard liquor were now scared away, fearing for their health. Of the 1,345 breweries running in 1915, only thirty-one were open three months after Prohibition's repeal. Those that remained consolidated, buying one another outright or joining in partnerships in a wave of mergers that continues today. In 1935 five companies divided 14 percent of the beer market among them; twenty years later those five had doubled their holdings to nearly a third. Today, corporate behemoth Anheuser-Busch InBev makes almost half of all the beer Americans drink.

These are dramatic changes but nothing compared to those happening to the drinker himself. If the bar killed the beer garden, the refrigerator now killed the bar. In 1920 about 1 percent of U.S. households had refrigerators, and fewer than half even had electricity. By the early '30s, however, a quarter had fridges, and brewers scrambled to pack them full of bottles and cans. Miller started canning its beer in 1936, its lines churning out two hundred a minute. Bar stools spun empty while La-Z-Boys (founded in 1927) groaned. Producer and consumer, first split by the bar itself, again parted ways. The drinker was home in his castle and the brewer, Wonka-like, ensconced in his factory. "With the capitalist principle of exchange," Shivelbusch wrote, the rituals that had governed drinking for millennia—toasts, buying rounds—"have generally lost [their] power in our daily lives."

Beer had become abstract, as soulless as any other can in the pantry. The bartender had been replaced by the grocery store cashier, the brewer by the ad man. And as drinking changed, the drink would too. Stocking those home fridges from supermarket shelves, shoppers (women, increasingly) had power. No longer bound by one or two tap lines at brewery-subsidized bars, they could choose what to drink. But brewers didn't quite know what that was.

By the 1950s advances in brewing science—water treatment, specifically—broke the last shackles of localism. When, say, Dublin's hard, carbonate-filtered springs could be softened to Pilsen's purity, when orders of grain and hops could be placed by phone and shipped by air, brewers could make anything. Place no longer dictated available ingredients, and so ingredients no longer dictated taste. A beer's story was told not in flavor but in advertisements. A beer wasn't fancier, and more expensive, because it used, say, a rare crop of dates or the season's last bit of saffron—it was fancy in image thanks only to a foil seal or a blue-ribboned label.

In the 1930s Miller was spending $7 million annually (in today's currency) on radio and newspaper ads across forty states. By the '70s, after being bought by Philip Morris, the figure was closer to $90 million. Beer, to a company that big, was just another line item. As Schlitz owner Fred Haviland said around the time of the Miller sale, "Beer to us is a product to be marketed—like soap, corn flakes, or facial tissues. We're Procter-and-Gamblizing the beer business."

The marketing salvo hit every consumer segment, from women (ads in *McCall's* and *Vogue,* dainty 6-ounce "gem" bottles) to men (Errol Morris's iconic Miller High Life commercials: "no salad"). From roughnecks (Coors's high country, cowboy swagger) to the "discerning drinker" (Michelob's fancy foil wrapper and distinctive "teardrop" bottle, designed to be recognized by touch in swanky, dimly lit lounges). Brewers scrambled for market share, probing all corners and hoping to hit a mother lode.

Then, a breakthrough. In a landmark article in the December 1951 issue of industry publication *Modern Brewery Age* titled, "In

Beer Character—What Does the Public Want?" the president of the Master Brewers Association posted a call to action. He proposed a "streamlined" beer with "an agreeable, mild hop flavor and no bitter aftertaste." Make this, he said, and we will reclaim our flock.

What did the drinker want? In this age of sweetened soda and ready-to-eat TV dinners, of microwaves and processed cheese, the drinker wanted something new, something bright and clean and modern. A collaborative study between baking industry scientists and the USDA, launched around the same time as the *Modern Brewery* article, found that Americans wanted their bread 42.9 percent "fluffier" and 250 percent sweeter than the current industry standard. Four years and a hundred thousand slices of test bread later, the bakers released "USDA White Pan Loaf No. 1," otherwise known as Wonder Bread.

Its beer equivalent? Wonder pilsner. If light lager saved beer in the century before, the thinking went, even lighter lager would save it now. And breweries around the country leapt at the challenge. They pushed their new brews with new slogans. "Extra dry!" they shouted. "Less filling!" "Sparkling clear!" And then the apex— or nadir—of it all: Miller Lite. A clone of a German brew called Diat, Miller Lite was released in 1975. Its sales doubled the next year, turning Miller, almost overnight, into the second biggest brewer in the country. By 1977 Miller Lite was just one of twenty light beers sloshing fizzy into the nation's pint glasses.

The original arguments for lager as a healthful tonic returned, couched now not in images of ruddy-checked Germans but in an odd amalgam of factory-made purity and natural grace. In an age of books including *Eating May Be Hazardous to Your Health* (sample chapter: "Cancer in Hot Dogs"), DDT-dusted apples, and diethylstilbestrol-laced cattle feed, ads for beer took on a verdant hue. Coors epitomized the irony. The beer was made from pure Rocky Mountain spring water—and a lab-grown strain of engineered barley. Even the revolutionarily light and durable, seamless, two-piece, all-aluminum cans were specially designed. Anheuser-Busch gave chase with Natural Light, "the only beer that truly could be sold in a health food store," according to one proud distributor. Natural Light, said the company's then president Augie Busch III, "exemplifies the company's dedication to completely natural ingredients."

Some skeptics weren't convinced brewers could have it both ways, natural and factory-made. Something was amiss. The 1970s OPEC embargo hit the grain market hard. Barley prices rose by 30 percent but, worse, brewers' beloved corn and rice rocketed 40 percent and 78 percent, respectively. To cut costs, Schlitz turned to corn syrup and hop extracts. Other brewers used high-oxygen "accelerated batch fermentation" or ABF to get their beers out faster.* And still they promised purity. Schlitz quickly renamed ABF "accurate balanced fermentation." In a fanatic pamphlet titled *Chemical Additives in Booze,* the microbiologist Michael Jocobson, a pal of Ralph Nader's, wrote that behind these new beers' "image of near holiness and purity" lurked gum arabic, caramel

---

* A similar shortcut, developed around the same time, revolutionized the baking industry. In a *Believer* magazine article about the invention of Wonder Bread, "Atomic Bread Baking at Home," Aaron Bobrow-Strain wrote, "Until the early 1950s, even the most cutting-edge bakers still fermented dough in much the same way as ancient Egyptians did: they mixed a batch and waited for it to rise." The high-heat, high-humidity "Do-Maker" accelerated fermentation process, developed in 1952 by the aptly named Dr. John C. Baker, produced, Bobrow-Smith wrote, "microbes on meth."

coloring, and seaweed extract. He was right about the seaweed: propylene glycol alginate helped Coors and Miller keep their foamy heads even after the rigors of highway shipping. And lest you sniff at seaweed, it's better at least than cobalt, a cheaper head stabilizer that killed three dozen drinkers in 1965. "If I want a belt of alginate, I'll ask for it," Mike Royko wrote in a series of muckraking articles in the *Chicago Daily News*. Royko and a few other journalists touted Pickett's Premium of Dubuque, Iowa, and Point Special pilsner from Stevens Point, Wisconsin, but nothing stuck. It'd be another two decades before the tide finally—if infinitesimally—began to turn against the corporate goliath beer had become.

Where are we now? Consolidation continues. Anheuser-Busch has almost half the market cornered, but the discerning drinker is back, and more discerning than ever. Foil wrapping won't cut it anymore. Over the past five years sales of once classy Michelob have crashed by 70 percent. President Jimmy Carter legalized home brewing in 1978 and many who picked up the hobby went on to open brewpubs (themselves illegal until the early 1980s) and the country's first microbreweries. From eighty-nine breweries in 1978, the craft industry has by now crested two thousand and is still growing. Anheuser-Busch alone sells eight times as much beer as all the country's craft brewers combined, but those craft sales rose by 15 percent in 2011, while overall beer took a bit of a dip. Craft production is booming so loudly—growing more than 70 percent since 2006—that some fear a bubble soon to burst, remembering another golden age in the early 1990s and the inevitable hangover that followed. Between 1996 and 2000 three hundred recently opened breweries shut down. But for now smaller is better.

In a move that echoes the greenwashing of the previous generation, the bigger brewers get, the quainter they act. They're mass-producing artisanal. The Brewers Association calls it "crafty, not craft." It all started with sweet and cloudy wheat beers. Sales of MillerCoors's "artfully crafted" Blue Moon and Anheuser-Busch's orange-slice-topped answer Shock Top are both still growing, years after their releases in 1995 and 2006. If Blue Moon counted as a craft beer, it'd make up 15 percent of the market by production volume. But brewed by an international conglomerate (MillerCoors is a joint venture between SABMiller and Molson Coors) it's not, according to the Brewers Association, technically craft. Neither is Anheuser-Busch InBev's Jack's Pumpkin Spice, Leffe, or ZiegenBock, nor are the Costa Rica–based Florida Ice and Farm Co.'s Genesee, Magic Hat, or Pyramid.

When big brewers aren't making up new beers—belt of Michelob Ultra Lime Cactus, anyone?—they're buying old ones. Miller-Coors took over the venerable family business Leinenkugel and bought a minority stake in the beloved Athens, Georgia, micro Terrapin, while Anheuser-Busch hopes it has a ringer in Goose Island, Chicago's favorite craft brewery, which it bought for $38.8 million in 2011. Goose Island's 312 Urban Wheat, named after the local area code, is now brewed seven-hundred miles away at the Budweiser plant in Baldwinsville, New York (area code 315). To these staunch older brands and experimental new ones, the big brewers are adding "premium" retoolings of classics. Budweiser Black Crown began life, enticingly, as "Project 12" and premiered at the Super Bowl in an ad campaign reported to have cost almost $4 million (not to mention the $1 billion Anheuser-Busch paid to buy the NFL sponsorship from Miller.) MillerCoors's Batch 19, from its Tenth and Blake series, is supposedly brewed from a "pre-Prohibition recipe" dug from a waterlogged crate in the brewery's flooded basement. At least, that's the story.

Sam Adams TV spots stand apart not just because they're commercials for a craft brewery in an industry notoriously skeptical of ads and image making, but because Jim Koch is actually *in* them. The brewer himself gabbing it up with forklift drivers, sniffing handfuls of hops—an actual person, actually making beer. Ads for the biggest brewers are cast if not with talking frogs or a snow-flecked team of draft horses, then with drinkers only: around a grill or at a ball game. The brewer is nowhere in sight. An exception is the ad campaign for MillerCoors's Third Shift, a "sweet malty, lightly toasted" amber lager. Those commercials promise "not just a beer . . . a story," with a moonlit tableau of a bustling brewery. The catch? It's all animated, staffed by cartoony avatars. The brewer of this craft-like beer might exist, the ads seem to be saying, but even he is computer programmed, factory built. If story is all this beer is, though, it's nevertheless a story I wanted to hear in person. So I went to Milwaukee.

Yelp reviews of the Miller factory tour are, to be blunt, as bland as the beer. "Kinda cheesey/hokey. But that's okay," one reads. "Better than I expected," says another. Bottom line? "It's free, people!" It has, one optimistic reviewer wrote, "the possibility of being fun." A potential, it was clear, based on the number of samples at the end. All agreed the free pours were the tour's best part, but adjectives were rare. Gone is the poetry heaped on West-vleteren or the rarest lambics. "Wonderfully cool," one reviewer wrote about his sample pour of Miller Lite—or was it the MGD64? Folks didn't seem picky. "Did I mention it was free?" Without fail, every review does.

I went to Milwaukee by ferry, nosing my station wagon into the hold of the boat with a few dozen other bleary tourists, doughnuts and drive-through coffee steaming up the windshields of their rental cars. Gray lake, gray sky, gray clouds—into the gloom we sailed. A fitting if faint echo, I thought, of Miller's glory days, when drinkers would ride trams up to the bluffs over Whitefish Bay for a day of Great Lakes sun.

In the nineteenth century a trip to the Miller brewery was a bucolic escape from industrial city life. For me, it felt the opposite. The breweries I had visited so far were quaint craft affairs. Some had reception areas, a few had gift shops, and some just a bar in front of the fermentation tanks with fresh beer, board games, organic burgers, and malted-grain pretzels. I'd usually show up unannounced. I'd find a wandering employee, and he'd call into the back—out would tromp a brewer in rubber boots. He'd dry his hands on the seat of his overalls, grab me a beer, and show me around. No safety glasses? No problem. "You're a home brewer?" he'd ask. "You're probably good." And then he'd lead me into the back, hopping over hoses, squeezing between fermenters, ducking into basement barrel rooms. He'd pull tastes from this tank or that or snag a freshly filled bottle right off the conveyor belt—watch your fingers. (The best way to taste it, said one brewer as he reached around a Lexan safety screen with a Mr. Bill doll masking-taped atop it, when the beer is still churned up and creamy from the filling process.) Things at these breweries were always under construction, being built or just barely hanging together. One Michigan brewery I toured boiled its wort in an army-issue coffee maker and fermented in a peanut butter storage tank snagged from a closing Quaker Oats bakery; another fed caps into its brand-new German bottler down a piece of vinyl gutter hung from the ceiling.*

Miller would be different. First of all, I had to call ahead (931-BEER). I had to get tickets. I had an appointment. I'd be chaperoned. When I began this journey at Dogfish Head in Delaware, I gazed across a wine-dark sea at a human hand. That Egyptian brewer, though long dead, still left his ghostly print on each bucket of honey, each discarded date pit. He felt real. At the other end of the bland grayness of Lake Michigan was a faceless factory.

The ferry ride was uneventful. The sky stayed gray and drizzly. I pulled off the boat without a map, a little nervous I'd miss my appointment. How strictly did they keep Miller Time? I shouldn't have worried. There's an old joke about St. Louis: "a large city on the Mississippi, located near the Anheuser-Busch plant." Even in Milwaukee's drizzly haze, I couldn't miss the giant Miller sign. Miller wouldn't be an escape from city life; Miller was the city itself.

At Founders Brewing Co., I had shared the parking lot with a Christian scooter gang. At Kuhnhenn's with a dusty pickup with local-pride bumper stickers ("Say Yah to Da U.P., Eh!"). Miller's lot was packed with RVs and tour buses. Rogue's was patrolled by chickens, Sierra's perfumed with hop dust. Miller's lot was strewn with hot dog wrappers and broken-off wrist bands. The beer garden was gone but its spectacle remained.

---

* Suzanne Wolcott of Goose Island told the *Boston Herald* that when Anheuser-Busch bought the brewery, you couldn't taste the change but you could see it. "There's a few more safety lines on the floor," she said, "so you don't run into a forklift or something."

On display, though, wasn't consumption—fields of picnic tables full of happy drinkers—but production. Instead of parading marching bands and waiters with silver trays, forklifts hefted kegs behind plate-glass windows. The Miller Garden's lookout tower once oversaw a lush, verdant river valley. Here, a four-flight climb, prefaced with a warning to the more, er, Gambrinus-built among us (they could sit it out and meet the group at the bar), revealed a set of boil kettles, gleaming under the fluorescents. Not a Ferris wheel or orchestra pit in sight; the bottling line was the star. The whir and whoosh of hydraulics mingled with the tour guide's midwestern drone, her vowels' rounded hills beaten as flat as the prairie. "Quality is *ahr* main *ahb*-jective," she recited as our group watched efficient machines efficiently be efficient. "This line fills two thousand cans per minute. As fast as you guys can drink 'em."

And where, among these mechanized marvels, where in this temple to capitalist efficiency, where was the brewer? Buried alive. The rain began to fall harder and we tramped down into the caves. It was here we conjured the ghost of Frederick Miller.

Carl Best built these lagering caves in the 1850s, chasing his big brother Phillip's success. The older sibling's Best brewery, soon renamed Pabst, was on track to be the world's largest, but poor Carl's Plank Road brewery tanked and, bankrupt, he sold the empty caves to Frederick Miller in 1856. Today, they're hallowed ground, vitrines of vintage bottles, illuminated relic-like by wrought-iron pendant lights. The Miller Girl in the Moon swings above like a censer. (My favorite piece of so-called breweriana, she's graced Miller's packaging, sometimes prominently, sometimes as a hidden Easter egg, since the early 1900s.) And then, the pendant lights dim and the man himself, Frederick Miller, appears. He's a hologram projected on the cave's back wall. I'm taken aback at first, but then I realize he fits in perfectly. Miller is all tech now, linked to the past in ghostly image only, and the brewer isn't a person, he's a marketing trick. That's the essence of Miller on display. Machines make beer; people sell it.

I didn't try to brew Miller myself. It felt to me a more authentic experience, and truer to the beer's story, to snag some paraphernalia at the gift shop and a bottle of beer at the corner store on the way home. The trail had run cold. There was no brewer I could channel. To truly understand the nature of Miller I had to buy it.

My six-pack of High Life cost $5.99; my Girl in the Moon magnet was only fifty cents. The beer tasted light and thin and sweet, with just a touch of surgary citrus—Sunny D, not fresh-squeezed OJ—like day-old cornflakes dusted with powdered Tang. It didn't conjure a story of its creation but rather hazy memories of collegiate consumption. It tasted just as it always has, surely just as it always will. The magnet remains on my bathroom mirror.

Back at Miller, the post-tour beers were, indeed, free. At the "Bavarian-style Miller Inn," we munched Chex Mix, we drank, we wrote some postcards. "Welcome to Miller Valley," they said, above an old-timey sepia photo—not of the factory or of a brewer but, naturally, of a salesman, proud and apron clad, peering out under a wide-brimmed hat and driving a pair of horses pulling a wagon laden with barrels. "Do you know what time it is?" I wrote to friends. As if they couldn't guess.

From the beginning, we find evidence of a deep continuity that is the legacy of an unimaginably distant past. . . . The nation itself represents the nexus of custom with custom, the shifting patterns of habitual activity. Below the surface of events lies a deep, and almost geological, calm. . . . We still live deep in the past.

—Peter Ackroyd, *London: A Biography*

EPILOGUE

It's always Miller Time but it's always, too, the Babylonian's time and the shaman's, the immigrant's and the monk's. At places like the Miller brewery, where my journey ended, history might be dusty vintage bottles and holographic magic tricks, but in the small craft operations where my trip began, the brewer's ancient spirit lives on, and it's as active as ever.

When I first started tracing beer's flavors through time, and reanimating the ghosts of brewers past, I had few companions. I met some similarly minded anachronists along the way but for the most part I was in wild new territory, exploring alone. Few had heard of, say, Nordic wormwood ale—fewer still had dared taste it.

Today, Anchor Brewing Company can release an herbaceous yerba santa–infused farmhouse ale alongside its perennially crowd-pleasing Steam, Boston's tiny Pretty Things Beer and Ale Project can reproduce a nineteenth-century recipe for IPA, and both breweries can be confident such experiments won't be wasted energy, assured they'll find drinkers curious to taste the past along with them. Even MillerCoors has re-created historic pre-Prohibition recipes with some success.

But brewers aren't just bringing back forgotten styles like salty gose and savory-spiced gruit, or strange old ingredients like tree sap. They're inventing new ones too. Each trip to the home brew store reveals an unfamiliar code on the hops packets in the fridge: YCR 5 one day, HBC 394 the next, with exotic flavors of blueberry and mango. The fateful bar visit that sparked this journey was overwhelming, but nothing compared to the array of beers I regularly see today, only a few years later. Tap lists runneth over, bottle shop shelves groan with imperial pilsners and sour stouts, white IPAs and black saisons, wines, ciders, meads, and unclassifiable hybrids thereof.

And drinkers are still thirsty. The more styles brewers create, the more flavors they conjure, and the more stories they tell, the more drinkers seem eager to keep tasting and listening. When even my parents, once a Rolling Rock–only household, now fill growlers at the grocery store with imperial stouts and IPAs, when my girlfriend's father's favorite beers are Bud Light Lime and Dogfish Head's honey-and-saffron Midas Touch, the future of beer seems as rich as its past.

Throughout its history, brewing has always been a balance of taste with *terroir*. Brewers learned to adapt their available resources to the desires of the time, whether that meant using American corn to make light pilsner or Kentish hops to make invigoratingly bitter IPAs. Some brewers are continuing the localist tradition. In San Francisco, for example, Almanac brews its Farm-to-Bottle series with northern California fennel, marionberries, and other produce. Others, though, revel in the fact that ingredients now can come from anywhere. Dogfish Head's Urkontinent used Australian wattleseed and African rooibos tea. New Belgium made an old-fashioned sour wheat beer called Berliner Weisse with the Asian citrus yuzu. As when the world's first spice routes opened a flood of flavor onto Roman tables so today, as our ability to create the exotic grows, our thirst for it follows apace. The more brewers can make, the more drinkers want to try. We have a new, simple answer to that infamous midcentury dilemma. "In beer character, what does the public want?" Everything.

Our tastes are wide open, and so is beer's future. Its story has always been one of reinvention. As the brewer traveled to new lands and new times, transplanting traditional recipes into new earth, he, his wares, and their drinkers would become something else entirely. As beer endures, it changes. My re-creations never hit their exact historical mark, but that was, in a way, the point. Beer is a moving target.

I gathered a lot of advice and insights from the brewers I met while working on this book, but the one idea to which I keep returning, that became in a way the mantra not only for this book but for all the beers I've brewed since I started it, is Ron Jeffries's remark about what he called the "fleeting art of the brewmaster." Each age has its tastes, each moment its perfect beer. The brewer adapts. His tale is still being told.

FURTHER READING

Stephen Harrod Buhner. *Sacred and Herbal Healing Beers: The Secrets of Ancient Fermentation.* **Boulder, CO: Brewers Publications, 1998.**

This was my ticket into the antiestablishment, hops-free brewing underground. The brewers I met there are all great characters and Buhner is a bit of a kook himself. His personality shines through in these recipes, peppered with anti-Protestant screeds and disclaimers on the "politically incorrect" medicinal use of henbane ale. Buhner's strange book was one of my first glimpses into the world of ancient meads as well. Under his spell, I brewed a mead from an entire hive I had raised, boiling up honey, pollen, propolis, wax, and live bees, venom and all. Floral, resinous, numbingly strong—to this day the best drink I've ever made.

Stan Hieronymus. *Brew Like a Monk: Trappist, Abbey, and Strong Belgian Ales and How to Brew Them.* **Boulder, CO: Brewers Publications, 2005.**

The story of monastic brewing is shadowy and convoluted, tricky to tell not only because it has evolved so dramatically over time but also because of the lore and hype swirling around it today. Fact, romance, and pure fantasy are tough threads to untangle. Hieronymus sets the record straight. If you seek the truth behind Westvleteren—or just want to try and make it yourself—this is your guide.

Patrick E. McGovern. *Uncorking the Past: The Quest for Wine, Beer, and Other Alcoholic Beverages.* **Berkeley, CA: University of California Press, 2010.**

McGovern is *the* expert on historic drinks and this is his masterpiece: a history of ancient brews, scraped from entombed pots and unearthed from bogs. McGovern's scope is wide and he covers much more than beer alone, moving from the first fermented beverages of the Near East to Greek wine, Viking grog, corn-based Incan *chicha,* and even African mead and yam beer. It's historically focused but not at all dry—a pun twinkle-eyed Dr. Pat would surely appreciate.

James E. McWilliams. *A Revolution in Eating: How the Quest for Food Shaped America.* **New York: Columbia University Press, 2007.**

Here is the most insightful explanation I found of what colonial America tasted like, from hasty pudding to persimmon beer. McWilliams spends less time on flavor and more on the social and political implications of what we ate and drank—what our food said about us—a path that inspired my own look at beer here.

Daniel Okrent. *Last Call: The Rise and Fall of Prohibition.* **New York: Scribner, 2011.**

I didn't dwell very long in this dismal chapter of beer's story, for obvious reasons. But Okrent's book, the corresponding Ken Burns documentary series *Prohibition,* and the wonderfully immersive exhibit "American Spirits: The Rise and Fall of Prohibition" at Philadelphia's National Constitution Center were fascinating histories. If you want to dive deeper into this dry pool, start here.

Wolfgang Schivelbusch. *Tastes of Paradise: A Social History of Spices, Stimulants, and Intoxicants.* **New York: Vintage, 1993.**

From liquor to licorice, Schivelbusch's book is a great explanation of the behavioral impact of all sorts of indulgences. His discussion of the changing architecture of bars is particularly fascinating.

William Littell Tizard. *The Theory and Practice of Brewing: Illustrated*. London, 1857.

Tizard was the foremost brewing scientist of his day, at a time when the objective study of beer was still coming into its own. The wonder, enthusiasm, and confusion of the nascent movement are palatable here, and the book still feels fresh and lively. Confident—dictatorial, even—though not always entirely accurate, Tizard's advice is as fun to read today as it surely was for him to write more than a century and a half ago, foaming mug in one hand, poison pen in the other. It's technical at times, but stick with it for the cheesy brewing metaphors.

WORKS REFERENCED

Arnold, Bettina. "Drinking the Feast," *Cambridge Archaeological Journal* 9:1 (1999).

———. "Power Drinking in Iron Age Europe," *British Archaeology* 57 (2001).

Baron, Stanley. *Brewed in America: A History of Beer and Ale in the United States*. Little Brown, 1962.

Bauschatz, Paul C. *The Well and the Tree: World and Time in Early Germanic Culture*. University of Massachusetts Press, 1982.

Behre, Karl-Ernst. "The History of Beer Additives in Europe," *Vegetation History and Archaeobotany* 8 (1999).

Bobrow-Strain, Aaron. "Atomic Bread Baking at Home," *The Believer*, February 2012.

Bottero, Jean. *The Oldest Cuisine in the World: Cooking in Mesopotamia*. University of Chicago Press, 2004.

Cornell, Martyn. *Amber, Gold and Black*. History Press, 2010.

Corran, H. S. *A History of Brewing*. David and Charles, 1975.

Craigie, William A. *The Religion of Ancient Scandinavia*. Books for Libraries Press, 1969.

Dietler, Michael. "Driven by Drink," *Journal of Anthropological Archaeology* 9 (1990).

Dugan, F. M. "Dregs of Our Forgotten Ancestors," *FUNGI* 2:4 (2009).

Ehret, George. *Twenty-Five Years of Brewing*. Gast Lithograph Company, 1891.

Fussell, Betty Harper. *The Story of Corn*. University of New Mexico Press, 2004.

Garwood, Paul, ed. *Sacred and Profane*. Oxford University Committee for Archaeology, 1989.

Gately, Iain. *Drink: A Cultural History of Alcohol*. Gotham, 2009.

Gayre, Robert. *Brewing Mead: Wassail! In Mazers of Mead*. Brewers Publications, 1998.

Gladwell, Malcolm. "Drinking Games," *The New Yorker*, February 15, 2010.

Glaser, Gregg. "Re-Creating Antique Beers," *All About Beer* 22.1 (2001).

Hagen, Ann. *Anglo-Saxon Food and Drink: Production, Processing, Distribution and Consumption*. Anglo-Saxon Books, 2006.

Hagen, Karl. *Economics of Medieval English Brewing*. Medieval Association of the Pacific, 1995.

Harrison, John. *An Introduction to Old British Beers and How to Make Them*. Durden Park Beer Circle, 1976.

La Pensée, Clive. *The Historical Companion to House-Brewing*. The King's England Press, 1990.

Loftus, William. *The Brewer: A Familiar Treatise on the Art of Brewing*. London, 1856.

Markowski, Phil. *Farmhouse Ales: Culture and Craftsmanship in the Belgian Tradition*. Brewers Publications, 2004.

McKenna, Terence. *Food of the Gods: A Radical History of Plants, Drugs, and Human Evolution*. Rider & Co., 1998.

Mosher, Randy. *Radical Brewing*. Brewers Publications, 2004.

Nelson, Max. *The Barbarian's Beverage: A History of Beer in Ancient Europe*. Routledge, 2008.

Nordland, Odd. *Brewing and Beer Traditions in Norway*. Universitetsforlaget, 1969.

Ogle, Maureen. *Ambitious Brew: The Story of American Beer*. Mariner Books, 2007.

Oliver, Garrett, ed. *The Oxford Companion to Beer*. Oxford University Press, 2011.

Orton, Vrest. *Homemade Beer Book*. Tuttle Publishing, 1973.

Pearson, Mike Parker, ed. *Food, Culture, and Identity in the Neolithic and Early Bronze Age*. British Archaeological Reports, 2003.

Redding, Cyrus. *A History and Description of Modern Wines*. Henry G. Bohn, 1851.

Ritchie, Carson I. A. *Food in Civilization*. Beaufort Books, 1981.

Rorabaugh, W. J. *The Alcoholic Republic: An American Tradition*. Oxford University Press, 1979.

Russell, John. *Early English Meals and Manners*. London, 1868.

Sambrook, Pamela. *Country House Brewing in England, 1500–1900*. Bloomsbury Academic, 1996.

Smith, Gregg. *Beer in America: The Early Years: 1587–1840*. Brewers Publications, 1998.

Sparrow, Jeff. *Wild Brews: Beer Beyond the Influence of Brewer's Yeast*. Brewers Publications, 2005.

Stack, Martin H. "A Concise History of America's Brewing Industry," *EH.net Encyclopedia*.

Steele, Mitch. *IPA: Brewing Techniques, Recipes and the Evolution of India Pale Ale*. Brewers Publications, 2012.

Stinchfield, Matt. "Getting Primitive: Trekking Beer Through Religion," *All About Beer* 32.4 (2011).

Turner, Jack. *Spice: The History of a Temptation*. Vintage, 2005.

Unger, Richard W. *Beer in the Middle Ages and Renaissance*. University of Pennsylvania Press, 2007.

Vitebsky, Piers. *Shamanism*. University of Oklahoma Press, 2001.

Wagner, Rich A. *Philadelphia Beer: A Heady History of Brewing in the Cradle of Liberty*. History Press, 2012.

Woodward, Roger D. "Disruption of Time in Myth and Epic," *Arethusa* 35:1 (2002).

ACKNOWLEDGMENTS

Beer is a social drink. It's made to be shared and its story is, more than anything else, a story about people. It's a story I couldn't have possibly told without the help of a barroom full of worthy drinking companions. First, all the brewers who helped turn what otherwise would have been a long slog through the library into an adventure of tastes and barstool yarns: Sam Calagione, Jeremy Cowan, Steve Dressler, Brian Hunt, Ron Jeffries, John Keeling, Ryan Kelly, Tom Kehoe, Jim Koch, Adam Lamoreaux, Dave McLean, Will Meyers, Jason Perkins, Rob Todd, and Rich Wagner. Then, the experts, those invaluable spirit guides who shone a light into the past: Stephen Harrod Buhner, Stan Hieronymus, Patrick McGovern, Dennis Pogue, and Mary Thompson. And all the tasters, friends, and brave co-adventurers on my journey: Alastair Bland, Daniel Bornstein, Aaron Britt, Daniel and Regine del Valle, Holly Gressley, Sarah Hotchkiss, Joe Lazar, Brett Martin, Dan McKinley, Dan Rosenbaum, and Jason Smith.

Thanks also to Matt Coelho, Abby Monroe, and Jim Woods, for sharing their bar with me as laboratory and sanctuary, and to

ACKNOWLEDGMENTS

Samuel Gill and Brendan Incorvaia, brothers at the brew kettle and on the shaman's path. To the smiling staff at Ritual Coffee for the office space, and to Shawn Magee and Brendan Thomas at Amnesia for the research assistance. To my agent Devin McIntyre for turning a dream into an idea, and to my editor Brendan Curry for making that idea a book. To my parents for their faith, my brother and sister for their love, and Jessi, for her light.

INDEX

narcotic plants, 30
NASCAR, x
Nation, Carrie A., 224
National Corn Growers Association, 214
Native Americans, 40, 210, 211, 212
near-beers, 228
Nefertiti, Queen of Egypt, 15
Netherlands, 137
nettle leaf, 46
New Belgium brewery, 51, 76n, 245
New England Farrier and Family Physician, 178
New England's Prospect (Wood), 175
New Monthly Magazine, 143
New York City, 185, 196, 199, 219
New Yorker, 40
New York Public Library, 165–66
New York State, hops industry and, 90, 145, 191, 208
New York Sun, 216
New York Times, 182, 218, 226n
Nietzsche, Friedrich, 223n
nightshade (belladonna), 36, 37, 60n
Nile River, 15
Ninkasi, 11–13, 16, 124, 135, 162
nixtamalization, 211, 215
Noel de Calabaza (beer, Jolly Pumpkin), 109
Nomura bank, 152
Nordland, Odd, 47, 63

Norse, 33, 34, 63, 178
  bog tombs and, 35, 37
  cauldron toasts and, 40–41
  herbal beer and, 44
  mead and, 38–39, 40–41, 62, 184
  sagas of, 38–39, 39n
  totenfloges and, 36
North Carolina, 68
North Clay hops, 139, 149
Northern Brewer hops, 148
Nugget hops, 148
nutmeg, 56, 165
nuts, 9
Nuzi, 15

oasts (drying rooms), 92, 92n
oats, 96
Oberhefenbier, 206
October beer (barleywine), 141, 142
Odell Brewing Company, 153
Odin, 39, 39n, 52
Oktoberfest, 40
Old English, 33
Oldest Cuisine in the World, The (Bottero), 9, 17
Ommegang brewery, 195, 220
On Evangelical Drinking (Haetzer), 63n
onions, 56
opium, 30
Orange Crush, 28
oranges, 67, 70
Oregon, hops and, 87–92, 145

turbid mash, 97, 105
Turkey, 143, 146
turkeys, 210n
Turner, Frederick, 31
Turnverein, 217
Twizzlers, 26

Ultra Lime Cactus (beer, Miller-
    Coors), 234
Underwood oysters, 197
Uneeda biscuits, 197
United States Brewers Association,
    90, 188, 224, 234
Urkontinent (beer, Dogfish Head),
    244–45
Uruk, 6, 62
USDA56013 hop strain, 149
Utopias (beer, Boston Beer Co.),
    188–89, 192, 194, 195

Vandervelde, Emile, 73
Van Roy, Jean-Pierre, 102–3, 105
Vedic religion, 38
Veltem Brewery, 77
Venice, glassmaking and, 138n
Veraldur, 39n
verticillium wilt, 191
Vienna Lager (Märzen), 205–6
Vikings, 48
    mead halls and, 38–39, 40–41,
    62, 184
Vina, Calif., 64, 65, 66
Vindolanda, Scotland, 32n

vinegar, 10, 11, 12, 107
Virgil, 30, 31–32
Virginia colony, 160, 174, 175, 184–
    85, 196
Virginia Company, 175
Virginia Gazette, 213
Vita-B, 228
vitamin B$_6$, 14
vitamin B$_{12}$, 14
Vitebsky, Piers, 35–36
Vivo, 228
Vleteren, Belgium, 49
Vogue, 230

Wadworth 6X, 130n
Wagner, John, 171
Wagner, Rich, 170–74, 177, 180, 186,
    187
Wahlberg, Mark, 189
Waits, Tom, 164
Walduck, Thomas, 176
walgbaert, 96
Wallace, Henry, 214
Wallonia, Belgium, 85–86
Wall Street Journal, x
walnuts, 67
Warhol, Andy, 195
War of the Spanish Succession, 123
Warren, J., 170
Washington, George, 177, 182, 183,
    187
    brewing and, 160–62, 164, 165,
    166–70, 171, 174